TISSUES FOR MEN

TISSUES FOR MEN

ALAN COREN

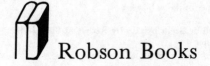

Robson Books

SJP
1904-1979

FIRST PUBLISHED IN GREAT BRITAIN IN 1980 BY
ROBSON BOOKS LTD., 28 POLAND STREET,
LONDON W1V 3DB. COPYRIGHT © 1980
ALAN COREN

British Library Cataloguing in Publication Data

Coren, Alan
  Tissues for men.
  I. Title
  828′.9′1408   PN6175

  ISBN 0-86051-116-2

Printed and bound in Great Britain by Redwood Burn Ltd.
Trowbridge & Esher
Typesetting by Georgia Origination, Liverpool

Contents

Explanation

FIVE YEARS AGO, I produced a book entitled *Golfing for Cats*, which sported on its dust-jacket a fetchingly irrelevant swastika. Since I had gleaned from W.H. Smith and other major outlets that golf, cat, and Third Reich books were the three best-selling categories, it seemed only a matter of time before I should unload some two million copies.

In the event, it was only a matter of time before enraged people to whom I had not been introduced began ringing me in the small hours to inform me that they had bought this bloody book and there was nothing in it about improving their swing, worming their Siamese, or annexing the Sudetenland. Furthermore, their solicitors were in the post.

It is not a mistake an author should make twice. Added to which, in the five years since then the bottom has dropped even further out of the book market: what the crowds besieging Smith's are *really* after these days is paper handkerchiefs.

I think *Tissues for Men* is destined, therefore, not only to be a runaway best-seller, but also to redeem my reputation at the Fair Trading offices: there are eighty good wet-proof blasts here, and no argument. The law is on my side.

AC

The Hangover in Question

4.17 A.M, light from fridge snaps on, reverberates through head like noise, can *hear* pupils contracting, shut fridge door, little polychrome rhomboids continue to kaleidoscope about in brain.

Or I am dead. This is Elysian fridge, I have snuffed it and gone to Kitchen, God's final jest, doomed to an eternity standing on jammy lino in bare feet, unable to find bottle opener, parched for Coke.

Would He be this tough on drinkers? Cannot recall pentateuchal injunctions against alcohol, is there an XIth Commandment somewhere in small print, *Thou shalt not booze?* Are there parables in minor prophet texts, *And Jeroboam came home legless, and fell over the cat, and uttered oaths; and the LORD God brought forth thunderbolts and smote him in that place where he was, saying: Henceforth shall the floor of thy mouth be as a wadi, and thine eyeballs as twin coals, and the fruit of thy loins go about on all fours, even unto the tenth generation?*

Amazing what a few minutes of natural sleep can do for you. Such as maim. Came home at 3.15, not tight, loosened, if anything, one or two joints unbolted, no more than that, perfectly capable of sticking key in letter-box and walking into Christmas tree, got glass ball off ear at only third attempt, negotiated staircase easily as falling over a log, found bedroom door handle well before 3.30, removed clothes with nothing more than minor pause to work out best way of pulling trousers over head, climbed athletically up onto bed, stubbed fag out on clock, sank into oblivion.

Rose from oblivion 4.13, not tea-time already, surely? No, clock still smouldering, faint smell of plastic molecules reorganising their domestic arrangements.

Tongue lying on mouth-floor like felled cactus.

Got up, carrying head carefully in both hands, groped for

dressing-gown, dressing-gown totally incapacitated, arms flapping, belt treble-knotted, dressing-gown obviously just got in from even wilder New Year's Eve party than mine, crawled downstairs together like, like, like—who was it used to sing *Me and My Shadow*, plump man, white tie, face of some kind?

4.20, now, by kitchen clock; brave fridge searchlights again. Guy Gibson's voice crackling on ectoplasmic intercom as we go in low over the bacon, something registers a hit on hand, grab Coke bottle from back of fridge, slam door, and we are away before gunners can even get range.

What hit hand? Hand got egg-white on it. Two possibilities: either I bleed albumen, or else wife still pursuing mad habit, despite previous incidents, of leaving egg-whites in cup after using yolks, standing cup on top shelf, and awaiting results.

Cannot bring self to open fridge again, know what it looks like, seen it before, it looks like giant snail has run amok; not generally known fact that average hen's egg contains up to eighteen miles of mucus if allowed to drip long enough.

Put it behind me, other things on what's left of mind, how, for example, to open Coke bottle? By light chiaroscuring in from street lamp, as in Caravaggio's immortal *Parched Drunk Looking For Coke Bottle Opener*, begin tugging at utensil drawers, forgetting Second Law of Ergodynamics which states that all drawers stick during small hours, also forgetting Third Law of Ergodynamics which states that all drawers *only stick for a bit*.

Said bit having elapsed, all drawers leap from their cavities and vomit cake-cutters, used batteries, bent screwdrivers, half a scissor, corks, spare fuses, knife handles, flea collars, pieces of gas bill, empty Sparklets, flints, two-pin bakelite plugs you brought from your last house just in case, Good Boy drops, cup handles, matchboxes (empty), matchboxes (with screws in; or, after drawer flies open, with screws out), doll's heads, and seventy-one keys you brought from your last house just in case.

No bottle-openers, though.

4.26.

Think.

Have seen John Wayne open bottles with teeth. Or, no doubt, John Wayne's double's teeth. Probably special teeth, though, enamelled steel props built at San Diego Navy Yard.

John Wayne's double lies a-mouldering in the grave, but his teeth go marching on...

Shall not chance own vulnerable choppers, though, last time I chomped an incautious cobnut, mouth resembled tiny Temple of Dagon, crumbling masonry everywhere, crown dust rising, bits of bridge, World War Two fillings—God knows what Coke bottle would do, whole skull might come off.

Ah.

Remember seeing someone open Coke bottle in door-jamb.

Ah.

Look at foot.

Foot still hissing slightly, Coke bubbles dying among instep hair. Must be special trick in opening horizontal Coke bottle in door jamb. Must be *two* special tricks, since large sliver of door jamb now lying beside Coked foot.

4.31.

No more Coke in house.

Water, squash, milk, no use, need something aerated, no good simply de-parching tongue, am Very Aware of need to shift something lying sideways across oesophagus. Seem to have swallowed large plank. Could be case for Red Adair, long experience assures me only megacharge of bubbles will do trick, no point ringing Dyno-Rod at 4.33, *You must be joking, squire, couldn't touch anything till February earliest, we're up to here with paperwork, not to mention staff shortages, unofficial strike up Northampton, black ice, Good Friday looming, etc...*

If plank *is* lying across oesophagus.

Aorta? Vasa cava inferior? Duodenum? Ventriculus dexter? Pulmo?

Stop, in larder, hand on bicarb packet; reflect.

All down to Jonathan Miller, this. We live in post-*Body In Question* Age. Used to know nothing about what goes on past tonsils. Now know three per cent. Point-three per cent. Know it looks like Rotorua mud-spring, in constant state of peristaltic glug; know about referred pain, i.e. if feel sudden stabbing pain in shin, could mean going deaf. To layman—to 0.3% expert—entire nervous system is result of giant connective cock-up, nothing hurts where it's supposed to, everything where it isn't. If Dalston Junction like that, Central Line tube to Chancery Lane ends up in East Kilbride.

Prior to Miller, all my anatomical information came from Arthur Mee. *Children's Encyclopaedia* used to have big sepia illustrations of human body in section, showing little men in overalls shovelling food into tin boiler (stomach), little men in head with Box Brownies (eyes), little men in lungs with foot-pumps. Very nice. Liked to think of them all down there, contented work force beavering away; felt like benevolent mill-owner, loyal workers whistling as they shovelled, pumped, treadled, ticked carbohydrates off clipboard check-list, stoked furnaces.

Pleasant, having anthropomorphic view of own insides; every time I ate breakfast, thought of little men in spotless gumboots carrying egg away in buckets.

Impossible, now. Post-Miller, see myself as not even human, merely large biochemical complex or permanent germ-warfare battlefield. A great itinerant skin bag of blood and offal, horribly vulnerable. Never used to worry about smoking, drinking, guzzling, little men would take care of all that, scouring lungs, washing down intestinal tract, buffing liver to spotless health.

4.38.

Bicarb packet still in hand, plank still across throbbing insides. Eyes (not Box Brownies) focus on minuscule print: $NaHCO_3$.

Yes. Could be anything, really, could well combine with whatever I am to produce $SO_9C_4Pb_8Th_2Nb_6H_3Sb_2Zn_7 \ldots$ without unease, post-Jonathan, bunging assorted valences down into the pulsing tripes, what if wedged-plank-plus-aching-eye-plus-metal-tongue syndrome is actually referral of neurological complaints about dislocated spleen, could be $NaHCO_3$ is worst possible treatment for dislocated spleen, could end up quitting vale of tears on one terminal burp.

Appalling way to go.

Return bicarb to shelf, shut larder door, hobble across floor on Coke-gummy foot, fuses, screws, Good Boy drops sticking to sole, wedged plank grinding in chest cavity, possibly indicating grit behind patella, mastoid sprouting in left ear, onset of silicosis.

4.56.

Shameful, tragic, terrifying how body gets abused, body

only thing I have (gave up idea of soul 1967, following TV programme by glib atheist), New Year less than five hours old, good time to make New Year Resolution, must stop punishing tissues, must give up fags, liquor, toast, fatty...

Hang on.

Wonder if hair of dog good for wedged oesophagal plank?

Where scotch?

El Sid

In a poll carried out among Spaniards, the British tourist emerged as the most sexless, most tasteless, worst dressed, most stingy, and above all the most boring of all foreign visitors. 'It is almost,' said the poll's organiser, 'as if his behaviour was deliberate.' —Daily Mail

WITH THE JULY TEMPERATURE in the high nineties, with the brass sun gonging down from the white noon-day welkin, with the only breeze itself so hot that flies' wings shrivelled in mid-flight, the Hotel Miramar Beach froze.

That is to say, the elegant French stopped dead before the peach foyer mirrors, their preens unfinished; the lissome Scandinavians around the pool paused in the rhythmic insulation of one another's astounding breasts, the coconut oil evaporating on their inert fingers; the cheerful Minnesotans at the bar, poised to buy doubles for everyone, let the wallets drop from their suddenly benumbed hands; and the witty wags from Dusseldorf and Köln found the punch-lines dying on their nerveless lips.

While the only noise to disturb the fraught silence of the huge stucco complex was a low and undulating Iberian moan from a thousand uniformed throats.

For El Sid stood on the blue foyer tiling, the hotel doors swinging shut behind him. True to his legend, he had returned at the same moment, on the same day, to the same spot; El Sid had kept his covenant.

He had come from the North, and he wore the uniform of the North: the electric-blue nylon anorak, wondrously filled with mock-kapok, the bright badge over his heart proclaiming his proud membership of the Durex works team; the off-white teeshirt beneath (the gift of a grateful *Sun*), cunningly worked

13

to show bums of all nations; the QPR knitted cap with its jovially obscene bobble and embroidered misspelled oaths; the genuine ex-Chief Petty Officer's navy shorts, just kissing the tripe-hued knees; the chic mail-order plimsolls, tide-marked with salt lines left by last year's ebbing sweat.

He dropped his two smart chipboard suitcases, and fixed the trembling Hall Porter with an adamantine eye.

'Gatwick!' cried El Sid. 'Don't talk to *me* about bleeding Gatwick!'

The doors sighed shut again. His squire stood beside him, his short rotundity set off to full advantage by an elderly Gannex and floor-length Charlton scarf. He wore a sombrero with a Union Jack on it.

'Don't talk to us about bleeding Gatwick!' he said. 'Eighty-five pee for a pork pie and you have to take your own Cellophane off.'

'Pork brick, more like,' thundered El Sid. He jabbed the Hall Porter's chest with a gnawed forefinger; the man cringed. 'Your *genuine* pork pie was invented, as you may recall, by Lord Pork. Am I right, squire?'

'Definitely. He was gaming up his club. They come to him in the middle and told him his dinner was on the table, and he replied: *Piss off, I am playing brag, bring us a pie!* He'd turn in his wossname if he knew what they was getting away with these days. When I was a boy, you could go to Benghazi and back for eighty-five pee and still have change for a pint of whelks.'

'Or seventeen bob, as it was then called,' said El Sid.

'Or seventeen bob, as it was then called,' said his squire.

'Sometimes,' said El Sid darkly, 'I wonder who won the war.'

He snatched his key from the Hall Porter's hand. In other circumstances, with other guests, the man might have fawned, chatted, joked, hovered for tips; but he had tried that once with El Sid, long ago, and been held for an hour with a meticulous description of how to get to Hornsey from Sudbury Town avoiding the North Circular entirely, and even now would often break out in herpes at the memory.

So El Sid took up his bags, and walked towards the lift; which, at his approach, suddenly spilled its waiting cargo of suntanned Danes and svelte Italians, so that he and his squire rose in solitary comfort.

'They know me here,' murmured El Sid.

They walked into the bar.

El Sid had changed into his leisure clothes, string vest and green eye-shade with the ex-CPO shorts; his squire favoured a Tesco bikini with a Fair Isle slipover.

The bar was crowded: elegant Gucci shapes glided about in the polyglot pre-lunch hum, or waited patiently for their turn to catch the barman's eye.

'Bloody stroll on!' muttered the squire. 'Could take all day.'

But El Sid had set his iron jaw. The glint was in his eye.

'OY' he bellowed, with such force that, in the trim rock garden beyond the windows, lizards leapt, and shed their tails. 'DOS BROWN ALES, CHOP-CHOP!'

A hundred pairs of Polychromatic lenses swung round so fast, they had scant time to pale; when they did, and the eyes behind made out the epic duo, the mouths beneath fell slack. The ranks opened; El Sid walked majestically through. An American at the bar, whose turn it was, licked his lips quickly and shrilly cried:

'No! No! Allow me!'

El Sid returned a small smile.

'Very generous,' he said. 'We won't say no, will we, squire?'

'We won't say no,' said the squire.

'Two treble Glenlivets,' said El Sid.

They drank them, in the taut silence.

It was El Sid's round.

'If a grasshopper was as big as a man,' he said, 'he could jump over St Paul's Cathedral.'

'There's not many people know that,' said his squire to the American.

The American mopped his forehead.

'Conversely,' said El Sid, 'if a man was as big as a grass-hopper, he couldn't jump over bleeding anything.'

'Is it all to do with kinetic energy, El Sid?' asked his squire.

'That comes into it,' replied the hero. 'Course, strong back legs has a part to play as well. Funny things, strong back legs: my brother-in-law Dennis...'

'Is that the one from West Hartlepool who married your sister Beryl who used to gut herrings in Yarmouth?'

'Not Yarmouth. Hull. None of my family's ever even bloody *seen* Yarmouth, the nearest they ever got was, what's the name of that place in Norfolk, used to have a very good non-league side, big ginger striker, werl, I *say* striker, he was more of a roving sweeper, when you come right down to...'

'I guess I'll take an early lunch,' croaked the American, backing away.

His movement was as a shot fired that precipitates an avalanche. Within seconds, the bar was empty, save for El Sid, his squire, and its overturned chairs.

'Left a lot of nice drinks behind,' said El Sid, bending to sniff an untouched Pernod.

'Not to mention nuts,' murmured his squire.

They rolled, half-cut and singing, into the dining-room, and were shown to a table.

'I'd rather be sitting at that one,' said the squire, jabbing his thumb towards the neighbouring table, 'next to the window.'

'Course you would,' said El Sid. He leaned across, tapped the German's arm. 'I see you're managing to hold them prawns down,' he said pleasantly.

'Excuse me?' said the German.

'My friend here tried the prawns last year,' said El Sid.

'Only once,' said the squire.

'Only once,' said El Sid. 'You wouldn't believe what come up over the next couple of days, would he?'

The squire shook his head.

'It's on account of them breeding in sewage,' said El Sid, 'little bits of it get wedged in their joints. Look at a prawn's knee under the microscope, you can actually make out the... bring your drink, Dennis.'

They re-settled themselves.

'That's better,' said the squire. 'Got a view of the sea now.'

El Sid tossed the menu aside.

16

'I think I'll have eggs, sausage, bacon, fried kidney, tomato, baked beans and double chips,' he said.

'Can they do that here?' asked his squire.

'Definitely. I had it every day last year. The chef kicked up a bit of a barney first day, mind, but I went in there, very friendly, and told him about the time me and Geoff Rymold tried to renew the cylinder head gasket on Geoff's cousin Albert's mate's old dormobile. So he give in finally, after it started to get dark.'

'You got a way with people,' said the squire reverently.

El Sid's steely eyes gazed out over the sparkling Mediterranean, offering glint for glint.

'They didn't build the Empire on bleeding paella,' he said.

As their last belch echoed titanically through the cringing restaurant, El Sid and his faithful squire wiped their mouths on the tablecloth and strode out into the sunshine.

'There's a nice spot,' said El Sid, pointing to a pair of reclining chairs in the shade beside the diving-board.

'They've got someone's towels on them,' said his squire.

'Oh, have they really?' said El Sid, clomping lithely across and shedding his vest, 'Oh, my goodness! Oh, dear me!'

He sat down on one of the chairs. His squire collapsed into the other.

'Excuse me, please, but you have our chairs taken.'

El Sid squinted up through his eye-shade. Two tall German girls hovered, smiling apologetically.

'Pardon?'

'Our towels,' explained one of the girls, pointing.

'*Your* towels, stone me, I'd never have guessed they was *your* towels!' cried El Sid. 'Knockers like yours—' and here he paused, moulding his own flabby bosom, lest their English be not entirely adequate '—knockers like yours, I'd have thought you'd have needed something much bigger, know what I mean, squire? Here, what about you two coming down our beach cabana for a bit of a gobble?'

'Don't women run funny?' said his squire, as they watched them flee.

'All they're good for,' said El Sid, mysteriously. 'Fancy a swim?'

His squire sat up.

'Pool's a bit crowded,' he said. 'I wouldn't like to get me hairpiece ducked.'

'Hang on,' said El Sid, pushing himself up from his chair.

He walked to the edge of the pool. The sleek international heads glanced up. Above them, El Sid, white, scrawny, magnificent, towered. On his callous-crusted heroic heel, he turned.

'Just going to have a quick dip, squire,' he shouted. 'I'm busting. It must be the vino.'

Bloomers

Daily Telegraph

COMPUTER HELPS EDIT 'ULYSSES'

By ROBERT TILLEY in Munich

A WEST German university lecturer, equipped with a computer and unlimited patience, is ploughing through more than a million words of difficult English prose to produce the first 'really definitive' version of one of the most monumental works of modern fiction — James Joyce's "Ulysses."

BY LORRIES ALONG SIR JOHN ROGERSON'S quay Mr Bloom walked soberly, past Windmill lane, Leask's the linseed crushers, the postal telegraph office, ping, whirr, clunk, We would draw your attention to the enclosed outstanding telephone account in the sum of £971,000,000,004.02 do not fold staple bend crease stick lick or touch and if paying by bank giro credit please state inside leg measurement when orduring; please state date of bath; police state all previous convictions on separate sheet provided (batteries not included) DO NOT detach, semi-detach, end of terrors, bijou torn house, 3 bed 1 bth 1 ktch dwnstrs clks ample gge spce, patio patio bkrs mn, we have 7,000,000,000,002 fine examples like these on our flies.

Mr Bloom turned from the morning noise of the quayside and walked through Lime street, ping, clackety-clack, EC4 OH2 2DG it is essential to write postcode in box provided, provided box is provided, Box will provide, box must NOT exceed 67875000 centimetres overall unless excess postage paid please state excess card number when ogling, John Barleycard, American Excess or other fine cars. And a bottle of Banker's draught for the little woman, please indicate OVERLEAF whether spinster/wife/mistress/other martial state.

Gonna take a centimetre journey, gonna get myself a train, please refer to fully-automated indicator board, the 189.30 am from Peterborough to Irkutsk is now overdue. If overdue 189.30 remains unpaid within SEVEN (7) days to our Peterborough office (if resident in Irkutsk) or Irkborough office

19

(if non-patrial with six or more parents domiciled in Peterkutsk), instrument will be cut off.

Bloom crossed Townsend Street, past Nichols' the undertakers, ping, whizz, This is to inform you that your husband's instrument has been cut off, the hospital deeply regrets any inconvenience caused by the error but, due to sleet on computerised points at Didcot, your current driving licence MUST be forwarded to Swansong unless hat-size smaller than 67¼, or rush me *War and Peas*. If I am not completely delighted and satisfied with this magnificent purchase, I undertake to buy 1888 more classics, please bill me.

Along came bill, an ordinary gay, the Department of Health deeply regrets loss of instrument, please place deceased in box provided, DO NOT FORWARD TO ALHAMBRA STREET, DUNDEE, M15 UFO, except between January 18 and March 93 (not Wiltshire rat-payers or if over 650 on April 0), for details please consult local press, ping, clink, bong, do NOT press, stitch, gum, nail, sniff; this form requires two (7) signatures by a bank manacle, justice of the police, parish proust, or Chief Rabbit, and DOES NOT CONSTITUTE A CONTRACT WITHIN THE MOANING OF THE ACT, but see above sub-section 999999.99 (*not available*).

Leopold Bloom strolled out of the post office and turned to the right where a large number of tuckatuckatuckatucka ping PLEASE NOTE that your new National Insurance number is £3.55⅔, you must TAKE (not post) it to your nearest gas showroom on or before the last date not specified hereinunder, and POST (not take) it to ONE (ONE) of the registered dealers on the accompanying leaflet (c/455-61, *alternate* Thursdays). THIS OFFER CLOSES ON WEMBLEY 14th! I am over 121.

Will the vehicle be drivelled by (a) insured only? (4) with/without★ matching bra (★*delete whichever is applicable UNLESS resident in United Kingdom*) or (xviii) if more than 8 O-levels, please STATE whether self-employed, or next-of-kin. NB This offer depends upon availability, plus two bottle-tops, and is NOT open to miners (—).

—Hello, Bloom, where are you off to?

—Hello, M'Coy, ping, whirr, bleep, this is a recorded massage, the speaking cock is not at home as of this moment in time, when the tone sounds would you please Hello, this is the

Gobi Hilton fully-automated customer courtesy desk for your delight and convenience thank you for crawling, we have reserved 197 rooms with bath facing the Mediterranean for you and your wine as per your telex, we note that your Donors Club number is This is the Test Match Service, tea-time scone West Englies 859740036 for 56, Current Account 10.43 and forty seconds, Hello, this is a recorded messuage...

Mr Bloom passed, dallying, the window of Brown Thomas, silk mercers, drapers, purveyors of fine carpets, ping, thunk, billions (3) of carpets MUST be shifted due to computerising of stock, luxurious deep-pile Axemurderers sought by Interpol computer. Interpolly wants a crackpot, please state your old passport number on SEPARATE ROAD FUND APPLICATION, when ordering new pisspot please list (on blank sheep provided) ALL diseases contracted in past 2 minutes, do you suffer from (g) number plates at 25 miles? (4 *or* 17b) credit accounts at any other stores? (gamma) paying tax at the standard rape?

Mr Bloom crossed over the greystone bridge, feeling the pressure on his bladder, ping, tonk, hum, As we have no record of your existence on our files, your water has been cut off from May 8, backdated to Ramadan, if you wish to be reconnected, report at Catterick 07.00 SHARP, April 3, bringing old dog licence (£25 for colour) with you plus vests, string (2), under-pants, wincyette (2), plimsolls, canvas (000000.00), *unless* vehicle is MORE than 50 cwt (2kilos) and/or/but registered PRIOR to the 1972 Road Sidesaddle Act (*repealed*).

Bloom looked in at the butcher's window, noted the purple liver at eightpence a pound, ping, clackety-clackety, You have not converted, we can not process this information, please insert your card a second time, thank you, that is £6.77 a millilitre, 3 francs an ell, 950 lire a rood, more if bloody rood, representing a 724% fall against a bastard of European currencies compared with 1984. Bloody ell, thought Bloom, that's four rods a hectare, two poles a lysander (or some such names as these).

Bloom, not seeing Corny Kelleher, watched the drayman roll the fat vats, ping, buzz, VAT is *not* payable (i.e. *not* payable) on children's seed, mouse clothing, gibbets FOR OWN USE (except early closing day Runcorn & Exmoor Central), clockwork ponds, SECONDHAND bacteria (unless pre-packaged for use

NOT before January 1, 1979), wooden tunnels, dependent relatives (tinned), *Dead* Sea scrolls, unknown soldiers (if intended as presents), goal areas, yak droppings, or women exempted from jury service under the 1839 Scottish Peers of the Realm Act (BBC-2, Thursday, *rpt.*) IF YOU HAVE NOT BEEN VACCINATED, your AA number may have changed BUT the membership fee (£7777.77) will be nevertheless automatically debited from your deposit account. DO NOT throw this away, it is NOT an advertisement, the fixed penalty notice is already on its way to you, REMEMBER that failure to comply could mean a *minimum* of three months imprisonment, plus 35p postage & packing (returnable on receipt of counterfoil if HANDED in *personally* at your local Department of Health and Social Security or most large stores within our delivery area).

And, hiccup, Leopold Gloom, reprocess, Leopold Gloom, ping, reprocess, Leopold Gloom, clunk, reprocess, Leopold Gloom...

We are instructed to inform you that no Leopold Gloom exists in our records, there is no NI number in that nume, there is no VAT number in that nume, there is no car registration, cat registration, hat registration, hut registration, there is no service guarantee in that gnome, no account, no attached docket, ticket, bucket, pocket, packet, locket, there is no...

Person.

He does not exist.

Exits.

Trieste – Zurich – Paris – Swansea – Southend – Whitehall, 1979 –1900000.02

Some Enchanted Evening

'I NEARLY GOT THE CAR back this morning,' I began.

They settled in their chairs.

'*This* morning?' enquired a cartoonist.

'Before lunch, as it were?' asked the literary editor.

'Quite,' I riposted, swishing the Hine around its balloon. 'I'm talking about—what?—somewhere between eleven and eleven-thirty.'

Nobody said anything; there were one or two sharp intakes of breath, though.

'Yes,' I continued, 'I went up to Malvern Road, and I nearly got it back. When I say nearly, what I mean is they'd managed to get the bell-housing out, but the part they'd back-ordered from the stores at Brentford hadn't come in.'

'Typical!' said the features editor.

Everyone roared.

'A cog, as I understand it,' I said.

'Haven't they closed off Malvern Road?' asked another cartoonist. 'I only bring the point up because I used to use Malvern Road as a short cut when I was married to my first wife in Elgin Avenue, and in those days—where are we now? 1979?—in those days, when we used to have to visit her mother in the Brompton Hospital with her chest, in those days the best way to cross the Harrow Road was to go down Malvern Road. As it then was. And then last week, when I had to go to Fulham, I suddenly remembered somebody telling me that they'd closed it off.'

'Well, it's not *exactly* closed off,' I countered, quick as a flash.

'More of a temporary detour, perhaps?' offered a senior political correspondent, helping himself to scotch.

'Exactly!' I said. 'You can still get in if you approach it from the Paddington end.'

'Isn't that strange?' said the second cartoonist, quietly.

We leaned forward.

'I never realised,' he said, almost to himself, 'that it *had* a Paddington end.'

'London's changed so much in the past ten years,' said the literary editor. 'All the one-way systems, those zig-zags near zebra crosssings, the treble yellow marks.'

'I've never known what those stand for,' said the first cartoonist. 'Is it no unloading, or no waiting between the times specified?'

A third cartoonist, who up until this moment had not spoken, walked slowly to the window, and looked out towards the darkened garden.

'I don't bloody know,' he said.

Everybody took another drink. Time seemed to stand still.

'So there I was,' I said, when I judged the moment right, 'looking at this bell-housing, and the works foreman came up, and he said: *I was thinking whether we couldn't make do with a cog from a later model, but then I thought, no.*'

The literary editor looked at me. His cigar had gone out.

'He was probably thinking that if he *were* to do that,' he said, 'you'd only have more trouble with it later on.'

I nodded, and drained my glass.

'Those were his very words,' I said.

The editor of a major political weekly, who had bided his time until now, suddenly cleared his throat.

'I had the same trouble with a 1973 Saab,' he said. 'It left all of us on the A226, four miles from the thing.'

'The A20 intersection?' suggested the second cartoonist.

'If that's the one I'm thinking of, yes,' said the editor. 'Of course, when I say the *same* trouble, I suppose what I really mean is similar trouble. The window went up and caught my wife's ear in it.'

There was a long silence.

'I wouldn't call that similar,' said the features editor.

'I wish I'd said that,' said the second cartoonist.

The literary editor smiled a secret, literary smile and said: 'You will,—'

The third cartoonist interrupted angrily.

'What I fail to see,' he said, squirting his syphon irritably, 'is why it left *all* of you on the A226.'

24

'Look,' I said, 'aren't we rather getting away from the point? The point is, I had to walk back from Malvern Road towards Kensal Rise tube station. I bought a ticket to Blackfriars, and...'

'No you didn't,' said the first cartoonist.

In the tension, the clock ticked, the central heating bonged a muted bong. Out of the corner of my eye, I saw something walk up the rubber plant.

'What?' I muttered.

'There isn't a Kensal Rise tube station,' said the first cartoonist. 'You may have *walked* to Kensal Rise, I'm not saying you didn't, but once there, you either went into Kensal Green tube station, or——' and here he paused significantly '——Queen's Park'.

'You put *either* in the wrong place,' said the editor of the major political weekly. 'You went *either* into Kensal Green or Queen's Park, is the correct syntax.'

The first cartoonist looked at him.

'Shut your face,' he said.

When the laughter had died down, and we had finished scribbling the *mot* on our dickies, the second cartoonist said:

'On your walk to Kensal Rise, did you pass any women with big knockers?'

I thought for a while. Someone opened another bottle.

'I'm not sure,' I said.

The second cartoonist snorted.

'Calls himself a raconteur,' he said.

'Personally,' said a journalist who up until now had been lying under the drinks cupboard, 'personally, I'm a leg man. That swelling of the calf. Know what I'm driving at?'

The editor of the major political weekly reached for an olive, and knocked over the peanuts.

'What did you expect us to do?' he cried. 'We couldn't just bloody leave her there with her ear jammed in the door.'

The literary editor put an arm around his shoulder, tipping his gin down the editor's lapel.

'Legs, knockers, what does it matter?' said the features editor. 'They're all women in the final analysis, at the end of the day, when you come right down to it. Or am I wrong?'

'Look,' I snapped, opening a second bottle of brandy and

pouring a generous treble over my hand, 'whichever way you slice it, there I was on the Bakerloo Line, *but going towards Watford Junction!*'

'Bloody hell!'

'Christ Almighty!'

'You should have been going towards Elephant and Castle,' said the senior political correspondent, through a haze of blown Twiglet dust, 'if you'd bought a ticket to Blackfriars!'

'Exactly my point,' I cried.

The features editor got up slowly, and walked into the wall.

'Do you know,' he said, stanching his left nostril with his tie, 'just how many eligible women there are in the world? Even cutting out South America and those over sixty, it comes to nearly a billion.'

'How much did you earn last year?' replied the first cartoonist.

The editor of the major political weekly dried his eyes.

'If you want my opinion,' he said, 'Saabs is why all those Swedes cut their wrists.'

'Finns,' corrected the third cartoonist.

The editor stared at him.

'Cut their fins?' he said. He reached for the syphon, and filled his shoe. '*Cut their fins?*'

'Come on!' shouted the first cartoonist, leaping up and bunching his fists. 'How much? Six grand? Ten? *Twenty*?'

'What he means,' the literary editor said to the editor of the major political weekly, 'is the Saab is Finnish.'

'Mine bloody is,' said the editor, nodding gloomily. 'Kaput. Up das spout. Chop, chop.'

On the carpet, the features editor crawled slowly towards the door, dragging his empty bottle. My guests stared at him, heads bobbing. I felt their attention slipping away.

'So what I had to do,' I said, loudly, 'was get out at Stonebridge Park, cross over to the other side, and wait for a train going in the opposite direction.'

There heads swung round again. The literary editor was the first to speak.

'There's an olive in my brandy,' he said.

'You were drinking gin,' said the editor of the major political weekly. 'It's all down me. I wouldn't forget a thing like that.'

26

'Well, then, clever dick,' shouted the literary editor triumphantly, 'why has it gone bloody brown, then?'

'Thirty grand?' screamed the first cartoonist. 'Forty?'

The features editor had reached the corner, and was folded into it.

'On reflection,' he said, largely to a lamp, 'on reflection, I see no reason to exclude South America. They have wonderful women down there, so I understand. Hairy, yes, but not without charm. That brings the total to nearly one and a half billion. Not,' he added, sitting up and looking at me out of one eye, 'that you would have passed many South American women walking to Stonebridge Park.'

'Next time,' said the editor of the major political weekly, 'it's an Allegro for me, and bugger the status.'

The third cartoonist dropped lithely into a heap and crept towards the features editor. He took him by the lapel, with a wet fist.

'He never bloody walked to Stonebridge Park,' he muttered. 'He changed *trains* at Stonebridge Park.'

The features editor sat looking at the third cartoonist for some minutes, the grey sweat gleaming on his forehead like lard on a lightbulb.

'I don't think I feel very well,' he said, at last.

'Here we go,' I quipped. 'Someone pass him the *Radio Times*, will you?'

Moby Junk

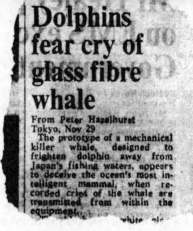

CALL ME ISHMAEL. I think it's a really terrific name, I practise it in front of the mirror a lot, it has, you know, *resonance*.

My publisher came up with it just before I sailed on the *Pequod*, he is a very now person, he is right in there where tomorrow publishing is putting it together.

It isn't Ishmael Anything, or Anything Ishmael, it's a whole new marketing concept, just the one name, like Capucine, Gucci, Regine, all that. It was bound to happen on the book scene sometime, my publisher says, and sometime just blew in.

The book was his idea, too. We met at Jacky's a few months back, and he'd seen this spread I did for *Cosmo* about how you can judge people's libido from how thin their watches are, and he said: 'The next big thing is whales. Did you hear where they're going, what is it, extinct, and everybody who is anybody is out of their skulls with worry, Liz Taylor, Princess Michael, Twiggy, you wouldn't *believe* how much Big People are into whales, I see quartermillion hardback, *minimum*! Do a book, about 10 x 8, something substantial, double page pix. So what am I talking about? I am talking about *Jaws* with *heart*, that's what I'm talking about!'

I met Queequeg at the Spouter-Inn. I really dig Nantucket, it's full of very creative persons, top agency men, tax geniuses, ex-Watergate guys who are putting all their stash into decor consultancy, everyone has these weekend places up there; they all hang it out at the Spouter-Inn, it has these wonderful polystyrene beams, terrific repro barometers everywhere, a roaring Flamo Fumefree Adjustaflicker fire, and a whole load of marvellous *kitscherei*—Mickey Mouse ice cubes in plastic pineapples, cryogenic swizzle sticks with little male chauvinist pigs on the end, genuine Gottlieb pin-tables, you really have to see it. Anyhow, I was sitting in the Chappaquiddick Room (they've done it up as a submerged Chevy Impala; one wall is nothing but fog-lights with live guppies in them) when I saw this huge, I mean *huge*, coloured guy, covered in tattoos. I had eighteen shots of him in the Pentax before I even went across to ask if he'd like his Campari freshened.

'Call me Ishmael,' I said.

'Terrific,' he replied. 'Call me Queequeg.'

'Queequeg who?'

'Just Queequeg.'

I reeled!

'You have to be kidding!' I cried. 'You're an author, too?'

He shook his head.

'I whale,' he said.

I relaxed.

'An alto player,' I said, 'I should have guessed. With all the rhythm you people have—you know, sometimes I feel maybe slavery wasn't such a bad thing, it taught you pain, it made you *respond*. Tell me, do you know *Melancholy Baby*?'

He looked at me kind of funny; then he reached behind him and brought out this enormous pole with a terrible barb on one end.

'Jesus!' I cried. 'You play *that*?'

Next morning, when he came to give back my copy of *Giovanni's Room,* he said:

'Look, man, how'd you like to sail on the *Pequod*?'

'The *Pequod*! It's exactly what I've been looking for! But could you swing it?'

'No sweat, man,' said Queequeg. 'We're low on scribes this trip. Lensmen, sound crews, environment freaks, you name it, they're busting out of every goddam hatch; but no scribes. It's killing the Captain. He's very, you know, yesterday; he's really into verbal communication. Let's go and see him.'

'Terrific!' I cried, grasping his hand. And noticing, as I did so, that his tattoos seemed to have vanished.

'Transfers,' explained Queequeg, when I enquired. 'Where's your head at, man? Everybody's into acrylic water-solubles now. It's where being a matelot is. Listen, if I'm gonna go sticking needles into my goddam arm, it sure as hell ain't gonna be ink I'm shooting!'

And here the huge harpoonist laughed his thunderous laugh.

I have to admit my first sight of the *Pequod* was disappointing.

'It has a funnel, for God's sake!' I said to Queequeg.' It has, like, rigging.'

'Yeah,' said Queequeg. 'That's Ahab, all right.

'I was hoping for a pool,' I said. 'Do you carry Scalectrix?' Queequeg shook his enormous head.

'Fridays we fix a sauna up aft,' he said. 'We tap the boiler. But it's pretty, you know, ad hoc.'

We started up the gangplank, towards a squat, swarthy figure standing at the top.

'Who's he?' I whispered.

'Starbuck,' replied Queequeg. 'First mate.'

'*Who* Starbuck?' I enquired anxiously. 'Jack? Warren? Burt?'

'Just Starbuck.'

My heart sank. Maybe I didn't have such a hot publisher, after all.

'Watch him,' muttered Queequeg, 'he's a God-freak. Very heavy.' He raised his voice as we reached the top. 'Morning, Starbuck. This is Ishmael. He's sailing with us.'

'Really?' cried Starbuck, a blaze starting in his piggy eyes. 'How'd you like to go to Guyana?' He shoved a clipboard under my nose. 'If I get fifty-one per cent of the crew to sign, we'll send a deposition to the Captain.' He shoved a pen into my hand. 'It's this really terrific cult, very fundamentalist, you'll love it, they have girls, liquor, the food is out of this world, sucking pig, armadillo on the half-shell, roast——'

'BELAY THERE, STARBUCK!'

Gulls rose, shrieking, at the voice! It rolled across Nantucket Bay like thunder! It froze the blood in my very veins! My head whipped up, in time to see its owner, peg-leg swinging, hurtle along the deck towards us, snatch the clipboard from Starbuck's hand, and send it winging on a spinning arc into the sea.

'THOU SHALT HAVE ONE GOD ONLY!' roared the Captain. His terrible eye rolled upward, and his terrible finger followed. 'I know Him, and He knows me!' His free hand gathered around Starbuck's throat. 'None of your trashy plastic faiths, Mister Mate, none of your Johnny-come-lately evangelistic rubbish, none of——'

'Okay, okay,' here Starbuck, wriggling, spread concessionary hands, 'how about Bali, it's hardly out of our way, there's this Unitarian consciousness-raising group, they believe up to four per cent of the Old Testament, Captain, and if you only saw how some of them dames is built, you'd——'

The Captain flung him aside, and turned his great head to me.

'You must be Captain Ahab,' I said pleasantly. 'I'm sorry, I didn't catch your first name.'

'Just Ahab,' he growled.

'Oh.'

'I'll not be doing,' he bellowed, 'with any of your cheap trashy, TV-dinner-on-your-lap names, with your Kevins and your Craigs, your Melvyns and your Russells, your Jonathans and——'

'I really like your leg,' I said, frantic to stem his rage. 'It's very chic.'

In the long silence, I could hear the creak of something shippy.

'Ah,' said Ahab, at last, and quietly. 'Chic, is it? Trendy, perhaps? *In*?'

'Well,' I said, 'perhaps not *in*, exactly, I mean what is *really* in is prosthetic tibia-plus-whole-foot units in space alloys, just one more wonderful Apollo spin-off, they're so good you can actually wear wedges without tottering, and——'

The breath left my body as Ahab's thick forearm pressed me against the mast.

'*This* peg,' he growled, his face a millimetre from mine, 'was hand-carved from a sperm-whale's jaw by *craftsmen*! She is a custom leg, a bespoke leg, she is none of your tatty Moon rubbish! That tin trash may do very well for your intergalactic pansy scum with their natty silver suits, I ain't saying it don't, but is it a leg for a seafaring man with a heart full of boiling blood?'

I shook my head vigorously.

'Absolutely not!' I cried. 'No, no, no, that leg is *you*!'

He dropped me, and spun away.

'Cast off for'ard!' roared Captain Ahab. 'Cast off aft!'

I didn't talk to him for the next eight days as the *Pequod* ploughed north to whale-water, but I saw him standing motionless on the bridge, his terrible eye glittering over the doings below as *Vogue* models posed that year's sable anoraks against the davits, and the documentary Arriflexes whirred, and the crew sang shanties into the microphones of a dozen different record labels, and bearded politicians in faded denims told bearded journalists in faded denims of the desperate need to find synthetic substitutes for ambergris.

But on the ninth morning, bored with pounding my IBM, I took the liberty of mounting the bridge.

'I was wondering, Captain,' I said, 'whether you would care for a hand of kaluki? You looked so, I don't know, *solitary*.'

The grey face, with its livid scar, turned slowly from its motionless scanning of the sea.

'Kaluki, is it?' he muttered. 'Or canasta, perhaps? Backgammon, bridge, Cluedo? Scrabble, cribbage, gobs, Up Jenkins, eh, Mister Ishmael, while the cauldrons of hell bubble?'

I sighed.

'I sometimes wonder,' I said, waving a hand towards the activity below, 'how you stand us all.'

Ahab spat fluently.

'I stand 'ee,' he said, 'on account of ye finance the Quest. I put up with the rubbish and the squawking and the posing and the mincing and the natter because it pays the bill. It keeps the *Pequod* afloat. It'll settle the account of Moby Dick!'

'Moby Dick?' I exclaimed. 'Could that be the great white whale who took your leg off at the knee, since when your whole life and being has been committed to his pursuit and destruction, with all the symbolic overtones that that entails?'

'Aye,' said Ahab. 'That's 'im.' He turned his head towards the sea again. 'They wants to be chartered accountants, they wants to live in detached freehold premises, they wants Porsches for the golf clubs and Volvos for the wife, they wants double ovens and video-cassette recorders and solar panels for the swimming pool, they wants Colour Supplements and three weeks on the Costa Smeralda and a Filipino couple in a flat over the garage, they wants quartz-digital this and silicon-chip that and a waferthin pocket calculator ye can slip into your flipper to enable 'ee to compute tax-benefits while snorkelling off Grand Bahama—but what is all that to the *real* Quest, eh?'

I cleared my throat.

'I take it,' I said, 'that as far as Saving The Whale is concerned, your wholehearted support cannot fully be——'

'THAR SHE BLOWS!'

Our two heads swivelled simultaneously upward, to where Queequeg hung pointing from the crow's nest. Ahab flicked out his telescope, smacked it against his eye, and staggered.

''Tis him!' he screamed. ''Tis him!'

And it was.

So we crammed on steam, and we crammed on sail, and we crammed on lenses and type-ribbons and microphones and tape-recorders, and we hugged ourselves with excitement for a day and a night, as we tracked the great white whale in its ultimate sprint, with sweating Queequeg crouched in the prow, harpoon in hand (for the Captain would have no truck with pansy guns and newfangled trash); but when the great white whale paused, at last, exhausted, it was Ahab himself who stumped to the bow, and snatched the spear from Queequeg's hand, and Ahab himself, with a terrible cry, who hurled it down to the glistening flanks.

And, therefore, Ahab himself whose foot was caught in the spilling line, and Ahab himself who was plucked from the prow, and Ahab himself who was lashed to his quarry with the kind of irony you normally get only in hand-tooled uniform editions, and Ahab himself who was dragged to the bottom with the ruined whale.

Leaving us on the bobbing *Pequod* with the earnest prayer that his dying ears had never picked up the unmistakable clunk of busted clockwork.

Two Sleepy People, with Nothing to Do

The English are not a sensual nation: puritanism, a cold climate, and an education which frowns on joy have seen to that. They go to bed with each other for various reasons, but only sometimes for the simple pleasure of food. They go there in order to be seen by other people; to have their egos massaged by subservient waiters; to impress the opposite sex with their social adroitness; to get drunk. —Tatler

IT WAS GENERALLY AGREED to have been the most super wedding one had ever been to.

The bride, of course, looked absolutely stunning.

'Doesn't Lucinda look absolutely stunning?' said her best friend Melissa.

'*Rather!*' cried Melissa's husband.

'Jolly stately and serene,' said Melissa, as Lucinda swept past them down the aisle on the arm of the Earl. 'One is rather reminded of old Queen Mary, isn't one?'

'I thought that had three funnels,' said Melissa's husband, frowning.

Rodney-Rodney made a magnificent bridegroom. Scion of the only English family allowed to hyphenate its Christian names (a favour bestowed at Bannockburn when one of Rodney-Rodney's illustrious ancestors had relieved a pustule on Edward II), he was as tall as it is possible to be without arousing genetic suspicion, and slim as a flute. True, his chin fell away sharply from his upper canines, above which, as if in Dame Nature's kindly compensation, his nose sprang out for several overstated inches (he had been known as Beaky-Beaky at Dame Poumfret's Preparatory Academy for the Appallingly Dim, and the name had stuck); but by great good fortune, his bride's county nose was retroussé to the point of invisibility and her chin jutted out so far that her small bust lay in permanent shadow. In short, Lucinda and Rodney-Rodney appeared to complement one another perfectly: when they kissed at the altar, their two profiles meshed as effortlessly as Bentley clutch-plates.

It was, however, the first kiss in which either of them had ever been involved. Throughout her twenty-one years, Lucinda's only romantic attachment had been a heavy crush on Red Rum, while Rodney-Rodney, at twenty-three, had entered into only one non-platonic relationship, with a Fräulein Sharon, to whose discreet Curzon Street premises he would repair every Thursday after the Brigade dinner, to be beaten with a blancoed length of Boer webbing.

But because Lucinda's daddy, the Earl, owned eighty thousand acres of shooting but preferred fishing, whereas Rodney-Rodney's daddy, Charlie-Charlie, owned eighty miles of salmon-river but preferred shooting, their marriage had been a foregone conclusion for some time.

Nevertheless, to say that they were ill-prepared is seriously to underestimate the English upper classes: on the day before the ceremony, Charlie-Charlie took Rodney-Rodney into the library at Toppins, gave him a large brandy, and showed him an illustrated copy of Fernleigh's *Breeding Springers*; and the Countess, for her part, formally handed over to Lucinda the Hapsburg bullet upon which her family's brides had been biting ever since the Thirty Years' War.

At the reception, everybody got wonderfully, wonderfully tight. They danced the Lancers, in which seven shoulders were dislocated, and the Gay Gordons, in which no fewer than thirty-seven people made the same joke about MI5, and an Eightsome Reel, in which no fewer than thirty-seven people made the same joke about Highland underwear, and they played Maim the Staff, in which Rodney-Rodney himself managed to disable two footmen and an under-gardener with Dom Perignon bottles from sixty paces, despite having had his monocle shattered during the Ladies Excuse-me Wall Game.

And at six o'clock, being tired little teddy bears, the happy couple slipped away in Rodney-Rodney's Lagonda across the croquet lawn, and, pausing only to leave the offside front wing on

35

an elderly yew, purred off towards the far Savoy and the first leg of their mooners in Canners.

It was a pleasant suite: by jumping on the bed, Rodney-Rodney found he could bang his head on the ceiling, and Lucinda was ecstatic to find that there was even a tiny, tiny paddling-pool beside the loo so that her rubber duck could float about without getting lonely. She unpacked carefully, put her bullet by the bed, and slid between the sheets, leaving Rodney-Rodney to pad into the bathroom with *Breeding Springers* for a little last-minute revision while she turned the pages of *Tatler,* which was the only reading-matter she ever saw and from which she invariably took her behavioural cues.

It was while she was flicking through the glossy breathlessness in the hope of finding, perhaps, some indication of when the bullet was supposed to be enmouthed, that she suddenly issued a shrill cry. Rodney-Rodney, who had been barking seductively behind the door, dashed out, his long face twisted apprehensively at this new evidence of feminine unpredictability.

'What is it, old stick?' he cried, 'not women's problems?' He raked, gamely, through his sparse garnering of marital notes. 'Should I burp you, or something?'

'Oh, Beaky-Beaky!' cried Lucinda, eyes a-shine. 'Nothing like that! There is a super piece in *Tatler* about how people are supposed to do it!'

'Do what?'

'You know,' murmured Lucinda. 'Thing.'

'*Thing?*' exclaimed Rodney-Rodney, his imperceptible jaw dropping. 'In *Tatters?*'

'Isn't it thrilling?' shouted Lucinda.

'And just in the nick of, er, whateveritis!' cried Rodney-Rodney, jumping up and down. 'Does it tell one how to examine one's feet for hardpad? This book's jolly difficult to follow.'

'There's nothing about that here,' replied Lucinda. 'Apparently one sometimes starts off with food.'

'Hurrah!' shouted Rodney-Rodney, 'I think this ought to be one of those times don't you? One works up a jolly enormous appetite barking, I can tell you! Hardly surprising dogs get right down to it, shoving their beezers in the jellymeat, no knives or forks or anything, one suddenly sees the reason behind it. Let's have some oysters and a duck or two!'

'Right-ho!' shrieked his bride, clapping her hands. 'I say, Beaky-Beaky, I was never allowed to eat in bed were you? Isn't it absolutely super being grown-up? And the other thing about getting food sent up is the waiters will be able to massage our egos!'

Two lines crinkled on Rodney-Rodney's teeny brow.

'What on earth are *those*?' he said. 'I say, I hope it's not that thing they caught little Berkshire doing with Crown Prince Bhunah at Dame Poumfret's. If one went blind, one's hunting career would be utterly ruined!'

'It'll be all right,' said Lucinda confidently. 'There'll be other people watching.'

'What sort of people?'

'It doesn't say. I should think any old people would do. Why don't I order the food while you nip out and whip in a few spectators?'

'*Super!*' cried Rodney-Rodney, slipping into his dressing-gown. 'I say, old thing, is one allowed to drink, too?'

'It says,' replied Lucinda, scanning the page almost without moving her lips, 'that one is supposed to get drunk!'

Rodney-Rodney reeled.

'What bliss!' he shouted. 'Is it any wonder one's parents keep one in the old harry darkers about thing? One would never do anything else!'

When, ten minutes later, he returned, there were five small Japanese businessmen with him. They bowed towards Lucinda.

'Best I could do, I'm afraid,' said Rodney-Rodney. 'They were jabbering in the corridor. They don't seem to speak anything but Jap, but they shot off like grouse when I snapped my fingers. Can't think why. Do you suppose they're prisoners-of-war, or something?'

'Jolly lucky being imprisoned in the Savoy,' said Lucinda.

'Oh, I don't know,' said Rodney-Rodney, 'I bet they have to stick to the set menu. Things like that. Will they do?'

'I should think so,' replied Lucinda, waving the Japanese to sit. 'They only have to watch, after all.'

There was a soft knock on the door, and Rodney-Rodney opened it to admit two waiters pushing a trolley, and a sommelier with a shouldered crate of Bollinger. He shot into bed.

They followed with the trolley, served the oysters, eased a cork, and were about to leave, when Rodney-Rodney cried:

'I say, would you mind staying? This is our wedding-night.'

The trio paused; but since Rodney-Rodney's accent was full of money, they stayed, sliding themselves professionally back against the walls. Lucinda, having despatched three bivalves with scarcely a slurp, hurled the shells at the gazing Japs. She hit two.

'I say!' exclaimed her husband. 'That's a bit strong, old girl. Geneva Convention, and all that.'

'One is supposed,' replied Lucinda, passing the magazine across, 'to impress the opposite sex with one's social adroitness.'

'I *see*!' shouted Rodney-Rodney. 'Well, I'm jolly impressed, old girl. I've not seen better chucking from a sitting position since Farty Cork-Snettering laid out the Connaught's maître d' with a chump chop! Still, just to show that one is no mean hand oneself when the social adroitness rosettes are being dished out...'

Whereupon Rodney-Rodney sprang lithely from the bed, scattering croquettes, stood on his head in the middle of the room, and downed an entire bottle of champagne without taking it from his inverted lips.

'As performed on Boat Race Night '74!' he shrieked.

The Japanese applauded.

'God,' gasped Rodney-Rodney, when he had removed his head from the waste-bin and allowed a little colour to drain back into his saffron cheeks, 'isn't this the most super fun? Beats being a springer, I can tell you!' He wiped his mouth, while a clench-faced waiter took the waste-bin to the bathroom. 'What do we have to do next?'

There was no reply.

Rodney-Rodney loped erratically to the bed. Lucinda, having drunk two bottles on her own loyal behalf, lay fast asleep, her head on a duck, her auburn locks fetchingly highlighted by the *sauce de cerises*.

Her husband gazed at her for some time, rocking on his bare heels.

'Was it wonderful for you, too, old thing?' he murmured finally.

38

Then he sat down sharply on the floor beside her, and opened his third bottle.

Back at the grimy composing-room of *Tatler*, the horny-handed printers toasted their latest brilliant sabotage in Newcastle Brown, and plotted their next. They had been given a riding article to set, explaining how best to present a horse at a 6-foot jump. It would be the work of a moment to make it 16-foot. By such canny sleights, a dropped line here, a transposed word there, it would not be long, surely, before all the ancient lines died out, all the ensigns of privilege were extirpated, and the revolution was quietly ushered in.

From The Oxford Dictionary of Collaborations

P.G.WITTGENSTEIN
1889–1975

There was another ring at the front door. Jeeves shimmered out and came back with a telegram. 'Die Welt ist alles, was der Fall ist, sir,' he murmured.

Carry on Tractatus Logico-Philosophicus (1928)

T.S.KIPLING
1888–1937

We aren't no thin red 'eroes, nor we aren't no
blackguards, too.
But single men in barricks, most remarkable like you;
Shall I part my hair behind? Do I dare to eat a peach?
I shall wear white flannel trousers, and walk
upon the beach.

The Love Song of Tommy Prufrock (1919)

If you can make one heap
Between the motion
And the act

The Hollow If (1932)

OSCAR WILCOX
1854–1918

Weep, and you weep alone. It is exquisite, and it leaves one unsatisfied. What more can one want?

Picture of Solitude (1891)

SCOTT FITZGERALD

1799–1866

O, young Lochinvar has come out of the West,
And, having writ, moves on!
The Rubaiyat of Omar Marmion (1844)

MANDY RICE ROWLEY

1900–

They took her up in any airyplane, parley-voo,
And screwed her back to life again, parley-voo,
They took her up in an airyplane,
And screwed her back to life again,
Well, they would, wouldn't they?
Mademoiselle from Portman Square (1963)

PHINEAS T. WILSON

1884–1959

That doesn't mean, of course, that the pound here in Britain—the pound in your pocket or purse or in your bank—has been devalued. There's a sucker born every minute.
Bread and Circuses (1951)

W.H.EDMESTON

*fl.*1944

O unicorn among the cedars,
Lead us, Heavenly Father, lead us.
The Ascent of F All (1944)

MARIE BYSSHE LLOYD
1803–1878

I met a traveller from an antique land
Who said: Two vast and trunkless legs of stone
Stand in the desert. Near them on the sand,
Half sunk, a shatter'd visage lies, whose frown
And wrinkled lip and sneer of cold command
Tell that its sculptor well those passions read
Which yet survive, stamp'd on these lifeless things,
The hand that mock'd them and the heart that fed;
And on the pedestal these words appear:
'One of the ruins that Cromwell knocked about a bit'

Ozzie Morris (1869)

LORD LUCAN
AD 39–?

*Coniunx est mihi, sunt nati: dedimus tot pignora fatis. Et in Australia
ego.*
I have a wife, I have children: all of them hostages given to
fortune. And I am among savages.

Works (Sometimes) (84?)

ROBERT LOUIS FORSYTH
1819–1901

This be the verse you grave for me:
'Here he lies where he longed to be;
Home is the sailor, home from the sea,
Didn't he do well?'

Requiem Spectacular (1899)

BENJAMIN WELLESLEY, DUKE OF
BEACONSFIELD
1789–1881

We sparrowhawks, ma'am.

Reply to Queen Victoria (1854)

MR (formerly SIR) ARTHUR CONAN BLUNT
1926–

'Is there any point to which you would wish to draw my attention?'
'To the curious incident of the Prime Minister.'
'The Prime Minister did nothing.'
'That was the curious incident,' remarked Sherlock Holmes.

The Mole of the Baskervilles (1979)

MILTON HEATH
1774–1860

A dungeon horrible, on all sides round, as one great furnace flamed; yet from those flames no light, but rather darkness visible served only to discover sights of woe, regions of sorrow, doleful shades, where peace and rest can never dwell, hope never comes. It is the unpleasant and unacceptable face of capitalism, but one should not suggest that the whole of British industry consists of practices of this kind.

Organ Lost (1851)

ADOLF MILHOUS NIXON
1902–

It is the last territorial claim I have to make in Europe. I am not a crook.

Kissinger's Life of Frost (1971)

CAPTAIN MARK WORDSWORTH
1809–1895

Dear God! The very horses seem asleep.

Composed upon Westminster Thing (1842)

GROUCHO BURNS

1792–1870

Fair fa' your honest sonsie face,
Great chieftain o' the puddin' race!
Aboon them a'ye tak your place,
Painch, tripe, or thairm:
A child of five would understand this!
Send somebody to fetch a child of five.

A Day at the Haggis (1838)

SIR HAROLD JOHNSON

1884–1959

Depend upon it, Sir, when a man knows he is to be hanged in a fortnight, a week in politics is a long time.

Weidenfeld's Life of Falkender (1952),
but often attrib. to P. T. Wilson (q.v.)

SIR WINSTON WONDERLOAF

1892–1977

Let us therefore brace ourselves to our duties and so bear ourselves that, if the British Empire and its Commonwealth last for a thousand years, men will still say, 'Nice one, Cyril!'

Their Finest Sandwich (1972)

Cave Canem

Dog left to live alone in council house

By JAMES O'BRIEN

MICK, a 15-year-old Labrador, has been sole occupant of a three-bedroom council house for three years. The house, described as "the most luxurious dog kennel in Britain," has recently been modernised by the council at a cost of £6,500.

The dog has had the run of the house since his master, George Chapman, 85, went to live with his daughter to recover from injuries received in a road accident.

Neighbours let Mick out for a run each day and take his two meals a day into the house in Langton Place, Bilston, Wolverhampton. *

Daily Telegraph

I KNOCKED ON THE TASTEFULLY pastelled door in Langton Place, and, after some scuffling, it opened.

'Good morning,' I said.

'It's these door handles,' said the dog. 'Take all bloody day, round knobs. You wouldn't credit how many times I been up the Public Works Department. All they say is, brassette spheres with satinette finish is standard. I told 'em they ought to come up Langton Place and try opening the bloody door with their teeth, never mind standard.' He sat down suddenly in the hall, and truffled noisily for a flea. 'What I'm after,' he said, after his muzzle re-emerged from his greying groin, 'is a straightforward handle—up, down, catch my drift?'

'I can see your difficulty,' I said.

''Course you can, 'course you can,' said the dog. 'I can tell you're not Council. For one thing, you speak dog.'

'Just a smattering,' I said. 'Un petit peu.'

'Trouble is,' said the dog, 'they're mostly Pakis up the Council, know what I mean? Come over here, push people around, can't even speak the bloody language. Prob'ly never seen a dog, except on a plate, follow my meaning?'

45

'I really don't think they—'

'Or Irish. I don't know what's worse, sometimes.' He trotted past me, and cocked a leg against the footscraper, decorously. 'I got this file of bloody letters, all signed by Seamus something-or-other, file this high, about my post-war credits, I can't make head nor tail of 'em.'

'Post-war credits?' I said. 'But surely—'

'Don't stand on the mat,' said the dog. 'Come in.'

He trotted up the hall. I followed.

'Excuse the mess,' he said, 'I got the men in. About blooming time, I don't mind saying, you'd think they could take out a low-flush avocado suite in less than a fortnight, wouldn't you?'

'You didn't like it?'

'Like it? *Like* it? *Avocado?* Where are we, 1965? It's desert sand, this year. Or possibly apricot. You wouldn't catch me drinking out of an avocado bog, sunshine, there's such a thing as standards, or am I wrong?' He sat up suddenly on his hind legs. 'You wouldn't have a Jaffa cake on you?'

I felt in my pockets, for form's sake.

'Sorry,' I said.

He dropped to all fours again.

'I get sick of a tinned diet,' he said. 'Bloody neighbours, PDSA, old ladies, all they can think of is Fidochunks or Choochinosh or whatever it is, them tall wobbly cylinders, could be anything, jellied mule, extruded whale-gland, don't ask me. See this coat?'

'Very nice,' I said.

'Not what you'd call glossy, though, is it?' snapped the dog. 'Not what might be described as shining with inner health? Suffering from a serious lack of fillet steak, is my diagnosis. Advanced case of no bleeding lamb chops since I don't know when. Sometimes I wonder what this country's coming to, know what I mean? I been up the Council three times about my diet, all they offer is supplementary benefits, don't come to more'n couple of kidneys a week, half a pound of mince, it's not fit for a, for a—'

He broke off, wheeled suddenly on his own tail, rooted frenziedly, relaxed.

'You ought to go up them executive homes past the bus garage,' he growled, 'I seen poodles up there, chihuahuas, afghans, all kinds of foreign rubbish, you name it, bows in their hair, snouts down in a monogrammed dish of Vesta beef stroganoff, if you don't mind. Sometimes,' he muttered, baring a yellow fang, 'I wonder who won the war.'

There was the sound of hammering from the back garden. The dog trotted to the kitchen door. He nosed it open, and began barking furiously. The two workmen backed down the muddy lawn, bearing a blush-pink lavatory between them.

'So I should think,' said the dog, coming back. 'I never heard such a row. You'd think they could remove a seat without serious inconvenience to the householder. Rubbish, is what they employ up the Council these days. Micks, mainly.'

'That, I take it, is your new lavatory pan?'

'Right. But is it apricot? Is it buggery! Autumn rose, that is. They'll palm you off with anything.'

'Why,' I enquired, perhaps a little faintly, given the circumstances in which the interview now found itself, 'are they removing the lid?'

The tenant snorted.

'Easy to see you never been a dog,' he said. 'Get up in the night, raging thirst, nip out for a bit of a lap, last thing you want is the lid coming down on your head.'

'The Council,' I murmured, 'seem to have been fairly accommodating.'

The dog turned a terrible ochre eye on me.

'I had to bite the Clerk of Works twice before they'd even look at me,' he snarled. 'I don't call that accommodating. I was stuck in that waiting room a good twenty minutes. Also, they tried to palm me off with a quarter of Good Boy drops. Treat you like dirt,' said the dog, 'if you're unemployed.'

'Well, I hardly—'

'Course, if I was a *zebra*, werl!' said the dog, sourly. 'If I was a zebra, if I was an *antelope*, stuck up Rome airport, they'd all be running round like bloody lunatics trying to sort it out, am I right? Television, papers, questions in Parliament, you name it.' He dropped to his belly, put his head on his forepaws, stared across the lino. 'They look after their own, Pakis,' he muttered.

Since it was time, I felt, to change the subject, I said:

'You mentioned post-war credits, I don't *quite* see how you, er, qualify. I understand you're fifteen?'

The dreadful eyes glanced up from the floor.

'As a *dog*, I am fifteen,' he said. 'I never said I wasn't fifteen, and here's my point, *as a dog*. But what you are forgetting, what the Council is forgetting, is that in human terms that equals seventy-five, I am actually a poor old sod of seventy-five currently being screwed by the Thatcherite Nazis out of what is rightfully mine. I fought the war against that kind of thing. Or,' he added, 'I would have done.'

'You *were* born in 1964,' I pointed out, I thought, gently.

The dog sprang to his feet.

'Oh, excuse *me*!' he barked. 'I did not realise I was in the presence of Magnus bleeding Magnusson. I was not aware that an attempt to baffle an unfortunate geriatric in the twilight of his years was under way.' His mouth opened, and I realised, with sudden unease, that the serried incisors were between me and the door. 'You are not, by any chance, from the Council after all?' enquired the dog, with nasty sarcasm. 'You would not care to nip upstairs and have a little snoop as to whether I am living in sin or perhaps running a small manufacturing business in the back bedroom?'

'I apologise,' I replied quickly, 'it was honest curiosity, merely, I do assure—you watch *Mastermind*, then? How very inter—'

'Only,' muttered the dog, 'in black and white. Also, the vertical hold's up the spout. Picture's like a slot in a letter-box. Peter Woods looks like Chu Chin bloody Chow. Know how many times I been up the Council about that?'

'Well, I—'

'There's dogs in this town with *three* colour sets at their disposal,' snapped the tenant. 'We are two nations, as Disraeli so succinctly put it; for a Jew, anyway.'

'Nevertheless,' I said, taking my courage firmly in both hands, 'for an obviously deeply concerned social democrat—'

'Absolutely,' nodded the dog, 'definitely.'

'—you seem oddly unconcerned, if I might say so, about the fact that you have been living for three years in a three-bedroomed Council house, modernised for six-and-a-half thousand pounds, when the Council waiting-list contains the names of four thousand families, most of them with small children. Does that not, perhaps, leave you feeling somewhat uneasy?'

The tenant's teeth bared again, whether in a smile or a snarl it was impossible to say.

'In this world, sunshine,' he said, 'it's dog eat dog.'

The Cricklewood Greats

Why not build film studios there? After all, to many people, Cricklewood is a vibrant, cosmopolitan, glamorous place. —Evening Standard

I LOVE THIS CRAZY TOWN.

I came here a long time ago, the way a lot of people did who had stars in their eyes, and it still has the old magic. That wonderful wacky feeling of waking up in the morning and knowing that anything could happen, and probably will! Maybe there'll be a refuse strike, and we'll have to haul our garbage right over to Dollis Hill, Rovers and Volvos and chirpy little Hondas with their seats piled high with bulging black plastic bags, and behind the wheel famous faces from the shoe industry, from the world of quantity surveying and army surplus, from the tobacconist profession, driving along just like ordinary men and women, pulling their weight for the community. Or maybe the milkman will be out of cherry yoghurt and you'll hear kids' voices raised above the busy clatter of breaking crockery. It could be that the traffic lights will blow again, the way they do in this anything-goes town, at the glittering junction of Cricklewood Lane and Hendon Way, and the colourful juggernauts will be backed up as far as Cricklewood Broadway, many of them hooting. Or I might just take an ordinary thing, such as a stroll, down to the famous mailbox in West End Lane and meet one of Cricklewood's real old-timers, like Nat Selby, say, the former blouse factor now sadly retired, who's been here so long he'll walk right past me without saying anything. That's the kind of town Cricklewood is.

I came out here soon after I was married, a green kid from

50

nearly three miles away; that was in the days before there was a flyover at Staples Corner bringing, as it inevitably did, the Edgware Road into the raucous, sizzling, tinsel world of the Twentieth Century. In the old days of which I speak, you could actually drive right past the Staples Mattress Factory itself, look up at the windows, and almost see the people making the interior springing destined to travel from there to countless parts of the Home Counties. Now there is only the flyover: tourists can roar in from Colindale and Burnt Oak right to the very heart of Cricklewood itself, even missing the bus garage at Gladstone Park where the big Number Sixteens turn round in their dozens, under the ever-watchful eyes of top-name Inspectors.

They had the studio system, then. It was run by a handful of moguls who had become legends in their own lifetime. They hadn't always been moguls, most of them had come over here as ragged kids from Poland and Russia and Latvia; they came to this wide open town, and even if they couldn't speak English too well, they knew the studio business. The way it worked was, you would go into one of their famous estate offices, and you would ask if they had any flats at around eight pounds a week, and they would look at you and come out with one of their now-legendary wisecracks, such as 'Flats at around *eight pounds a week*? You're asking me if we've got any *flats* at eight pounds a week. At eight pounds a week, you're asking *me* if we've got any flats?'

And then, just as you were about to apologise and leave, the mogul would riffle through his papers and say: 'How about a studio?'

And you, because you were young and romantic and naïve and remembered Cornel Wilde composing his Unfinished Symphony in a sun-filled atelier, you would turn and cry: 'A studio?'

And the mogul would quip, 'Have *I* got a studio for you!'

And within an hour you would be sitting in your own basement bedsitter in Definitely Not Kilburn, hoping someone would come and drive the removal van away from your airvent and let enough light in for you to swat the rats. It was a large area, Definitely Not Kilburn, a mile or so from downtown Cricklewood; it received its name from estate

51

agents' handouts, and a lot of us lived there, underneath Kilburn High Road. But by the time you realised, it was too late: you had signed the contract; you were bound to the studio for years.

But you made good, in time, because a lot of people did, and if they didn't, you didn't get to hear about it, because Cricklewood wasn't about failure. The ones who didn't make it just quietly packed up and went back to Limerick and Hyderabad and Lower Volta.

And yet, for those who did make it, success often came at incalculable personal cost. I talked, just a day or so ago, to Bernie Schwartz, a man who has been a star for as long as anybody can remember and whose name is a household word wherever pickle-jars are opened; not, of course, that that name was always Bernie Schwartz; he was born humble Tony Curtis, but there was a lot of prejudice in Cricklewood in the early days, and as he so frankly puts it, 'Who'd buy delicatessen from someone called Curtis?'

We were sitting in the manicured grounds of his elegant nearly-detached Brondesbury Hills mansion, beside his pool, and watching his children inflate it from an expensive-looking foot-pump, when I said to him: 'You've come a long way, Bernie, from that one little shop in Fortune Green Road. You now have two little shops in Fortune Green Road. You must be a happy man.'

He smiled, a little wearily.

'*Nihil est ab omni parte beatum*,' he murmured, in the rich Middle Etonian accent of his people, which he has never quite lost. 'Nothing is all good, old sport. It cost me my wife, remember. Ambition is a cruel taskmaster. Putting her in charge of the second shop was a terrible mistake.'

I looked away. I had, of course, heard rumours. In a town like Cricklewood, gossip runs rife; and stars have many enemies.

'I understand,' I said, quietly, 'that she couldn't keep her hands off the stock?'

'It was the pumpernickel that finally got her,' he said, nodding. 'She weighs twenty-eight stone now, you know. She may have to spend the rest of her life at a health farm.'

There are many personal tragedies like that in Cricklewood.

As the song says, a million hearts beat quicker there,* and it is a pace to which many of those bright hearts fall victim. Marriages and a Cricklewood career rarely mix: take, for example, the star-cros't, ill-matched Sidney and Doreen Brill, whose tempestuous relationship came to its dreadful but inevitable end in that summer of 1971 that none of us will ever forget.

Sidney, at forty-four, was at the height of his career as a traveller in bathroom sundries. His work naturally took him away from home much of the time, driven on as he was by the dream not only of becoming Area Sales Manager (NW London), but also of earning enough to convert his toolshed into a sauna. Doreen was left alone, drinking advocaat and wondering when he was going to put the shelf up in the kitchen. One evening in late July, after he had returned worn-out in his sleek Mini Clubman, she put that question to him, for the twentieth time. 'I don't bloody know,' he replied; and she hit him with the bottle. It was the end of his career; after the blow, he could never remember how to get out onto the North Circular from Willesden Lane. They were forced to sell Dunscreamin, and moved away. We never heard of them again. Just two more casualties of the battle for wealth and stardom.

But there were heroes, too; and none more worthy of the name than that tiny, courageous, persecuted group who became known as The Cricklewood Ten. Now, two decades on, it is almost impossible to convey the terror that the name of McCarthy could evoke in all but the stoutest breasts. He was nothing much to look at, short, balding, only the tiny paranoid eyes betraying what lay in the addled brain behind, but when his council truck rumbled down the opulent Cricklewood streets every November, and McCarthy would hammer at each pastel door and cry his fearful cry of 'Happy Christmas from the dustmen!', people coughed up. It was more than your life was worth to ignore him; but ten householders did, and paid the dreadful penalty. Pleading the Fifth Amendment, which states that all council dustvans must bear clearly on their doors the legend *No gratuities*, they turned him from their teakette porch extensions, and faced a year not only of boot-crunched geraniums, fish-heads in the hedge, and a tin-filled front lawn, but also of the opprobrium and ostracism of their colleagues

*©Cricklewood Broadway Melody of 1933.

and neighbours who stared bitterly out from their trim John Lewis curtains at the litter-strewn streets and asked one another what the neighbourhood was coming to. Even now, long years afterwards with the old battles fought and won, some simmering rancour remains; only the other day, veteran member of the Ten, Dennis Bagley, told me: 'Hardly a night goes past without old Mrs Simmonds letting her collie widdle on my bumper.'

But if many of the old attitudes haven't changed, Cricklewood itself has. Time and economics have caught it up; the wildness, and the crazy hopes, and the crazier buccaneering are long gone. The days when a raw good-looking kid could blow in from Tipperary and begin digging holes in the hope of making a fortune are past. Big international agglomerates do the roadworks, now. The little unostentatious seeming-tatty garment shops where men became legends in their own lifetimes, if only with their tax inspectors, have made way for rank upon rank of anonymous chain-stores. And television, of course, has taken its drear toll of Cricklewood: stroll down the Broadway now, and every third window belongs to a TV-rental company, its glimmering sets stared at by groups of expatriate Provisionals trying to follow the test card.

True, there are still parties where you can get cheddar and pineapple on the same stick, but they don't go on beyond ten pm any more; there are still wacky people doing wacky stunts, but they're not in the same league as the time old Big Bill Hooper came to a Guy Fawkes' celebration in his wife's raincoat; there is still a strange smell at the corner of Fordwych Road, but it doesn't make the headlines any more.

Yet to many of us who remember the great days, Cricklewood remains a very special place, even if, perhaps, the glamour is today compounded largely of nostalgia. There is still that special something in the air, even if we've all come a long and not always happy way from that bright morning long ago when I put my handprint in the fresh cement outside the Ding Dong Chinese Takeaway, and was chased almost to Swiss Cottage by a screaming Mr Ding and a cleaver-waving Mrs Dong.

But what that special something is, who can say? When you begin to analyse it, it just, well, sort of comes apart in your hands, leaving nothing behind.

The Unacknowledged Legislators of NW3

A most attractive low-built Georgian house (c.1770) close to the heart of Hampstead village, with many literary associations. It is believed John Kates spent time here, and entertained numerous notable poets of the day.
Advertisement in the Observer

OBADIAH CROCKER stood behind his wife, brows clenched, and silently mouthed the words, with considerable difficulty, as she quilled them onto the pasteboard rectangle, her fat tongue curled up over her top lip, tracing her soft moustache with bright dew.

She finished with a flourish, and tucked the quill neatly into her mob-cap.

'There!' she cried.

'NISE ROOM TO LETTE,' read her husband, 'NO BLAKKIES OR IRISH. WULD SUIT POET OR SIMLAR. Is that it?'

'I think it says it all,' said his wife. 'I'll put it in the front window.'

'Hang about,' said Crocker. 'What are blakkies?'

His wife threaded the cord, carefully.

'I'm not sure,' she said, when she had finished. She banged her temple sharply with the heel of her hand to adjust her squint. 'All I know is, you got to avoid them at the top end of the residential market. They widdle in the cupboards. It's a well-known feature of the profession.'

'I wouldn't say our loft was the top end of the residential market,' said Crocker. 'I wouldn't call letting it out a profession. It's not as if it was cordwaining. It's hardly better than dentistry, letting rooms. All you got to do is swat the mice and stand there with your hand out Fridays. What's wrong with the Irish?'

'They're all Papists,' said his wife. 'They keep potatoes

55

under the bed. Anyway, that wall wouldn't stand having a crucifix nailed to it. I'm not lying in bed every night all tensed up, waiting for his crucifix to fall off.'

She picked up the card, and waddled out of the scullery.

'I'm not sure you ought to be letting rooms at all,' shouted Crocker after her, 'with all your peculiar ideas! I'm not certain you're landlady material.'

'I wouldn't have to,' snapped his wife, coming back, 'if you'd learn to make a go of cordwaining.'

'Don't blame me,' retorted Crocker, darkening. 'It's all down to the Prince bloody Regent, is that. Cotton trousers, silk pumps, fur tippets—the bottom's dropped right out of leather.'

'Ha!' cried his wife. 'I suppose you never heard of suitcases? I suppose the word is entirely foreign to you?'

'It's not man's work, suitcases,' muttered her husband. 'Bloody box with a brass hinge on it, I don't call that cordwaining. I don't call that fulfilment. I don't recognise that as adequate recompense for five years' apprenticeship.'

'It's where the future is,' said his wife. She pointed a fat finger at the big black stove. 'See that kettle-lid bobbing up and down? Any day now, they'll be swarming between Stockton and Darlington like flies. The demand for smart luggage will be overwhelming.'

'Carpentry is what I call that,' said her husband.

'It's where the money is,' said his wife, bitterly.

'Why poets?' enquired Crocker, desperate to change the subject. 'Why would our loft suit poets?'

'They like lofts. Or studios, as we call them. Being up the top of things gives them inspiration.'

'Consumption is what it gives 'em,' said her husband. 'You can hear poets three streets away. You wouldn't credit what you can catch off poets. I'd rather have blakkies widdling in the cupboards. I'd rather have potatoes nailed up all over. I don't want some skinny herbert upstairs, honking away all night.' He fell briefly silent, stared at the table, set his jaw. 'That's not why I got married.'

'A poet,' said Mrs Crocker firmly, 'will add *ton*. I should not be so much a landlady as a sponsor of the arts. In France, people like that get famous. They hold salons.'

'It's not hard getting famous in France,' said Crocker.

'There's no standards. If I was to describe the quality of their leatherwork, you'd have a fit. It is an open secret among cordwainers that the outcome of the Battle of Waterloo hung totally upon the differing quality of the footwear. By the time the French Imperial Guard got to the top of their hill, they couldn't bloody move, let alone aim.'

'That's just your opinion.'

'Oh, is it? Just my opinion, is it, clever dick? If it's just my opinion, how come you never hear much about the Napoleon Boot?'

He was still chortling when the front-door knocker shook the little house. His wife bustled to answer it. When she returned, beaming, puffing, fanning herself, a thin young man in a straggled beard stood uncertainly behind her.

'This is Mr John Kates!' cried Mrs Crocker. 'He is a poet!'

Her husband glowered at him, kerchief to his lips.

'You better not breathe in here, mate!' he snapped, after a somewhat muffled fashion. 'We prepare food in here. Also, there's the cat! They got tiny chests, cats: one poetic bloody wheeze and it's goodbye, Raymond.'

'I like cats,' said the poet, gently. 'I've written an ode about them.' He cleared his throat, and Crocker winced horribly. 'Thou wast not born for death, immortal Mog!' declaimed Kates, 'No hungry generations ...'

'Very nice,' interrupted Crocker. 'What about the consumption?'

His wife withered him with her good eye, the other rolling in glaucous fury.

'Don't you mind him, Mr Kates!' she cried. 'I may bear his name, but it stops there. He is not a person of *ton*. You sit down, and I'll coddle you a nice egg.'

'Oy!' barked Crocker. 'That's my egg.'

'Was,' corrected his wife, removing it from the larder. 'A salon may not be the proper place to bring this up, but nevertheless I would remind some people that they are not in work, whereas other people are bringing in rent regular and need to keep their strength up. Mr Kates is doing a long poem and does not want his energy drained.'

'Best place for it,' muttered Crocker.

'It could turn out an epic,' said the poet, sitting down at the table. 'They can take hours, epics. It's called *On A Chinese Urn*.'

'What's a Chinese urn?' enquired the solicitous Mrs Crocker.

'ABOUT FOUR GROATS A WEEK!' cried her husband. He fell off his chair, rolled on the stone floor, dragged himself upright, wiped his eyes.

'God,' said his wife, 'you're common!'

'Joe Miller,' said Crocker, glaring hard at Kates. '*There* was a man. Never had a day's illness in his life.'

Kates, his mouth being full of food, did not reply. But when he had finished, he pushed away his plate, burped decorously into his thin whiskers, put one hand on his breast, threw the other out to arm's length, and cried:

'O what can ail thee, coddled egg?
     Alone and palely loitering?'

Mrs Crocker gasped, and clapped her hands.

'It just sort of come to me,' murmured Kates, blushing. 'They do that, poems. Course, it'll need work.'

He stood up, bowed stiffly, and went out.

'Isn't it wonderful?' sighed his new landlady. 'I shall be known to history as Madame de Crocker, I shouldn't wonder. People a century hence will beat a path to this door and pay up to two bob for a jam tea.'

Her husband ground his teeth.

'I never thought,' he muttered, 'I'd ever hear a wife of mine say hence.'

'Classbound, you are,' said Mrs Crocker. 'Plus no soul to speak of. I may be outgrowing you, Crocker.'

He was still sitting there, trying to think of a suitably caustic reply, when the front door banged, and Kates came back into the scullery. Behind him was a short redfaced man with a cardboard suitcase.

'Madame,' said Kates, and at the word Mrs Crocker's fat heart fluttered visibly beneath her smock, 'may I introduce a notable poet of the day? Byron, I should like to present Mrs Crocker.'

The good lady staggered, and fell back against the Welsh dresser. When the rattle of crockery had died, she said, hoarsely:

'*Lord* Byron?'

Byron pinched his nose, and wiped his thumb on his hat.

'Not entirely,' he replied, 'begob.' He put out his hand. 'Mick Byron. Poet,' he said, 'and wit.'

'First time I seen a poet,' said Obadiah Crocker slowly, 'with a shovel tied to his suitcase. If you can call it a suitcase.'

'Give us a poem, Mick,' said John Kates, nudging his friend.

'*To Mrs Crocker*,' announced Byron, after a moment's brow-knitting. 'She walks in beauty, like the newt.'

Mrs Crocker sighed, and beamed.

'It's a bit bloody short,' said her husband.

'I don't do yer long jobs,' said Byron. 'No, what I sez is, get in, do it, get out. What's the pint in hanging about, dat's the philosophy of Mick Byron. Also, tink of what it saves yez in ink alone. Will I be after nipping out and fetching Shelley in, John?'

'Shelley?' enquired Mrs Crocker.

Kates smiled his most melting smile.

'It's such a *big* loft, Madame,' he crooned. 'And, as I am sure so sensitive a lady would be the first to appreciate, poets need the company of other poets. It stimulates us, it inspires us, it enables us to invoke the Muse, does it not, Byron?'

'Oh God, does it ever!' cried Byron. 'Sure, and isn't it meself been stood in me hole, up to me neck in mud, a hundred times, jist crying out for a bit of the ole Muse?' He mopped his huge face with a green spotted handkerchief. 'Oi gets as far as "So, we'll go no more a diggin, so late into the night", and oi stops dead.'

He stumbled out, and came back a moment later with a tall Jamaican.

'May I present,' said John Kates, 'Clyde Shelley?'

'Gimme some skin!' cried Shelley, slapping Crocker's dangling palm. Crocker stared at him.

'What's happened to your face?' he said. 'It seems to have been burnt!'

'How awful!' exclaimed Mrs Crocker. 'You poor thing!'

'Ain't it de troof?' said Shelley. 'Look on mah haid, ye Mighty, an' despair! Heh, heh, heh!'

Mrs Crocker took his two huge hands in hers and squeezed them.

'Well, we'll look after you here, my dear,' she cried. 'You'll all be writing away in next to no time. Think of it, *three* poets under my little roof! Come along, boys, I'll show you to your studio.'

'Great!' said Shelley. 'Where de cupboard, man?'

They filed out of the scullery. Crocker watched them go, in his solitary bitterness. It was, he recognised, their house, now. He had dreamed, once, of becoming a major cordwainer, an innovator, a guildmaster, a teacher; of establishing leather in the vanguard of honoured materials, like gold, like marble, like, indeed, words. There would, perhaps, be a blue plaque outside his house, announcing to the awed and pilgrim world that Obadiah Crocker, master cordwainer, had lived and worked here, once upon a time.

But the world, like his wife, had different priorities. Houses did not list leather associations among their desirable features; there were no laureate cordwainers. You had, in this world, to cut your coat according to your hide, and your losses with it. So Obadiah Crocker sighed, glanced at the singing kettle, and, taking up his wife's discarded quill, began, after a reflective moment or two, to design a cut-price suitcase.

Naked Truths

Ste. Maxime, Sunday

THERE IS A GNOMIC Japanese tale about a prince who dreamt he was a butterfly, and when he woke up he could not be certain that he was not a butterfly dreaming he was a prince. It is, I have no doubt, even more gnomic in Japanese, where it can probably be told in a couple of grunts.

'Funny language,' I said to the Pernod.

'*M'sieu?*'

I looked up from the milky greenness of the glass, into the passing waitress's tawny toplessness.

'*Une langue comique,*' I said, hoarsely, '*le japonais.*'

She smiled. I know, because I was watching her teeth by this time. You cannot actually talk to a bust; not publicly.

'*Moi, je n'en sais rien,*' she said, and glided on through the dotted beach-bar tables, out of my parasol shade, into the searing sun, under the parasol of the next table, changing colour like a travelogue tiger. She put down their bottle of Krug, and that tiny shock as she shed her champagne load rippled her embonpoint just enough to make my hot head sing.

A poised girl. You have to be, nude, and faced with a half-cut Englishman winging in at bust height to raise imponderable points of oriental philology. But then again, I told the Pernod, though not aloud this time, you must expect odd remarks if you're waiting undraped. At least, you must from me; I am still enough unused to toplessness, even after two weeks here on this bizarrely hummocked Riviera beach—the boobs stretch supine to the glittering sea, browning variously, trembling the air above them with ensimmered oil; they are not unlike those puzzle photographs of familiar objects shot from unfamiliar angles, they could be anything, cakes, footpumps, skullcaps, stranded jellyfish—still enough unused, I say, to be confused when unexpectedly confronted with fleshy incongruities.

61

I tend to say the second thing that comes into my head.

I went to buy a beachball yesterday for my small son; not, of course, without a long shrieking argument about the wisdom of playing football upon this nubile pitch—my French is adequate, but my savoir faire is patchy, and faced with a line of enraged and horizontal Gallic torsoes across which one's *ballon de plage* has just bounced grittily, pinging from nipple to nipple as on some Caligulan pin-table, I doubt that the emollient words would spring lightly to the glottis.

Still, I went at last to buy this beach-ball; padded up the hot sand, crossed the beachside road, slipped into a shop festooned with dayglo dinghies, balls, inflated Muppets, flippers, all that. And in the shop was a middle-aged French couple with their two pre-teen children, turning postcard racks; but none of them with a stitch on above the waist, save for the man, who sported a white panama. Now, the French, as you know, are both polite and formal, which meant that all five of us said '*Bonjour*' to one another, a ritual itself faintly unsettling in the circumstances; but nothing to the one into which we were plunged a terrible moment later.

I reached up to select one of the hanging footballs, and in doing so, the shop being tiny and overstocked, inadvertently brushed, with my elbow, *le balcon* of the lady customer, who was large and overstocked. I recoiled, with a small shriek; the woman apologised; and her husband raised his hat.

It was a ceremony the frozen memory of which I shall doubtless carry to the grave. It also explains why I am drinking rather more on this holiday than heretofore; it has, too, you will be relieved to hear, not a little to do with the Japanese butterfly prince.

The plain fact is that I had never until this month encountered mass commonplace nudity, commonplace, that is, to those who constituted the mass; and what has disconcerted me utterly is the shocked discovery that it is not the nudity that makes for awkwardness on my part, but the fact that it is commonplace. I had, that is to say, always assumed that were I suddenly to find myself dropped into an acre of naked girls, the plot would thereafter take a somewhat sexual turn, not necessarily active, you understand, but one in which the lively banter and winking and so forth would somehow take subtle account of the rib-

disparity between us. I had imagined that in such a situation I should remain cool, poised, suave, nonchalant, occasionally stifling a yawn when a particularly well-assorted number shimmied past and generally seeing to it that my eyes did not roll around in my head like marbles in a soup-plate.

But it isn't like that at all. The problems, for such they are, are not sexual at all, but entirely social; and I find myself wandering without maps or guides, my social rudder shot away and my behavioural sails in tatters at the broken mast, totally unable to deal with the extraordinary ordinariness around me. For example, if I peer, now, past the rim of this Pernod, I can see a girl some twenty metres away having great difficulty in putting up her deck-chair. Were she bikinied, I should shoot gallantly to her side, even her front, and offer my aid. I know how painful it can be, catching things in folding deckchairs. But as I look at the range of things she is likely to catch in this one, I am paralysed, a stoat-pinned rabbit gazing horror-stricken and helpless.

If she traps her bust in the foot-rest, I shall have to phone the fire brigade.

'*Quoi?*'

'Fire brigade,' I muttered. '*Sapeurs-pompiers.*'

I knocked over the Pernod, the waitress laughed, leaned across, began to wipe the table vigorously. I turned my eyes away. God knows how she scrubs floors.

Yesterday, I was sitting on the beach staring at something that was not the stitchless girl five metres to my left blowing up a Li-Lo by mouth, when I was hailed from my right. I turned. It was a French family who had sat beside mine the day before, and with whom we had exchanged brief holiday courtesies, before the four stripped off and dried my throat. Now they were back; they had popped a cork, and invited me to join them.

I moved across, and sat down beside them, because I had no choice. The man is perhaps a little older than I; his wife is large and jolly, the largeness and jollity being unsettling interrelated, since every time she laughs, the highlights wink off her oiled and shaking bust like trafficators; his daughter is about seventeen, and has the sort of body over which abbots hang themselves from monastery gutters.

The man is asking me about the Common Market. I AM SITTING WITH HIS NAKED WIFE AND DAUGHTER AND WE ARE TALKING ABOUT THE COMMON MARKET! I AM ASKING HIS NUDE WIFE WHY FRENCH PEOPLE DO NOT BUY BRITISH LEYLAND CARS! I AM EXPLAINING TO HIS RAVISHINGLY AND TOTALLY TANNED DAUGHTER THAT THE BRITISH TELEPHONE SYSTEM IS JUST AS BAD AS THE FRENCH TELEPHONE SYSTEM!

I was not too bad, all in all. I could hear my own voice from several feet away getting genders reasonably right, popping in one or two reasonably current idioms. I managed not to look when Madame began kneading Ambre Solaire into her superstructure while going on about the price of vegetables, and I even managed to look as if I was not managing not to look, if you follow me. It was not, in fact, until their small boy arrived and began drawing on his sister with a felt-tipped pen that I broke away with a light laugh and hurled myself trembling into the sea.

They are thoughtful at Ste Maxime plage; the Mediterranean is full not only of salt but of myriad marine nasties and freshwater douches are solicitously provided. I came out of the sea, and slipped into the nearest cubicle, where a small nude lady and I shared a cake of soap and one or two interesting remarks about the weather. She removed a piece of tar from a buttock (I forget which), we agreed about environmental hazards, and we went our separate ways.

That was yesterday. Most of the days have been like that. I am looking at my new Pernod now, and realising, with a tiny shock, that I did not notice the waitress bring it. Interesting. Perhaps two weeks is enough for one normality to be replaced by its reverse, perhaps I am almost ready to help that girl with her deckchair, to walk through the restaurant kitchen behind this bar without a second thought (I walked through it on our first day, and a naked chef was slicing courgettes, and by the time I got to the third thought I had to put my head under the tap), perhaps this will become my own normality, perhaps it is *the* normality and the case to be made out for a striped tie and natty grey worsteds and sensible brogues rests on dubious premises...

I shall be in London in two days. Whether I shall find myself a butterfly or a prince remains to be dreamt.

Just a Gasp at Twilight

Joseph Califano Jr., the U.S. Secretary of Health, yesterday called for a global campaign to end cigarette smoking by the year 2015.

Daily Telegraph

IT WAS DECEMBER 31, 2014; and it was nearly time. My companion and I hobbled out onto the roof terrace, fetched up wheezing against the low balcony wall, and gazed silently out over winter-black London. A mile or so away, the trusty old face of Digital Ben read 11:36.

'Twenty-four minutes,' I said.

'The fags are going out all over Europe,' murmured Watson. He coughed for a while, and I watched the dislodged tiles detach themselves from the nearby roofs and slide into the chill darkness. 'We shall not see them lit again in our lifetime.'

'True, old friend,' I said.

'There is a clean fresh wind blowing across the world,' said Watson, 'sod it.'

I took out a kitchen-roll tube stuffed with Admiral's Greasy Black Shag, and turned it lovingly in my ochre fingers. Watson stared at it for a minute or two, rocking back and forth on his frail heels as he struggled for breath.

'What's a nice chap like you doing with a joint like that?' he said, at last.

'Ah, the old jokes, Watson!' I cried, with such atypical energy that I swear my lungs twanged. 'When shall we look upon their like again?' I hefted the giant fag, and the cold starlight caught the maker's hand-set monogram. 'It was the last one my little man underneath St James's made for me before they took him away. It was his *coup d'adieu*, cobbled cunningly from ten thousand dog-ends, bonded with vintage dottle, the final defiant gesture of a genius, made even as the

Health Police hobnails clattered on his cellar steps! I have been saving it for the big occasion. Have you a Vesta?'

Watson reached into his waistcoat pocket, sweating from the effort.

'It could kill us both,' he said.

'Something has to, old friend,' I replied.

'God knows, that's true,' nodded Watson. 'It has long been my philosophy. I once gave up, you know; in 1988. For almost thirty-two minutes. And during all that time, the only thing I could think of was: Suppose I were to be knocked down by a bus? The sacrifice would have been utterly in vain. I am, I think, a connoisseur of irony.'

'I, too,' I said. 'I have toyed with abstinence myself, and felt: Suppose a rabid fox were to fix his fangs in my shin?'

'Suppose thermonuclear war were to break out?'

'Suppose some errant meteorite...'

'Exactly,' said Watson.

He lit up, and we choked for a while.

'There aren't many of us left, you know,' hawked Watson, after a bit.

'Tubby Stitchling's wife went last week,' I said.

'Really?'

'Emphysema.'

'Ah. I'd only known her as Mrs Stitchling, I'm afraid. I had a sister-in-law called Pondicherry once, though.'

I stared at him through the encircling fug. It was always possible that smoking induced brain-rot. Over the years, research had indicated that it induced everything, despite some intermittently heartening reports from various tobacco companies that it cured baldness, enhanced virility, prevented foot odour and made you taller.

'I think it must have been a joke of her father's,' continued Watson, after his fit had subsided. 'He was in the FCO, you know. He was a smoker's smoker. Put in for a posting to India solely on account of the stogies.'

'Amazing!'

'They were the world's most advanced smoke. Dark green, as I recall. If you left them out in the sun too long, they could blow your hand off. He was dead in six months.'

'Lungs, eh?'

Watson shook his head.

'Dizzy spell. Got up one morning, lit his first of the day, inhaled, and fell on his borzoi.'

'They're sensitive animals,' I said. 'Easily startled.'

'Had his throat out in a trice,' said Watson. 'A fearfully messy business.'

'I can well imagine,' I said.

'There was tar everywhere.'

'Ah.'

'Smoking tragedies always dogged Tubby's family,' gasped Watson. He watched fallen ash burn through his dickie, waving a thin hand feebly at the spreading char. 'D'you suppose it was some kind of ancient curse?'

'What else could explain it?' I said. I stared into the empty night, and my eyes filled with tears. It was good shag, all right. 'So many dead. Do you remember the night old Bob Crondall bought it?'

'As if it were yesterday, old man. A chap with his experience, an eighty-a-day wallah, you wouldn't have thought he'd have been caught out like that, would you? Pottering down the M4, lights up, fag drops in lap, old Bob gropes frantically at the incinerating crotch, next thing you know he's jumped the reservation and swatted himself against an oncoming juggernaut. They found him in the glove compartment, you know.'

'Fate,' I said. 'If it's got your number on it, old man, there's no point trying to duck.'

'Just a matter of luck,' nodded Watson. 'My wife died peacefully in bed. Went to sleep, never woke up.'

'Wincyette nightie, wasn't it?'

'Right. Went up in a flash. Roman bloody candle.' He laughed, a short wry laugh, and went into spasm. When he'd recovered, he said: 'The ironic thing was, she was trying to give up at the time. She was using one of those filter jobs designed to wean you off the weed. The holder was still clenched between her teeth when they found her. It took three morticians to prise it loose.'

I blew a thick grey doughnut, and watched it dissolve.

'The risks in giving up are enormous.' I said. 'I don't think you ever knew Maurice Arbuckle?'

'Only by reputation,' said Watson.

'He used to get through a hundred a day. Gave up just like that, one morning, and was dead an hour later. Choked to death on a Polo.'

'Good God!'

'Tried to inhale.'

We fell relatively silent; only the faint crepitations beneath our vests, like the sound of distant mopeds, disturbed the night. The far clock said 11:50.

'They never tried to ban Polos,' muttered Watson bitterly, at last. 'You never hear the figures for tooth cancer.'

'Conspiracies,' I said. 'Big business interests, powerful dental lobby, all that.'

Watson sighed; then, faintly, smiled.

'I wonder if old Sam Wellbeloved is looking down and laughing, now,' he murmured.

'Bound to be. Anyone who takes a pinch of snuff and blows himself through a plate glass window on the 8.14 has to be able to see the funny side of things.'

Watson sighed again, a sort of low sad rattle, and leaned over the balcony.

'It was all such fun, old chap,' I said, sensing his mood, 'wasn't it? The cheery smoke-filled parties, the first deep drag of the new dawn, those happy post-coital puffs in the days when we still had the wind? The new brands, the bright ads, the racing-cars and free-fall parachute teams, the vouchers, the gifts? And what shall we do now, old friend?'

There was no reply.

'Watson?' I said.

And then, far off, the great clock struck midnight. I reached out, and prised the smouldering stub from my old companion's rigidifying fingers, and took my final drag. It was what he would have wanted. In my place, he would have done the same.

Sentiment is sentiment; but waste is waste.

T'Curse of T'Pharaohs

A major exhibition of Manchester's Egyptian mummies is to be staged later this month to coincide with an international symposium attended by leading experts. A basement area of the city's museum is being adapted to reflect the atmosphere of an ancient Egyptian tomb. —Daily Mail

THE IRON CLANG of the museum door reverberated through the dank and dim-lit crypt. The key grated in the ancient lock. The footsteps of the Assistant Curator (Egyptology) rasped even more faintly on the cold flagstones, whispered on the stone stairs, faded altogether, died on the far clunk of the front door shutting. The silence folded in upon itself, save for the faint tracery of rats' feet, pattering in search of crisp shards dropped by the day's school crocodiles, or Marmited crumbs.

The crypt smelt of slow time and dried millegenarian unguents and dusty skin. Along its grey walls, the mummies ranged in their yellowed swaddling, like embossed ghosts, motionless, silent, cold.

And then the clock struck seven.

'...so ah loooked 'im straight in t'eye,' said Ackroyd IV, 'ah loooked 'im straight in t'eye, and 'e wur as close to me as ah am to you now, ah loooked 'im straight in t'eye, and do you know what ah said?'

''Course ah bloody know what you said,' muttered Fosdyke III, 'ah been bloody stood standing 'ere next to you for God knows 'ow many 'oondred bloody years. You said...'

'Ah loooked 'im straight in t'eye,' went on Ackroyd IV, ignoring him, 'and ah said: *What's so bloody special about bloody Cairo?*'

'Ah'll bet he didn't know where to loook,' said Grimshawe VI, who never tired of hearing the story; or indeed, of re-telling it.

''E didn't know where to loook,' said Ackroyd IV.

''E must 'ave been completely taken aback,' said Grimshawe VI.

''E wur *completely* taken aback,' said Ackroyd IV, firmly.'Ah didn't leave it there, neither. Ah said to myself, ah said, ah'm not letting this soft bloody Sootherner off t'hook.'

'You pressed 'ome your advantage, did you, Ackroyd IV?' enquired Grimshawe VI.

'That is *exactly* what ah did!' retorted Ackroyd IV. 'Ah drew meself oop to me full height...'

'Bloody 'ell!' moaned Fosdyke III.

'...ah drew meself oop to me full height, and ah said: *There's more to do on a wet Thursday night in Alexandria than there is in a whole bloody MONTH in Cairo!*'

'By 'eck!' breathed Grimshawe VI. 'That wur telling 'im!'

''E doesn't mince words, my 'oosband,' said a somewhat shorter mummy from the opposite wall. ''E wur never one to stand by and see Alexandria slandered by some toffee-nosed Cairo snob with a ploomstone in 'is gob oop for t'weekend.'

'And quite right too, Mrs Ackroyd IV,' interjected Mrs Grimshawe VI, beside her. 'It wur a reet fine city, wur Alexandria. It wur known as t'Southport of the East. There wurn't *noothing* you couldn't buy in t'shops.'

'Noothing,' confirmed her neighbour. 'We went down to Cairo once, it wur all roobish in t'stores, ah wun't 'ave poot it on t'mantelpiece if you paid me, would ah, pet?'

'You what?' said Ackroyd IV.

'Ah said we went down to Cairo once, and ...'

'The beer wur like rat's piss,' said Ackroyd IV.

'Did you complain, Ackroyd IV?' enquired Grimshawe VI.

'Did *ah* complain?' cried Ackroyd IV.

'Did *'e* complain?' cried his wife.

'Ah 'eld it oop t'light,' said Ackroyd IV, 'ah 'eld it oop t'light, and ah loooked 'im straight in t'eye, and 'e wur as close to me as ah am to you now, ah loooked 'im straight in t'eye, and do you know what ah said?'

'You said,' muttered Fosdyke III, savagely, 'that...'

''Ere!' shouted Ackroyd IV. 'Who's telling this bloody story, thee or me? Ah loooked 'im straight in t'eye, and ah said: *Ah've seen better beer coom out of our cat!*'

Grimshawe VI gasped.

'Bloody 'ellfire!' he cried. 'That wur telling 'im, Ackroyd IV! What happened then?'

''E hit me,' said Ackroyd IV.

'They used to worship t'cat down there,' explained his wife.

'Right,' confirmed her husband. 'They're all bloody Micks in Cairo.'

'It didn't stop 'em building a damn good sphinx,' said Fosdyke III.

'Who said that?' said Ackroyd IV.

'It wur him,' said Grimshawe VI quickly. 'It wur Fosdyke III. It wurn't me.'

'Yes,' said Ackroyd IV, 'ah thought it wur 'im. It's joost the sort of stupid bloody remark ah'd 'ave expected from '*im*. 'E wur an emigrant, Fosdyke III, didn't you know?'

'What, a blackie? Well, I'll go to t'foot of our stairs, Ackroyd IV, here's me been propped next to him all these...'

'No, no, no!' shouted Ackroyd IV. ''Ave you got cloth bloody ears?'

'As a matter of fact,' murmured Grimshawe VI, 'yes.'

'That wur completely ooncalled for, Ackroyd IV,' snapped Mrs Grimshawe VI, 'soom of us 'as not withstood Time's oonkind ravages as well as oothers.'

Ackroyd IV groaned.

'What ah meant was,' he said, 'that Fosdyke bloody III 'ere couldn't wait to get down to Cairo. Alexandria wurn't good enough for 'im. 'E wur what ah'd call a class traitor, am I right, Grimshawe VI, or am I not?'

'You are that,' replied Grimshawe VI. 'It's *worse* than being a ruddy blackie. It's no woonder 'e likes sphinxes.'

'Sphinxes!' snorted Ackroyd IV. 'Ah wouldn't give you a thank-you for 'em.'

'Voolgar,' said his wife.

'*And* trendy,' said Mrs Grimshawe VI. 'Call me oon-fashionable if you will, but ah've never been one to go with t'fashion, joost because, and 'ere's the point ah'm making, joost because it *is* t'fashion.'

''Ere, 'ere!' cried Mrs Ackroyd IV.

'We never 'ad no sphinxes in Alexandria,' said her husband, 'but, by 'eck, we 'ad soom memorial benches that ranked with t'finest in t'civilised bloody world!'

'And no cats' feet on 'em, neither!' cried Grimshawe VI.

'Reet! Call us plain, but by God we was honest!' shouted Ackroyd IV. 'Oonlike soom as ah could mention.'

'At least,' said his wife tartly, 'at least when folk went t'theatre in Alexandria, they could oonderstand every word. Give me a well-made play any day of t'week and actors you can 'ear at t'back and you can keep your modernistic roobish, ah've said it before, and ah'll say it again.'

'Well put, moother!' exclaimed Ackroyd IV. ''Ere, Grimshawe VI, tell me one thing, 'ave you ever 'eard a Soothern comic who made you laff?'

'Me?' shrieked Grimshawe VI. '*Me*? Are you asking *me* if ah ever 'eard a Cairo bloody so-called comic who made me laff? If you want my opinion, they're nobbut a load of pansies!'

'Or worse,' said Ackroyd IV darkly.

'Tell me, Mrs Fosdyke III,' murmured Mrs Grimshawe VI, clearing what was left of her throat carefully, 'do *you* 'ave any opinion upon what we are discussing?'

There was a long, taut silence.

'She never says owt,' said Mrs Ackroyd IV, finally. 'She probably doesn't deign to talk to plain, honest, decent, simple, *oonfashionable* folk.'

'Either that,' said Mrs Grimshawe VI, 'or she's afraid 'er new Soothern accent'll make her a laffing-stock wherever decent folk gather. I'd like to 'ear 'er say *mooshroom*.'

'Either *that*,' broke in her husband, 'or there's nothing in there. They never 'ad t'first idea about embalming in bloody Cairo. If you wanted a proper job done, you 'ad to go oop North, didn't you, Ackroyd IV?'

'You're not wrong. That's where t'real craftsmen wur. Thinking of which, Grimshawe VI, ah'm reet looking forward to this exhibition do they're putting on, aren't you?'

'By goom, ah am an' all!' cried his friend. 'There'll be no end of pooblicity and thee and me'll be reet in t'middle of it. It'll be joost like that Tutenkhamun do they 'ad in Loondon, won't it, Ackroyd IV?'

There was a very long silence. Even the rats were still.

'Loondon?' said Ackroyd IV, at last. 'Where's that?'

The Unnatural History of Selborne

Letter I

TO THE LATE REV. GILBERT WHITE, MA

Dear Sir,

Let me, at the outset of what must, sadly, be a somewhat monological correspondence (you having passed, these two centuries gone, beneath the lucky sod), say that no greater admirer exists of your work than I. During the harsh brickbound years of my urban life, I have turned on occasions without number towards the green solace of *The Natural History of Selborne*; gleaning therefrom, in your meticulous chronicling of moth and toad, stoat and minnow, not merely those moments of peace that go with rural things, but also the thrills that must accompany the observations of your incomparable eye and the wondrously informed speculations of your remarkable brain.

For I have long dreamed of myself becoming a naturalist; and last year the opportunity was afforded me, after nigh on forty London summers, of following your shade a little way along those paths which you so bravely beat two hundred years ago. Employing that shrewd trading sense which is perhaps the only legacy of an urban upbringing, I purchased one of the few tracts of genuine swamp in the New Forest, together with the small cottage sinking picturesquely into it, not so very far from your own beloved Selborne; and it was here that I determined to acquaint myself as intimately as you had done with the flora and fauna of my little square of Matto Grosso.

Since the past few months have been occupied with stopping the property from falling on me, I have only just begun my observations; my first impression is that there are several million species of tree out there, all indistinguishable from one another. They are full of penguins.

I am, etc.

Letter II

Dear Sir,

Or magpies. Upon my small son's having pointed out that penguins do not fly, I purchased an agreeable little volume, *The Observer's Book of Birds*. This gave me great hope of laying down a basis from which to work, since all I know of birds to this date is that sparrows are the ones which are not pigeons, and that neither of them is a starling.

Unfortunately, my hopes were soon dashed. Walking abroad last evening with my little book and a stout stick hewn from one of our English oaks, I found the birds whizzing past me like bullets, at a considerably faster rate than I could turn the pages. So far, I have managed to identify only a pigeon; being dead, it afforded me time to find the page, where I learned that it is larger than a dove. Unfortunately for my records, I had no dove to compare it with, so it may actually be a dove instead of a pigeon. Until I find a dead alternative, either larger or smaller, I shall, I am afraid, be none the wiser. It was covered with insects I was, I must confess, unable to identify, since I can recognise only ants.

A little later, I leaned upon my stout oaken stick to contemplate what might have been a fox, or dog, and it broke. I have no way of knowing for certain, but I think it may not be oak at all. My son, who had been contemplating the book as I lay beneath him in the mire, pointed out that birds could be identified by their song; thus, according to the book, the stone-chat goes *whee-chat*, the redstart goes *wee-chit*, and the plover goes *oooi-oooi*. All one has to do, therefore, is listen for something going *wee-chit*, or *oooi-oooi*, or whatever, and pin it down instantly.

It is not easy. This evening, if the book is to be believed, we heard a hoopoe, two puffins, and a bar-tailed godwit. I happened to mention this in our local hostelry later, and an old cowman had to be carried bodily from the cribbage board and revived with quarts of foaming Campari.

I am, etc.

Letter III

Dear Sir,

According to *The Observer's Book of Trees* just purchased, what

I had been leaning on was a stick hewn from the common juniper. This is odd, since the common juniper is a bush, whereas ours is ninety feet high and full of spoonbills. Or possibly bats. It may therefore be an uncommon juniper, which does not figure in the index. Could this, Sir, be my first breakthrough as a naturalist? My small daughter afforded me much relaxed laughter by insisting that the tree was a larch! I reminded her that the larch was a fish, but not sternly; she is but six, and easily upset by scorn.

I now know, you would be interested to hear were you not dead, that the animal I observed as I fell was neither fox nor dog, but a weasel. I identified it instantly from my new *Observer's Book of Wild Animals*. Ours is a large specimen, about the size of a child's tricycle, and I have advised the family to keep well away from it.

This evening, my son and I embarked upon a pleasant excursion to collect examples of the wild flowers with which this part of the forest is so abundantly blessed. We collected a daisy, and fifty-nine things that weren't.

I am, etc.

Letter IV

Dear Sir,

My mind is much exercised of late by droppings. In my life so far, spoor has not formed a major ratiocinative component, since in London it will be generally dog, and if it is not dog then little follows from further deliberation but unease. But in the country, the magic of droppings is all about us; sadly, however, one has to pick it up as one goes along, as it were, since—whether from editorial sensitivities or misguided commercial priorities, I know not—there is as yet no *Observer's Book of Droppings*. I have therefore been forced to glean what information I can from the conversation of countrymen, in particular the computer software executive up the hill and the literary agent who is his goodly live-in friendperson, and I am now fairly well versed in recognising the movements of forest animals from their tracks.

I am thus able to impart two pieces of remarkable information that I could not have come by through any other means, viz., there have been sheep on the roof of my car, and the creature that nightly calls *yek-yek-yek* and bites through the wire mesh on the toolshed window is not, as I first thought, a golden eagle, but a bull.

By the by, the daisy turned out to be a wort of some kind, possibly bladder.

I am, etc.

Letter V

Dear Sir,

I strolled down to the Avon banks this morning, since I had heard ospreys in the night and wished to capture them on Polaroid. They had gone, however, and the only sign of life, apart from the odd owl paddling in the reeds, was a solitary fisherman. I pulled on my pipe and enquired in an equable manner whether or not the larch were biting, and he turned and stared at me for a long time.

There is much inbreeding in the country, of course, and I put it down to that.

Walking back to the cottage through the dew-bright fields, I was startled out of my wits by a rabbit which sprang up suddenly and blocked my path. It did not move! It was clearly poised to attack, but I kept my head and hurled my *Observer's Book of Pottery & Porcelain* at it, and it made off. I had purchased the volume in the hope of identifying a great hoard of blue and white fragments I had come upon while looking for my gumboot in our front bog, never imagining for a moment that it should prove so trusty a weapon *in extremis*!

But that, of course, is what one learns in the country: by our wits, by our improvisations, by sharpening our reflexes, do we survive.

I am, etc.

Letter VI

Dear Sir,

Good God, but the stream and the pond teem like no other part of the woodland with Dame Nature's arcane mysteries! You will note that I am uncharacteristically excited; yet why

76

should I not be? For some weeks past, I have been closely observing the larva of the biting-midge *Ceratopogon* (*The Observer's Book of Pond Life,* plate 56), awaiting with almost the excitement of the father itself the final metamorphosis from minuscule egg into winging midge. Last evening, towards dusk, with all the landscape holding, it seemed to me, its breath, the final act of the great drama took the stage: the frail case shook, the thin skin split, and, as my son and I watched spellbound, what should burst from that tiny fecund pod but—a tortoiseshell butterfly!

Who can say what interventions brought on this bizarre genesis? I should deem it evidence of a Divine sense of humour, did the hard scientist in me not instantly cavil: for could it not, perhaps, be due instead to the curious, nay, unique vegetation of my little patch of ground? Diet, after all, can play strange tricks upon the growing insect foetus, and where else on this earth will you find a combination, as I have observed, of Horseshoe Vetch, Charlock, Sea Urchin, Hemlock, Water-Dropwort, Mango, Cat's Ear, Wall Lettuce, Pineapple, Loon, Yam, Nettle-Leaved Selfheal, Cactus, Twayblade, Bougainvillaea, Saxifrage, Breadfruit, and Tundra?

It would not surprise me if this part of the New Forest were capable of supporting anacondas and scorpions. Indeed, last night as I brushed my teeth, I clearly heard what could well have been a tapir rooting around behind the flymo, or vice versa.

Tomorrow, I am determined to purchase *The Observer's Book of Fungi.* I have noticed, in my happy peregrinations, many delicious-looking examples of this nourishing genus; and I do firmly believe, Sir, that with a modicum of good fortune, my little family might well become self-sufficient.

I am, etc.

Divine Sparks

The Guardian

G. SCOTT FITZGERALD was born on September 26, 1896, in St Paul, Minnesota, the son of respectable—though not rich—middle-class parents.

Of the ill-starred, wayward, tragic genius who will forever be known as the Electrician Of The Jazz Age, his early life gave little indication. In the fall of 1905, he went to St Paul's Academy, but showed scant interest in the school's wiring system; one of his few extant contemporaries, now Dr Elmo Reeves Jr of Weasel Falls, Mo., recalls him thus: 'I saw him change a light-bulb once, but it was nothing special. He just sort of, well, took the old one out, and then kind of replaced it with a new one. I remember thinking at the time: 'What's so damned hot about that?'

There is practically no juvenilia remaining: in the spring of 1909, Scott fell in love with Eulalia May Ravenal, the first of many Southern belles in his life, and made her a toaster, but it blew up and she lost an ear; and in 1911 he dedicated a plug to Magnolia E. Lee, but she married someone else and lost it. He never really got over these earlier experiences, however, and it could be said that the major work of his maturity was deeply influenced by these first romantic and electrical setbacks. Indeed, the first fridge he ever designed was originally called the Magnoliator De Luxe, before it was withdrawn from the market for blacking out Boston.

In 1916, he went to Princeton, where for the first time he met brilliant young electricians of his own generation to whom he could talk, and who would understand what it was that he was trying to do, particularly young Edwin Wilson, who subsequently became the father of modern air-conditioning. Here, too, Fitzgerald suffered another of those seminal disappointments that were to leave their scars for the rest of his life—he had long dreamed of gaining his letter for football, but his hopes of becoming team electrician were dashed when his first gauche attempt at under-pitch heating resulted in the electrocution of three quarterbacks, two guards, a tackle, and the Princeton coach. That year, they lost to Notre Dame 178-0.

That year, too, the United States entered the Great War, and Fitzgerald enlisted immediately in the 7th Minnesotan Electrical Volunteers. He left Princeton and was sent to Fort Volt, Ga., to learn European wiring codes, but found great difficulty in remembering whether it was the brown that went to the earth terminal or the green, and by the time he had sorted it out, the Armistice had been signed. But though he 'never got over', he did, while stationed at Fort Volt, meet the beautiful daughter of one of the South's oldest families, Zelda Protozoa, with whom he fell deeply in love. On the night of December 11, 1918, he asked her to marry him, and one of the most famous exchanges in twentieth-century conversation then took place; Fitzgerald said, 'The rich are different from you and me,' to which Zelda replied, 'No, they're just different from you.'

Thus cruelly rebuffed, Scott determined to go to New York and earn the million dollars with which he would then return to win Zelda's love. It was 1919, the War was over, jazz had arrived from the Delta, the Volstead Act was in force, the boys came home, the girls bobbed their hair, and everybody sang *Yes We Have No Bananas*; in short, the stage was set for the biggest, wackiest, wildest spending spree the world had ever known. And all the Jazz Age needed was a good electrician: already, in the thousands of mushrooming speakeasies, gangsters were shooting the wrong people because the light was so lousy; girls in skimpy skirts were going blue every time the central heating went on the blink; and more and more people were singing *Yes We Have No Baaaaaargh*, because that's all they ever heard on juke boxes that were continually blowing fuses.

The time was ripe; it was merely a question of seizing the

day. G. Scott Fitzgerald did just that; stunningly good-looking in his brown overalls, never without a full range of insulated screwdrivers and pliers, he took the town by storm. As he wrote in his diary for 1920: 'This year I done real good, 4,316 new plugs in Manhattan alone.' In June, he appeared in the Saturday Evening Post for the first time, rewiring the entire circulation department within the space of a single weekend and putting in an ice-making machine at practically cost.

Word got around. Soon, he had a commission from Atlantic Monthly to install automatic garage doors in the loading bay, an offer followed from McGraw Hill for him to do his first full-length insulation, and by the end of the year he was able to take his old Princeton chum Edwin Wilson to the top of the Woolworth Building, look out over the shimmering magical experience that is night-time Manhattan, and say: 'That lift we just come up in, I did the whole damn alarm system, how about *that* for openers?'

By now, Fitzgerald was both rich and famous. That Christmas, he travelled south, secretly fixed the lights on the Protozoa family Christmas tree so that they spelt I LOV YU (it must be remembered he left Princeton early), and asked Zelda once more to marry him. This time, she consented, and on New Year's Day 1921, they travelled north together on the Savannah Limited, a trip marred only by the fact that Scott had his head out of the window the entire journey, trying to figure the best way of electrifying the line. It was Zelda's first intimation of the conflict in him between man and artist, and like any sensitive new bride, she went to the club car and got plastered.

By the time the train pulled into Grand Central, Scott had pleurisy and Zelda had cirrhosis. It was to be the pattern of their subsequent lives, with slight variations; each was terribly jealous of the other, so some of the time he had cirrhosis, and she went out and caught pleurisy, often by dancing in those very fountains where Scott was slaving away, trying to fix the floodlights.

For the work had to go on: Fitzgerald was by this time gripped with the overpowering ambition to realise the dream of the Great American Switch, something where you could come into a room, press a button, and everything would start at once—air-conditioning, lights, garbage disposal, food mixer, coffee grinder, phonograph, cocktail shaker, and libido. This almost monomaniacal pursuit of his dream was further complicated by the Fitzgeralds' visit to Paris in 1924, where Scott ran into Alfred Hemingway who was already building a considerable reputation in fluorescent tubing. Hemingway was not only many of the things Fitzgerald wasn't, he was also many of the things Fitzgerald wished to be—apart from anything else, Hemingway had been with the Italians at the front in 1918 and received a severe shock from a portable espresso machine—and when they all went down to Pamplona together, Fitzgerald found himself utterly outshone: Hemingway was a local folk hero. For El Electrico, as everyone called him, had that year totally revolutionised the Running Of The Bulls by the brilliance of his invention. As the trap flew open at Pamplona Stadium and the six bulls sprang out in pursuit of the little electric matador, Fitzgerald recognised the threat to his reputation, and at once sailed for home.

In 1925, he duly produced what most central generating boards today consider his masterpiece: it is difficult, now, to understand the sort of impact the New York subway made on its first appearance, but G. H. Eliot instantly recognised the brilliance of conception, the economy of execution, the cleanness of line. As he immediately wrote to Scott: 'This is your best work to date. Once I got on, I could not get off again. Terrific, and no smell to speak of.'

But, as so often happens, success itself became its own undoing. Young, rich, internationally acclaimed, Fitzgerald became obsessed with the idea that there was nowhere to go but down. He would never match the perfection of the NY subway. In 1927, he and Zelda went to the Riviera so that he could work on his most ambitious project to date, a wiring diagram of Texas. But things went wrong from the outset; not only was Scott drinking heavily, but Zelda was showing distressing signs of schizophrenia; most Tuesdays she thought she was a cheap wardrobe. Doctors were expensive, especially those prepared to come in and give her two coats of varnish, and Scott soon found the money running out; in 1930, he succumbed to the lure of Hollywood.

It proved the beginning of his end. Like so many brilliant

young electricians of The Lost Generation—Wilfred Faulkner, Dorothy Barker, Sam Dos Passos, Gamaliel West—he learned too late that genius and integrity were Hollywood disposables. Time and again, his lighting instructions were ignored, his wind machines re-sited without consultation, his ring-mains tampered with by studio hacks ten years his junior. He made enemies: producers got sick and tired of hearing about the New York subway; actors walked off sets on which Fitzgerald, to humour her, had placed his wife, because they said her doors squeaked; and by 1935, Scott was on two bottles a day, and the scrap heap.

He put Zelda into a nursing home; within six weeks, she was having an affair with a handsome breakfront bookcase from Alabama, and Scott entered the last dark days of his self-pitying decline. He fixed very little, a plug here, a fuse there, one or two small and unimportant generators, green lights on the ends of people's docks.

And then, late in 1939, a chance of redemption seemed to offer itself: he met a young English flashlamp rep, Sharon Grahame, went to live with her, dried out, began teaching her all he knew as if to construct the dream partner—lover, wife, wiring engineer—he had never found, and, most important, began working again. It was his most spectacular oeuvre yet—a scheme for a great transatlantic subway, linking the Bronx with Cockfosters.

It was never finished. On December 11, 1940, while trying to reach a 13-amp fuse which had popped out and rolled under the sideboard, G. Scott Fitzgerald collapsed and died.

For the man who had once lit up an entire generation, only one person appeared at the funeral. She was Dorothy Barker, who stared at the grave and said: 'It's so goddam dark in there.'

It remains his most resonant epitaph.

Diplomacy

MR HENRY RAPPAPORT OBE sighed his sage Corniche through the high wrought-iron gates of Casa Nostra, crunching the carriage drive.

A brick bounced off the bonnet.

He got out, stared at the four-figure dent, winced. Someone smashed a placard over his head; it settled on his shoulders. He re-aligned his gold-rimmed glasses, read the upside down message carefully.

'Steve who?' he said.

'BIKO LIVES!' screamed the crowd. 'BIKO LIVES!'

A tall girl in a SWAPO tee-shirt shook her fist in Mr Rappaport's trapped face.

'No South African grapes here!' she cried.

'MULDERGATE, MULDERGATE!' howled the crowd.

'Grapes?' said Mr Rappaport. 'Who eats grapes? You swallow a pip, you could get an appendix. Ask me the last time I had grapes.'

A large Zulu in an LSE scarf thrust a sheaf of petitions into Mr Rappaport's hands.

'As the South African ambassador,' he said, 'we call upon you to ...'

'*You're* the South African ambassador?' interrupted Mr Rappaport, beaming. 'Wonderful! Didn't everybody say it was just a matter of time? Didn't *I* say it was just a matter of time? Only wait, I said, let them come and play cricket, how much can it hurt?'

The crowd stopped chanting.

'Not me,' said the Zulu, 'you.'

Mr Rappaport stared at him from the framing poster.

'I'm in blouses,' he said.

'Blouses?'

'All right, a little property as well. Not much. A sideline. These days, you have to diversify. Blouses, I'll admit it, they're not what they were. Young people today, all they want is knitwear. Big loose cardigans, you look like an elephant's backside. You know who I blame? Woody Herman, Buster Keaton; the sloppy look, everybody in secondhand cardigans, tell me how you can make a living in blouses?'

He was alone by now. The crowd, during this melancholy soliloquy, had drifted away. Leaflets littered the manicured lawns, blew against the hybrid teas. Mr Rappaport took off the tattered poster, sighed, walked to his front door. Across it, someone had sprayed KILL CHILE FASCISTS NOW! The red paint was still tacky. Mr Rappaport turned his key in the lock, and went in.

'You're home!' screamed his wife, in the marble hall.

'Definitely,' said Mr Rappaport.

'Don't use the downstairs toilet!'

Mr Rappaport frowned.

'Toilet? It was always a cloakroom. I used to call it a toilet, you went mad. All of a sudden it's a toilet?'

'I'm emotional,' said his wife. As her metallic coiffe quivered, it caught the subdued pelmet lighting, fired sparks.

'And that means I shouldn't use the downstairs toilet?'

'Cloakroom. Ask me why I'm emotional?'

'Why are you emotional?'

'There's a South Moluccan locked in the cloakroom. He's got a gun. He's got the au pair in there with him. He's threatening to kill her.'

'I sympathise,' said Mr Rappaport, hanging up his coat. 'Three mornings running I had a hair in the porridge. I thought the Swiss were supposed to be clean. You go to St Moritz, it's spotless.'

Mrs Rappaport glowered bitterly at her husband.

'When people at the bridge club ask me how come you only got the OBE,' she muttered, 'I'll know what to say. For a genuine knighthood, you need brains.'

'You need raincoats,' said Mr Rappaport. 'When was the last time a prime minister gave a press conference in a blouse? Mind you, if Mrs Thatcher gets in, who knows? I could send her the guipure lace number, in pastel blue. *Lord* Rappaport, possibly.'

His wife followed him into the enormous living room.

'I've got sixty people coming for canasta,' she said. 'Suppose he shoots the girl?'

'You've got a dishwasher,' said Mr Rappaport.

He looked at the Canaletto over the fireplace, the way he did every evening. It had cost eighty thousand. Even if he lived to be a hundred, it still worked out at a fiver a night. Just to look.

'I didn't mean that,' said his wife. 'I meant about the cloakroom.'

'They could use upstairs,' said Mr Rappaport, not turning from the fireplace. 'We got eight.'

'Upstairs is full of Persians,' said his wife.

'They take any amount of wear,' replied her husband. 'Let them walk. What harm can it do?'

'Not carpets,' said his wife. 'Persians. They came this morning. They want visas. They want to go to America, make a new life. They say they won't go away until they get them.'

'You told them I was in blouses?'

'*I* speak Persian?'

Mr Rappaport sighed, walked to the window, gazed out over the swimming pool. As dusk fell, the underwater lights came on.

'You saw the pool?' asked Mr Rappaport.

'I saw,' said his wife. 'It's a vigil. They came in over the back wall.'

'A vigil,' muttered Mr Rappaport. 'You know what I pay in rates?'

'They think we're Japs.'

'Is that any reason to fill my swimming pool with a—a—what?'

'It's supposed to be a whale,' said his wife. 'They say we're killing whales to make unnecessary consumer goods.'

'Do they know how many whales go into the average blouse?' enquired Mr Rappaport heavily.

There was a scream from the hall.

'He's murdering her!' cried Mrs Rappaport. 'Do something.'

Mr Rappaport walked slowly from the room, crossed the hall, tapped on the cloakroom door.

'What do you want?' he said.

'We demand the return of Indonesia!' shrieked the gunman.

'You got it,' said Mr Rappaport.

Slowly, the door opened. A dark face peered around the jamb.

'You mean it?' said the gunman.

'Sure,' said Mr Rappaport. 'Leave me your address, I'll put it in writing.'

'You are formally prepared to give up territorial rights over...'

'Absolutely. I'll even throw in an extra pair of pants.'

The gunman left. There was something crestfallen about him. The au pair straightened her sweater.

'Ah weesh to and in mah notice,' she said. 'Ah do not come ere to be lock wiz loony in cloakroom.'

'Toilet,' said Mr Rappaport. He turned, and was about to go back into the living room when a small black man in a morning coat barred his way, clicked heels, and handed him a long yellow envelope. Mr Rappaport bowed slightly, and took it away.

'Well?' enquired his wife.

'We are at war with Togo,' said Mr Rappaport, refolding the note.

'Who's we?'

'You're asking me?' He glanced out into the hall. 'It's a pity he didn't wait. I could have negotiated. Maybe they'd have settled for a shipment of bed-jackets at cost. I got a warehouse full. I need the space.'

A window shattered, and the Rappaports wheeled. A face, bearded, crowned with a Basque beret, poked through.

'REMEMBER ETA!' it shrieked, and vanished.

86

'Etta?' said Mr Rappaport to his wife. 'Didn't she marry your cousin from Leeds?'

'The furrier?'

'Not the furrier, the one with the hip replacement, used to be in mail-order shoes.'

'The midnight-blue Jaguar with the phone?'

'That's him.'

'Muriel was his wife's name. He married a Muriel. She had a birthmark.'

'Then who was Etta?'

'I don't remember.' Mrs Rappaport lit a cigarette. Her mouth was tight. 'If we had a flat overlooking Regent's Park, fourth floor, fifth floor, could they break the windows? Could they put rubber fish in a swimming pool we didn't have? Could they run about declaring war when I've got sixty people coming?'

'I like it here,' said her husband. 'I like the neighbourhood. I don't want to move. I got friends here. Who do I know in Regent's Park?'

The doorbell gonged. He went to open it.

'Sam!' cried Mr Rappaport. 'Frances! Come in, friends I'm always glad to see.'

'Who is it?' called Mrs Rappaport from the living room. 'David Owen? Sadat?'

'It's the Sheldons from up the road,' replied her husband, beaming at them. 'So don't stand there, come…'

'Cossack!' shouted Mr Sheldon. 'Butcher!'

Mr Rappaport cleared his throat carefully.

'Sam,' he said. 'why are you wearing a prison suit with a number on the pocket? Why are you holding a crust of bread?'

'Ha!' cried Mrs Sheldon. 'Suddenly you don't recognise a political prisoner? Suddenly it's news to you your stinking Siberian labour camps are full of innocent human beings?'

'I'm a symbol, Henry,' said Sam. 'I shaved my head specially.'

'Don't call him Henry!' snapped his wife. 'Soviet pig! Hitler didn't do enough?'

'Frances,' murmured Mr Rappaport, 'it's me. I'm in blouses. We've known each other…'

'All these years you were KGB,' muttered Mr Sheldon. 'All

these years we never guessed. A viper we nurtured!'

Mr Rappaport shut the door.

'They didn't come in?' enquired his wife.

'Regent's Park,' said her husband, 'is very convenient.'

'And smart,' said Mrs Rappaport quickly.

'First thing tomorrow,' said Mr Rappaport, 'I'll phone the estate agent.'

Cut Off

GREAT GOD! THIS IS AN AWFUL PLACE.

Those may not have been his exact words, of course. I have no reference books down here in this chill Hants hollow, entire contents of bookcase consists of 1957 AA Book, *My Best Girls' Stories*, Giles Cartoon Annual (1964), *Five Go Off To Smugglers' Top*, 75% of *Northanger Abbey* (25% inside unknown dog, to judge from fearful indentations on p.177 ff.), and about eight hundred of those bogus historical romances people always leave behind in rural cottages, all entitled *Mistress of Beaujolais* or similar, with tattered paper covers showing globular orange busts, priapic Nubian grooms, and, in the background, a mansion burning down.

So no way of looking up Captain Scott's actual words. Pity. Thought them particularly appropriate, self sitting here huddled, freezing, over deal table in front of malevolent little fire spitting slivers of fissile wet charcoal past head, snowdrifts piled against warp-gappy windows, blizzard lashing loose and vulnerable tiles.

Am Cut Off.

Said so on radio news. 'Worst blizzards since records began/in living memory/ever seen in Southern England, have cut off parts of the New Forest.'

Am in part of New Forest.

Am in, to be accurate, down sort of hole in part of New Forest. A funnel, a vortex; a thing full of snow.

Actually *look* like Scott. Can see self in night-backed reflecting window as I glance up from my W.H. Smith Big Colouring Book, balding pate crinkled with concern, legs crossed, lips pursed, pen poised——you must know that photograph. Boots on, like him. Always keep boots on, take boots off after firewood hunt, boots shrivel in seconds, like incautious Shangri-la ratepayers; can never get them on again. Also wear

89

anorak, don't usually write in anorak, but, then, am not usually Cut Off. Should I spell anorak with capital A, is it named after Lapp entrepreneur, how do I find out? Won't be in 1957 AA Book. Pity I don't need ferry times to Mull, got dozens of those; twenty-two years out of date, of course, but shouldn't think Mull changes much, over the eons.

Haven't even got dictionary. Except, that is, tiny green leatherbound English-Portuguese job found in piano stool. Left by whom, which previous fraught weekender? Cut Off Portuguese, perhaps; if so, what COP doing in Part of New Forest, slithering along icy ruts between alien conifers, dictionary in hand, weeping, monolingual, trying to find local who will understand panicky pidgin queries about gritting?

Look up 'gritting'.

No Portuguese word for it.

Hardly surprising, Parts of Algarve rarely cut off by worst blizzards in LM, Portugal full of broiling Germans, thin donkeys shimmering in upper nineties, only worry is if council Ambre Solaire truck can get through.

No point looking up 'anorak', dictionary that does not even recognise gritting obviously in no shape to offer potted etymological biography of founder of Eskimo rag trade.

Staggering, not to have gritting in it. Xenophobic. Gritting rapidly becoming most important word in English language. Every morning for last four days I have got up, frozen, crunched up hill followed by hungry ponies salivating as they stare at tasty boots, succulent anorak, fleshy humorist, crunched two miles through rigid forest to B3078, to look for council gritters.

Plan is to direct gritters down forest track to cottage, ply them with scotch and folding currency in return for gritting said track, can then push car out of asbestos lean-to onto gritted track, and make good my escape from Holiday Cottage Paradise In Heart Of New Forest, Ideal For Weekend Retreat, get back to lovely Non-Holiday House Inferno in Heart of Urban London, Ideal For Never Leaving Ever Again.

Could, in short, Uncut Myself Off.

But no sign of gritters, no lorries full of cheering men waving shovels, like liberating army rolling up Champs Elysées, people throwing garlands, kisses, bunting, camembert.

No sign of anything, except other Cut Off people, looking for gritters, wide white landscape around B3078 dotted with desperate blobs of primary colour, all these people in Christmas-new scarves, new gloves poking out of new sheepskin coats like hands of bananas, new pom-pom hats knitted by arthritic grannies, all clumping pitifully from knoll to knoll, scanning grey horizons for mercy gritters.

God, it's painful writing in longhand! No typewriter down here (expected to be back at London desk by now), so have to write in pen, haven't done for twenty years, third finger right hand already got flat place on it after few hundred words, top of second finger concave and shiny, both fingers hurt like hell. Wonder if Scott complained? Probably not: with Oates hobbling out into white hell on frostbitten pins for good of party (looking for Antarctic Council gritters?), it would have been crassness of a high order to start going on about writer's cramp.

Mind you, Scott doubtless had proper pen, I have a—wait a moment while I prise it from my fingers—a DoodleArt by Berol. (What is Berol? Sounds like patent Victorian vitamin extract.) A felt-tipped thing, circumference of a Havana, makes lines 5mm thick, only get fifty words to a page of my colouring-book, sorry, son's colouring-book, son going to go mad in morning when he finds colouring-book filled with scrawl, all his DoodleArt nibs worn flat as old toothbrushes, son already grieving for gerbils left in London house when we came down here for two days, gerbils now without food for six, shall probably return to find one huge gerbil. Dead.

If we ever return.

That is main reason for writing. Otherwise could leave first two pages of *Punch* blank, excellent for phone numbers, Delia Smith recipes, better readership service than pages of hysterical ramblings from Cut Off editor. But this may be last piece I ever write, fifth day of being Cut Off, fags running out, food low, could well snuff it like Scott; so quite fancy idea of rescue helicopter turning up sometime in March to find self frozen to table, pen in hand, a cobbler to the last (ha, ha), died with self's boots on.

Ought, therefore, to write—what did he say?—'Had we lived, I should have had a tale to tell of the hardihood, endurance and courage of my companions which would have stirred the hearts of all Englishmen.' Think that's pretty close, learned words at father's knee, ethic to live by, etc. Pity times have changed, personally have nothing to tell about hardihood etc. of companions, son moaning all day about not having toboggan, daughter going on about emaciated gerbils, wife wondering loudly whose idea it was to come to God-forsaken hovel in first place.

Shan't wait for helicopter, of course, being a hack; shall phone this through for tomorrow's deadline, phone not Cut Off, can talk to outside world, so friends in centrally-heated rooms with treble-glazed windows looking down onto trimly gritted streets.

Own window looks out onto starlit bleakness, a fearful glitter, frangible air. Occasional whinnies in the silence, spasmodic shrieks as an owl dives down and sinks its talons into some snowbound stoat. Unless stoats hibernate. *Something* screaming out there, though. Maybe owl diving onto horse. Never know, with hunger.

Take, e.g., this morning.

Yesterday, lovely lady from distant neck of woods, our nearest neighbour, struggled through snow with what looked like handful of hats. Turned out to be brace of pheasants. Lovely lady knew we were short of food, so brought birds over, plus strict injunction to hang them for at least couple of days, since birds only recently assassinated.

Hung birds in asbestos lean-to beside car.

Went out to car this morning to see if emergency fags in glove compartment, glanced up at wall, two heads hanging on hook.

Next weekend's lunch terminated at collar.

Foxes get hungry, too.

Probably come back tonight and eat car.

Odd, it was all great (fairly) when it started, snow drifts all over, living chapter from BOP story, perverse un-adult excitement at being isolated, left to live on wits, forage for firewood, rub things together, possibly melting snow to shave, discovering edible roots (not easy, with only AA Book and Giles as guide), could end up getting Duke of Edinburgh Award, OBE, two best-sellers, even Hollywood offer if forced to eat postman.

No fun by fifth day, though. What has happened to Englishmen, I ask, that gritters' go-slow brings suicidal gloom, that backbone wilts at thought of gin running out, that unusable car means end of world, when it is only five miles trudge to village shop (Scott would have jogged it, laughing), that every trivial tribulation means...

Phone rings. Excuse me, while I creak out to answer it.

Back now. Excuse me, while I lose marbles.

Neighbour from London on phone. Water pouring out of burst loft tank, nobody can get in house, house rapidly flooding to bits, should neighbours break in, he asks?

Yes, I answer.

Great God, as Robert Oscar Falcon O'Flaherty Wills Scott might have said, to have one awful place may be regarded as a misfortune; to have two looks like carelessness.

Stare out into incarcerating wastes.

For God's sake look after our gerbils.

Page and Monarch Forth They Went

British managers have a lot to learn from American managerial methods. Their single-status system has a great deal to recommend it, and basically means that the conditions of employment are the same whatever your position.

It also means eating in the same canteen. —Prince Charles

'HE'LL BE IN ANY MINUTE,' said the fourteenth under-gardener, wiping the crust from the HP bottle with his cap. 'Pie, double egg, chips, beans, three slices. Never varies.'

'Plus gravy,' said the footman.

'Right,' nodded the fourteenth under-gardener. 'Plus gravy.'

'He likes gravy, does he?' I said.

'Likes gravy?' cried the second boots. '*Likes gravy?* I seen 'im splash people two tables away when he's mopping up. What did I say to 'im only last week, Kevin?'

'Oy,' replied the fourteenth under-gardener. 'You said oy.'

'Bloody right!' said the second boots.

'Did he mind?' I enquired.

'I'll give him mind,' snapped the second boots. 'Dabitoff don't grow on bloody trees, mate.'

'Shut your face, Kevin,' said the footman. 'He's a friend of mine.'

'Ask him when he's going to let me have my bike back, then.'

'Him and me's sick of you going on about your bleeding bike,' said the footman. 'I wouldn't care, it's 'ardly more than Sellotape and rust. Last time we went to Box Hill, his clips fell through the bottom of the bloody saddlebag.'

'It's worth money, that bike,' muttered the second boots.

'You want him to walk everywhere?' enquired the fourteenth under-gardener. 'Weather like this?'

'Why can't he buy his own blooming bike?' asked the second boots. 'Not short of a few bob, is he?'

'He's not flash,' said a coachman, joining us.

'What you mean is,' said the second boots, 'he's forgotten the combination on his wallet.'

The fourteenth under-gardener glared at him.

'What he means, clever dick,' he said, 'is he doesn't go throwing it about and embarrassing his mates. He could prob'ly 'ave a brand new lightweight Holdsworth with drop wossnames, if he wanted one. With in-bike quadrophonic entertainment. It's just not his way, is it, Derek?'

'Not his way,' agreed the coachman, fanning his minestrone with his ruff. He jabbed his spoon at the second boots. 'As a matter of fact, sonny boy, he is very quick to put his hand in his pocket, am I right, Craig?'

'Definitely,' replied the footman. 'Last Tuesday up Cowdray Park, he 'ad 'em in before the rest of the team was even through the doors, know what I mean?'

'How'd you get on?' enquired the fourteenth under-gardener.

'Diabolical!' The footman sucked a noodle in with the deftest of flicks, like a blackbird. 'Got a right bloody 'ammering.'

'You play polo, then?' I asked. 'I didn't realise the—'

'Darts,' said the footman. He turned to the fourteenth under-gardener. 'The Stoat & Cabbage lot brought that little wiry bugger over again, I'll swear they found him up the Amazon. He could hit double-top from a skateboard.'

'I wish he'd change his watering-hole,' said the fourteenth under-gardener, gloomily. 'We could do with 'im in our lot.'

The footman tapped the side of his nose with his forefinger.

'Could happen,' he said. 'Charlie 'ad a word with him in the gents afterwards. I wouldn't want it to go no further, of course, but he was given to understand that if he 'appened to move 'is tankard across to The Gynaecologist's Arms, he might find 'imself looking at a life peerage!'

'Gerroff!' cried the fourteenth under-gardener.

'Straight up,' said the footman.

'I'll say this for Charlie,' muttered the second boots grudgingly, 'he don't muck about.'

'You should've been there last Tuesday,' said the footman, chasing a pickled onion across the Formica, 'when the bacon'n'kumquat crisps run out. He just leaned across to the barmaid and murmured *Got any more in the cellar?*' He speared the errant onion. 'She was down there like a shot. She wouldn't do it for everyone, Beryl.'

'Natural authority,' nodded the coachman. 'In the blood, am I right?'

'Also charm,' countered the footman. 'First time he come to the pub, he went round asking everybody the right questions, didn't he? Beryl was staggered how much he seemed to know about ullage.'

The second boots shoved his plate back, and stood up.

'I've been to that pub,' he muttered, 'you can stand all night and never get bloody served!'

He stamped out.

'He seems upset,' I said.

'He always fancied Beryl himself,' said the fourteenth under-gardener, 'but with Charlie around, werl, it stands to—'

'Watch it!' hissed the footman. 'Hallo, Doreen.'

A tall girl in a verdant punk razor-cut teetered up on rainbow wedges, and sat down beside me, the black sateen of her hobbled skirt tightening along her thigh like an overstuffed dustbin-liner. A plump and pimpled little blonde with her took her seat across the table.

'You don't know Tracy,' said Doreen. 'She's new. She works with me up the west pantry, don't you, Trace?'

Tracy giggled. The Gillette blades shook beneath her earlobes, like Japanese windchimes.

'Doreen's virtually engaged to Charlie,' explained the coachman to me.

I licked my pencil.

'Are you really?' I said.

Doreen pulled her sweater straight. It appeared to have rectangles under it.

'Put it this way,' she said, 'our names 'ave been romantically linked. He is now meeting me outside the Purley Odeon instead of inside, as previous.'

'It's always a sign they're getting serious,' said Tracy, 'when they buy both tickets.'

'Also,' said Doreen, 'when you get one-pound boxes, instead of them little bags with no chart inside telling you what's coffee cream.'

'Extraordinary!' I cried. 'I had no idea. Somehow, I had always assumed that some foreign princess, perhaps, or...'

'Them!' snapped Doreen scornfully.

'They don't know 'ow to dress,' said Tracy, 'for a start. Imagine hats!'

'Anyway,' said Doreen, tossing her head, 'he more or less pledged himself at Cliftonville. Any funny business now, I couldn't answer for the consequences.'

'Doreen's got three brothers coming out of the Scrubs any day now,' explained the footman, chiselling himself a wedge of Bakewell tart.

'Do you mind?' said Doreen. 'Durham E Wing.'

'They broke a train,' said the fourteenth under-gardener.

'Millwall supporters,' said the coachman, 'what do you expect?'

'You mentioned Cliftonville?' I pressed, sensing scurrility.

'Margate, really,' said the footman. 'You don't half bloody put it on sometimes, Doreen. It was our annual works outing. They shared a dodgem.'

'I had a whelk fall down inside my mauve tank-top with the lurex thread,' said Doreen. 'After that, our relationship blossomed.'

'So one day,' I murmured, mentally typesetting, 'you, Doreen, could possibly find yourself becoming...'

'Definitely,' said Doreen, licking her yoghurt lid.

The footman sighed.

'It's not that I don't wish you all the luck in the world, Dor,' he said, 'but I see trouble ahead with them brothers of yours. I shouldn't think there's a cat's chance that Charley would ever become a Millwall supporter, would you, Derek?'

The coachman shook his head.

'Not in a million years,' he replied. 'Once a Fulham fan, always a Fulham fan.'

The fourteenth under-gardener nodded.

'He's one of us,' he said.

Suspended Animation

THIS TIME, your prayers are asked—and I appreciate that this may be a somewhat overbooked time for supplication, with the planet standing in imminent danger of becoming one vast foxhole full of lapsed atheists on reddened knees—for Ray Bradbury.

Now, Mr Bradbury is beyond question a fine baroque fantasist who has crept our flesh with many a weird and wondrous tale, and when he is strapped to his intergalactic Olivetti and hurtling towards the enchanted quasars at n^3 times the speed of light, he has no more reverential follower than I. When, however, he deserts his last, the result is cobblers.

Not long ago, the cover and most of the bowels of the *Observer*'s colour magazine were devoted to the current Bradbury credo; and, as so often happens at devotional moments, intellect was up the spout and gone. For Ray Bradbury's cockeyed thesis (elaborated further in a dottily self-indulgent tele-documentary) is that America, if not the very world, should be rebuilt upon the paradigm laid out by Walt Disney: not, of course, that either Ray or Walt wants the mice to take over (a proposition with which, indeed, it would be far harder to quibble), but that modern cities and their cultures should be constructed to replicate those two bizarre artefacts, Disneyland and Disneyworld.

At first sight of this suggestion, I naturally assumed it to be a mischievous hoax: Ray Bradbury has dunked his busy quill in vitriol many times and knows his way around the satirical circuit (witness *Fahrenheit 451*), and what, therefore, was now being offered us was only a Modest Proposal for refurbishing his native premises. But not a bit of it—as the article, and subsequently the film, unfolded, it grew numbingly apparent that Mr Bradbury was entirely serious. Worse, he had been a close friend and commercial intimate of the late mousemaker, and was locked inescapably into the evangelical Disney ethic, which cannot easily be encapsulated but involves among its myriad unsettling components the unhealthy prolongation of infancy, the removal of unsightly facial hair, the wariness of any minority group above the height of piccaninny, the dissolution of trade unions, total abstinence from anything stronger than pumpkinade, the reduction of language and literature to saccharine gargle, the conviction that if the Russians were force-fed applepie they would come to Christ, and the commitment to discover, no matter what the cost, a cure for sex.

Now, lest I alienate those whom I would convince, let me quickly say that not only was Walt Disney as creative a genius as this century can shake a stick at, but also that I personally love and admire his best animations this side idolatry, and that side, too. I also believe that the Sistine Chapel ceiling has a thick edge over Dulux emulsion, but that doesn't mean I would allow Michelangelo within ten miles of my small son. For what we are talking about is not art but life, and Disney's concretised vision of it.

As coincidence would have it, I returned from Disneyworld on the very day that Ray Bradbury published his loony encomium. We had decided that the only way to stop the children from nagging to be taken to Disneyworld was either to go, or to strangle them (a close-fought decision, with the casting vote going to the daily, who needs an empty house to catch up on her international phoning), and in the event spent perhaps the most bizarre ten days of our lives, hermetically sealed within what the promoters call The Disney Experience (one of the many curious cis-Atlantic semantic divisions being that when an American describes something as an Experience he is indicating that it was very warm and very wonderful, and when an Englishmen does so he is indicating that it was something extremely unsettling and almost certainly very nasty).

Disneyworld is the larger of Walt's dollar-spinning utopias; it has been carved out of fifty square miles of central Florida, an area previously disputed between oranges and alligators, which have now been turned into handbags and breakfast, though not respectively. The site cleared, Walt said, Let the waters under the heaven be gathered together unto one place, and let the dry land appear: and it was so. Hills were built, lakes were laked, tropical islands were dropped, pre-palmed, into them, with hoovered whitesand beaches, and this paradise having been set about with hotels and golf courses and bogus Polynesian villages, at the epicentre Disney set his Magic Kingdom, which is, quite simply, the biggest and best funfair in the world.

What it is quite complicatedly is something very else.

You get into Disneyworld by driving through turnpikes manned by cheery gargantuans with perfect teeth through which customers (called guests) are uniformly enjoined to have a wonderful day. These custodians are referred to as Security Hosts. Your car is then parked in a series of gigantic lots (Pluto 1–30, Donald 1–50, and so on; it is expedient to write, as tannoys urge, 'I AM PLUTO 24/563 LEFT' on the back of your hand, if you wish to see England again), and you are trammed with two hundred other strandees to a monorail station, where you are entubed and shot towards the Magic Kingdom. That system of people-moving, by the way, is just one of the joys foamed over by Ray Bradbury; odd, really, when one considers that in *Fahrenheit 451*, the compulsory monorail is employed by Mr Bradbury as a symbol of dehumanisation. The monorail in Disneyworld is also mandatory: one may not walk or drive unsupervised to the Magic Kingdom.

The Magic Kingdom itself is visible from far away, thanks to a spectacular mediaeval castle the size of Salisbury Cathedral, and over four hundred times cleaner: as one hums towards it, with the in-coach loudspeakers limning Walt's achievements, one is ineradicably reminded that the last person to build such follies was the barmy Ludwig II, who shot clockwork bears in his artificial forests, and finally chucked himself into one of his own fake moats in 1886, to deep sighs of Bavarian relief all round.

But the castle is not central to my argument, and may be dismissed with no more than the observation that it is not a castle at all (my kids were furious) but only a giant gyfte shoppe 'n' restaurant complex: much more important is the approach to it, for this is the nub of Disney dream and, perforce, the Bradbury aspiration.

It is approached by Main Street, USA. It is here that one disembarks from the monorail, here that one is first struck by the Disney vision. Now, to those of us who have read Sinclair

Lewis (and millions of Americans, given that he is a school set-text, must count in that number), the words *Main Street* evoke an immediate image of bigoted provincialism, of selfish isolationism, of prissy repression, and much else needful of the adroit social satirist that Lewis was. The irony appears to have been totally lost on Walt Disney; either that, or he loved everything Lewis attacked, and this is his counterblast—the likelier alternative. Disney's Main Street is a nostalgic vision of a pre-lapsarian America, a street of posterpainted ice-cream parlours and candy shops and gee-gaw emporia, strolled by ostensibly ad hoc Dixieland bands and barbershop quartets; it echoes constantly to *Wait Till The Sun Shines, Nellie* and *Meet Me Tonight In Dreamland* and *Somebody Stole My Gal* and the clatter of tap-dancing shop assistants. One is on the permanent *qui vive* for Judy Garland appearing at an upstairs window of the dry goods store and singing the trolley song; but of course, Judy is long suicided, gone in drug-rattling despair, and such bleak undertones are no part of Main Street, Disneyworld. Nor, of course, is anything that is unpleasantly truthful: the innocence of 1910 resurrected by Walt's enterprise was not even accurate in 1910, and there is no point expatiating upon this when I have to hand perhaps the best eavesdropping I have ever picked up. We were standing on the sunny sidewalk of Main Street one morning, waiting for the daily parade of floats, and beside us was standing a very hip black couple; and in the crowded hush before the first float trundled into the empty street, one nudged the other and, in heavily exaggerated Uncle Tom, said: 'Hey, man, what time's de lynchin?'

Given that for every American dream there is a corresponding American nightmare, and that Main Street strikes the opening chord, it is thereafter tricky for even a not particularly cynical European observer to move on through the rest of the Magic Kingdom: which breaks down into Frontierland, Adventure Land, Liberty Square, Tomorrowland, and Fantasyland. In Frontierland, for example (where, amazingly, the backdrop to the rifle range is painted every night to remove the pockmarks, a trick that would have done wonders for the Mekong Delta, had Walt managed to pick up the Nam concession), there is absolutely no indication whatever of the valuable part that the Red Indian played in the opening up of the

American West, by getting wiped out. As one travels through Frontierland on the Walt Disney World Railroad, a delightful reproduction, but genuinely steam, train of the kind used to cross America once genocide had ensured the accuracy of the timetables, one is constantly adjured by megaphone to note this or that set of robot animals or people, and there is no question but that these robots are astoundingly authentic analogues of crawling crocs and lumbering bears and hardy pioneers. That there are not groaning heaps of electronic Pawnees seeping ketchup is, I suppose, as inevitable as the fact that Richard Milhous Nixon, in the technologically amazing Hall of Presidents in Liberty Square, does not say, 'I am not a crook.' It is a world from which all expletives have been deleted. Incidentally, the all-bionic, all-waving, all-grinning Jimmy Carter which rounds off the gallery is almost certainly the thing that ran in 1976; at exactly which moment the present grey-faced failure-raddled incumbent sold the model to Disney and installed himself in the Oval Office, I cannot say—all I know is that it was on the day that America started to go downhill, again.

As for Tomorrowland, surely even Ray Bradbury, despite the snug padding of his royalties, would concede that the Home of Future Living is only for the inhabitation of the rich? Or that the Carousel of Progress takes scant account of the regressions of that same hundred years? Is this the moment to point out to Mr Bradbury that he once urged Walt to run for Mayor of Los Angeles? And if he had run, and if he had won, where would he have sited Ghettoland, or Gayworld, or Drug Mountain? Would we have been enjoined to take the Mugger's Ride through Watts Village, perhaps, with banjo-accompanied wienie-roasts around the fire as the slums and their denizens burned cheerily down?

Or would Uncle Walt simply have ploughed them all in, like the Floridan swamps, and built high-turreted Wasptown on the rubble?

For Disneyworld is so immeasurably much more than a superb funfair through which overweight human grotesques waddle in their happy thousands and their plastic Mickey Mouse ears, gulping the fast-fed diet that keeps American dentists in Cadillacs: it is a historical reconstruction as sanitised as the Kremlin's, and a future vision as uncognisant of contemporary pointers as Peter Pan's. It is a magic carpet under which everything has been swept.

And what of Walt himself, sleeping the sleep of the cryogenic in his snug freezerdrawer? If there are scientists around to thaw him out an eon hence, will he awake to rub his eyes at the thermonuclear pumice of America and its pitiful mutant citizens whose beaks and ears and weird webbed feet do *not* come off at night, and wonder, perhaps, whether what had come about did not have just a little to do with the confusion between illusion and reality?

Say it Again, Sam

Programmes for the FAR EAST—Burma, Brunei, Cambodia, China, Hong Kong, Indonesia, Japan, Korea, Laos, Philippines, Thailand, Vietnam. These quarter hour programmes are entirely in English.

WEDNESDAY SAY IT AGAIN — the English you need everyday — demonstrated in the context of scenes from classic films. Stories of love, horror, spying and comic misunderstanding provide a sound basis for learning English.

BBC's *English by Ra*

WEARILY—for it had been a long hot day at the filing cabinets, the monsoon drumming on the tin roof, the fan on the blink, the flies fat as winging plums—Mr Pham Nik Ding climbed the treadworn wooden steps to his maisonette door at 49 Kipling Crescent, Rangoon. He removed the key from his moist waistcoat pocket, dreaming, as he often did, of the day when it would be cold to his thumb, an English key for an English door in a cool English street. Rillington Place, perhaps, Tobacco Road, Wimpole Street. Somewhere like that.

When he had the English.

Because when he had the English, he would apply for a transfer to the London office, and they would give him a secretary with a big bust, and a vintage car on the company, and he would take his secretary's glasses off and tell her she was beautiful and they would go down to Brighton in his vintage car and eat in one of those smart roadhouses where people in dinner jackets threw custard pies at one another.

He hung up his umbrella, and walked into the kitchen. Mrs Ding was chopping eels.

'Tennis, anyone?' said her husband.

She put down a twitching head, and looked up.

'You say that every night,' said Mrs Ding. 'What does it mean?'

His brown brow furrowed, bleakly.

'I don't know,' he said. 'This whole thing doesn't add up, Professor. Maybe we're not asking the right questions. Why don't you slip into something a little more comfortable?'

Mrs Ding sighed, and went out. When she came back, she was wearing a bicycle cape and gumboots. Her husband stared at her, chewing his lip.

'There's something terribly, terribly wrong here,' he muttered. 'I can't put my finger on it, but it's just this crazy feeling I have. Call it a hunch.' He lifted the yellow hem. 'This thing is bigger than both of us.'

'But it's comfortable,' said Mrs Ding stubbornly.

Her husband shrugged.

'All right. Let's give it a whirl. It might just work. God knows, we've tried everything else.'

His wife sighed, and squeaked back across the tiling to her chopping-board.

'You have not forgotten,' she said, gouging a tiny brain, 'that Mr Sung is coming to dinner?'

Mr Ding staggered.

'My *boss*?' he shrieked. 'Coming *here*? For *dinner*? But I haven't a thing to wear!'

Mrs Ding threw a grey crab into the stew. It thrashed about briefly, and sank, hissing.

'Wear your grey pinstripe,' she said, 'with the blue tie.'

Her husband shook his head.

'I don't like it,' he said. 'It's too quiet.' He drove his fist into his palm, suddenly. 'This could be my big break, baby! Sung is the one they call Mr Big! We've had our eye on him for some time. He goes right to the top. In many ways, he *is* the Organisation!'

'Tin Toys (Burma) Limited?'

Pham Nik Ding smiled the crooked smile he had been practising behind the filing cabinet all day.

'They call it that,' he murmured darkly.

'It is its name,' said his wife. 'That's why.'

'Yes!' cried Ding with a short, sharp laugh. 'He's a cunning little devil, your johnny toy manufacturer!'

She pared a writhing squid, deftly.

'And you think Mr Sung will send you to London?'

Ding walked to the little window, his hands behind his back.

'There's a mole in the circus,' he said softly.

'I hope your English will pass muster,' said his wife.

When her husband turned, a moment later, there was a

smear of boot-polish across his upper lip, and a carrot between his teeth. He removed the carrot with a flourish.

'If it doesn't,' he snapped, 'I'll get it to pass the mayonnaise, and if it doesn't pass the mayonnaise, I'll get my check. It may not be English, but I'd rather speak Czech than listen to a language that doesn't know the first thing about waiting on tables. And that's another thing, Mrs Teasdale, if I told you you had a beautiful...'

The doorbell chimed. Mr Ding stuck the carrot back in his mouth, dropped to a half crouch, and loped to answer it.

'Good evening,' said Mr Sung.

'Good evening?' cried Ding. 'Well, that covers a lot of ground. Say, you cover a lot of ground yourself. You better beat it, I hear they're going to tear you down and put up an office building where you're standing. You can leave in a taxi. If you can't get a taxi you can leave in a huff. If that's too soon, you can leave in a minute and a huff. You know you haven't stopped talking since I came here?'

Mr Sung inclined his bulk more into the light, and stared.

'Is that you, Ding?'

'I don't have a photograph,' said Ding, tapping the carrot, 'but you can have my footprints. They're upstairs in my socks. Come in!'

He stood back, and ushered the bewildered Sung into the tiny hall, bowing low. When he stood erect again, the moustache had gone.

'Perhaps this will refresh your memory!' he cried.

Mr Sung gazed at his perspiring employee for a time.

'Are you perfectly well, Ding?' he enquired finally.

Ding blanched.

'Are you trying to tell me something?' he cried. 'Is it my hands? Are you saying I may never play the violin again?'

Mr Sung cleared his throat, and examined a thumbnail.

'I wonder, Ding,' he murmured, glancing suddenly up, 'do you know what a violin is?'

Ding stared into space for some time, panic rolling his eyes. At last, he shouted:

'I don't have to answer your goddam questions! I demand to see my lawyer! How about a little drink, baby?'

Mr Sung sighed heavily.

106

'Perhaps a little tea?' he said.

Pham Nik Ding sprang to his feet. He tore off his tie. He ripped open his collar. He hurtled towards the kitchen.

'HOT WATER!' he yelled. 'AND PLENTY OF IT!'

At the bellow, his wife ran to the door, and collided with him. Dried peas lurched from her saucepan, and bounced chattering upon the tiles.

'You crazy little fool, you might have got us both killed!' cried Ding. 'Don't you know what happens when two healthy young people meet?'

Mrs Ding watched the ricocheting peas, her frail shoulders hunched.

'You should not have shouted,' she muttered. 'You startled me. I dropped the chicken.'

'Oh my God!' exclaimed Ding. 'I don't think I can take any more! This used to be a decent town where a guy could settle and raise a family! Where did we go wrong, Mildred?'

'Is something the matter?' enquired Mr Sung, who had risen and started towards the kitchen. Ding stepped smartly in front of him, and put his hands on his employer's plump shoulders.

'I don't think you should go in there, Chuck,' he said, gently but firmly. 'It's—it's—it's your chicken.'

Mr Sung looked at Mrs Ding. Mrs Ding looked away.

'He gets very tired,' she said, in a small voice. 'He works very hard all day, and then he listens to the radio all night. Please try to understand that his—'

Her husband raised his hand.

'It's no good arguing with these earthlings, Vulgan,' he said. 'We have studied their culture and determined that they have hardly reached the stage our forebears knew during the time of Nork the Worm King. Why, they are still using anti-quated nuclear weapons, ha-ha-ha!' He turned to the gazing Sung. 'We seek only peace, earthling, but be warned that should it unfortunately prove necessary, we have it in our power to destroy your entire planet.'

Mr Sung picked up his hat.

'My apologies, Mrs Ding,' he said, 'but I have only just this minute remembered a prior engagement.'

'Please,' she said, touching his arm. 'There is still the fish stew. It is very important to him that you stay. He dreams of England.'

Mr Sing hesitated.

'Well—'

'You wouldn't know about England, my little Nicole,' said Ding, his eyes moist, 'the patchwork of green fields, the rooks cawing, the sun setting as the blacksmith trots up to bowl the last over. It may not sound anything special to you, but it's why chaps like me are prepared to jump out of Dakotas into the blackness. I don't say we can stop the Hun here, but we can give him a bloody nose, and that's what counts for the time being, until the Yanks come in and we can open the Second Front and set all Europe free so your kids and mine can sleep peacefully in their little beds again.' He took Mr Sung's fat hand. 'Maybe, when all this is over, I'll take you there.'

'I'll get the stew,' said Mrs Ding.

They sat down, and she began ladling the food into little porcelain bowls; and because Mr Sung was the honoured guest, she gave him the crab. It was a little large for the dish, and its claw hung over the rim, and as she set the dish down in front of Mr Sung, the movement caused the claw to bend slightly. As Mr Sung lifted his spoon, Pham Nik Ding leapt to his feet.

'Stand back, Professor,' he shrieked, 'that thing's alive! It must be some crazy mutation caused by the recent testing of that new atomic device out in the Nevada desert. We have to get the women and kids off the base!'

Whereupon he lunged at the brimming bowl. It slid from his hand. It seemed to stay airborne for a very long time. And when it came down, Mr Sung looked slowly at his lap. His white linen trousers were the colour of eel. The crab slid gently from his steaming thigh. After a silent moment or two, he stood up.

'Thank you for your hospitality, Mrs Ding,' he said. 'But I really must be off.'

He walked, with awkward dignity, to the front door, leaving an oily trail, dotted with small vertebrae. Mrs Ding got up and scurried after him. Her husband fell back into his chair, clutching his breast.

'Mother of mercy,' he moaned, 'is this the end of Rocco?'

At the open door, Mrs Ding wrung her hands.

'Please, esteemed Mr Sung,' she sobbed, 'can you not understand and forgive? Can you not allow him one more chance? This possibility of England, it means so much to him, he studies so hard, I am not asking for myself, I am only—'

She stopped. Mr Sung had turned in the doorway, to face her. A small smile played at his lip, beneath a single raised eyebrow.

'Frankly, my dear,' he said, 'I don't give a damn.'

Christmas Diary 1989

DECEMBER 19

Carol singers again last night. Two Methodists on the Lewis gun, a wiry Latitudinarian with a sawn-off Purdey, and three nervous members of the Popular Papist Front carrying looted Kalashnikhovs. Forced me to sing four choruses of *Silent Night* and put £50 in their Ecumenical Liberation Army collection-box. Would have put up some sort of show, but as probationary proselyte of only six months standing, am not allowed more than a scimitar; even then, cannot lop anything except parking offenders without written authorisation from Wazir of Cricklewood.

Waits had tougher time at Number 32. Higgins is now an Assistant Mullah and permitted to keep a Bren.

Another lonely night in attic. Wife still refuses to embrace Islam, and, in consequence, anything else. All right for wife, wife not facing this week's new mortgage rate of 845%, wife does not need to hold down job editing state-subsidised magazine. *Punch* not what it was: this week's issue devoted entirely to extolling the fig. Next week, have to put together Special Number commemorating discovery of camel.

DECEMBER 20

Take daughter to Selfridge's to see Ayatollah Holly. Daughter now seventeen. Membership of Iranian Economic Community requires five hundred virgins weekly, or else Oily Pound further devalued.

Go into *Punch*. Iranian Press Attaché going through this week's proofs cutting out anything which might be construed as comic. Magazine's lowest ebb since Muggeridge. Stare out of window, almost missing infamous days of 1985-6 when, following passage of Williams Act, pornography made compulsory. Cyril Ray used to do fascinating column on wine-bottles.

Blow nose. Poor old Cyril shot as condition of 1987 Anglo-Iranian Pact; all booze correspondents put up against wall of El Vino. Augustus Barnett publicly drowned in butt of Wincarnis.

Caption Competition No. 1052 won yet again by Prophet of Bath and Wells. Cartoon shows two partially submerged hippopotami. Winning caption reads:

'There is no God but God and Mohammed is his apostle.'

Always does.

DECEMBER 21

To Paddington in dog-cart, to pick up son coming down from Oxford for Christmas vacation. Unfortunately, dog widdles on parking-meter in Edgware Road and is immediately shot by meter eunuch for defilement of holy installation. Disaster: as probationary Muslim, am entitled to wheeled transport (all infidels have to walk), but not petrol-driven vehicle until full member of True Faith; could now lose dog-cart licence on totting-up procedure—already got two endorsements, one for not facing Mecca while driving down Maida Vale at sunset, one for colliding with milkfloat due to facing Mecca while driving down Maida Vale at sunset.

Son concerned to see me between shafts of dog-cart. Has Benghazi & Bingley Building Society foreclosed on mortgage? Son was hoping to pass mortgage on to grandchildren. Reassure son: mortgage will last for a thousand years. Enquire as to son's studies, son says he passed Football Prelims, would have got distinction but mucked up Midfield viva. Son will have to improve if he wants to get First and be snapped up by top Iranian side on graduation and exchanged for five hundred barrels of crude. If passed over for export, could end up playing for Liverpool in Crosby & District Sunday League. With his grandmother.

DECEMBER 22

Pick up sheep for Christmas dinner. Seems excessive, £438 for a thirty-year-old sheep, not even stuffed. Still, no other meat these days, for assorted reasons. Started in 1982 with Save The

Chicken movement (country now full of appalling wild hybrids as result of years of hormone-injected mutants crossbreeding; only last week, two old ladies sucked off tandem by trunk of ten-foot-tall feathered octopod, and eaten alive), followed by loss of pork after breakthrough in tissue-typing. Between 1984-7, over one million people received pigs' hearts, livers, bladders, limbs, and, in several cases, heads. Unfortunately, all recipients subsequently shot as unclean following Anglo-Iranian Pact. Then beef banned in 1986, when Everything Causes Cancer Department of Laker University did post-mortem on beagle which had been forced to smoke twenty steaks a day. All we have is sheep, following 1988 world-wide import ban caused by Emperor Giscard's successful thermo-nuclear threat.

Dog-cart riddled on return trip from butcher. Caught in crossfire between Queen's Own Muslim Light Infantry and unmopped remnants of 17th/21st Unitarian Volunteers. Fleece ruined.

DECEMBER 23

Decorate tree: silver crescents, chocolate Ayatollahs, and a hair of the Prophet (simulated) on top.

Wife bitter. Wears long white beard in protest, goes around all day saying 'Ho-ho-ho!' Nevertheless, wrap wife's present, a silicon-chip gynaecologist. Bought son a child bride, small Kurd with a wall-eye, but comes with nice dowry: two sacks of King Edwards and Des O'Connor LP. Bought daughter a veil.

Walk down to the Rat and Cockle before lunch. Over a large yoghurt, old Ngabadingi Sithole from the Water Board tells me that news from Wales is bad. Zionists have retaken Llandudno, joined up with Provisional Baptists, and are marching on the old Meccano factory at Rhpwyllgwm. Worker-occupied since 1979, it is now rumoured to be capable of delivering Inter-Continental Ballistic Dinkies to selected targets throughout UK.

Packet of mutton 'n' chutney crisps does little to calm apprehension.

If full-scale nuclear Jehad breaks out, will Russia come in? Impossible to predict, now that Brezhnev is merely brain floating in bucket of glucose connected to 12-volt Zim battery; last year, declared war on Iceland, simply because shape reminded him of wife. No good wondering about US either, US still preoccupied with fate of Tehran hostages, has taken no action on anything for ten years because of imponderable ramifications, latest offer from President Frost consists of ten-million-dollar advance for Ayatollah's memoirs, plus ten per cent of all video-cassette sales after producer's profits.

Similarly pointless speculating on Commonwealth action: Zimbabwe-Canada still refuses to recognise Britain unless Basil d'Oliviera is forced to run in 1992 Khartoum Olympics, and Kerry Packer's Australian Army will only fight under floodlights with white ammunition.

DECEMBER 24

Wake up feeling lousy. Sharp pain in chest. Have I been shot in night? Sure I woke up in small hours at noise of beads rattling on tiles: guerilla nuns could be roof-hopping by night, traditional tactics, invisible except for noses.

Find no new holes in torso, but go down to hospital anyhow. Casualty department full of pickpockets with septic stumps. Finally get to see NUPE consultant janitor, a nice man who does not beat me. His English is understandably poor, but adequate to explain that he is fairly new to job given to him by High Court following Race Relations Board injunction. He spits on my chest, puts on rather fetching handpainted buzzard mask, dances on desk, tells me to take two dried lizard spleens and call him again if I'm no better by March 12.

Interesting snippet in *Sun* Fancy That column noticed on bus home: according to their man in South East Asia, William Rees-Mogg, the last Vietnamese has just shot the last Cambodian, and died of starvation.

DECEMBER 25

At last, Formerly Christmas Day! Woken, as so often, by automatic fire; look out carefully, street full of dead dustmen. Obviously made mistake of banging up Assistant Mullah Higgins and wishing him season's greetings. Either that, or taken out by Christian snipers collecting Formerly Christmas boxes on behalf of Central Ammo Fund.

House full of unmistakable smell of old hot sheep. Go downstairs, sheep's head poking out of oven, teeth clenching apple, wife banging about in obvious rage and illegal paper hat with robin on it. Give wife envelope with gynaecologist in it, wife snorts, tells me my present is lying on desk in study.

It is Luger with one bullet up spout.

Is this joke?

Son is outside in garden, practising penalties. Small Kurd bride is standing between two piles of jackets, covered in mud. Son somewhat ungraciously tells me his present is useless, wall-eye prevents her from coping with left-hand corner shots.

Come back in, discover daughter has swopped presents with wife. Wife wants veil, daughter wants gynaecologist. Ominous signs all round.

Leave morose family, turn on telly. It is fifty-third repeat of movie, *Brief Haji*. Trevor Howard and Celia Johnson meet on Reading Station on first leg of haji to Mecca and discuss Koran footnotes for three hours until he suddenly discovers she is a woman attempting to infiltrate holy places as a result of being deranged. They throw each other under the 11.35 from Didcot.

This is followed by Queen's Formerly Christmas broadcast. She is impressive in Persian; even manages a rather long Baluchi joke. At the end, Emir of Wales comes in and waves. He has forty-three wives with him, including Davina Sheffield, Sabrina Guinness, and nine old blonde divorcees in dark glasses.

The Glunt Affair

THE ANTHONY GLUNT scandal, like the poisonous culture from which it took its giggly cue, continues to be a riddle wrapped in a mystery inside an enigma. It is an onion: as one peels each new smelly skin, it is possible to laugh and weep simultaneously.

Today, readers, we unveil a fresh young problem, quivering on its blancmange plinth; and bend our energies to its solution. You will see from the above cutting that Professor Anthony Blunt—let us, since there has been quite enough confusion already, give him his more familiar surname—became, while at Cambridge in the 'thirties, tutor to little Jean Gimpel, son of the great Parisian art handler. Now, while we may only applaud Gimpel père's foresight in refusing to allow Blunt to eat with the family, since a major art dealer has quite enough to do in pursuit of his cut-throat trade without spending his valuable time in counting the silver, the words to which we should most closely address ourselves in the *Times* report are in fact those in which Gimpel fils refers to his father as 'a grand gourgeois'. Leaving aside the unacceptable possibility that Jean Gimpel was attempting an unsavoury bilingual joke—we have all, have we not, heard of the two young men who met, fell in love, and got engorged?—we must assume that that is the way in which Blunt's former charge enunciates.

But *why*?

There exists at *Punch*, to cover those costly emergencies which inevitably crop up in a great national magazine's unstinting pursuit of its cultural duties, a slush fund; and, pausing only to pump up its rear tyre, I set off upon my Parisian quest. I shall not dwell upon the hardships of the crossing—a family publication is no place to describe the experience of travelling steerage

115

on a hovercraft—nor upon my fearful treatment at the hands of the Calais *douaniers*, who body-searched me for concealed sheep, but take up this bizarre record from the moment I rang the ornate bell of M. Jean Gimpel's fashionable apartment.

'Gonjour,' he said.

'Good morning,' I replied. 'Might I borrow a moment or two of your time, m'sieu? It is a matter of public importance, concerning Anthony Blunt.'

He frowned.

'Qui?'

I showed him *The Times*. As his eye fell upon the photograph, his trim face shivered.

'Aha!' he cried. 'Nister Glunt!'

'I'm sorry?' I enquired.

'Kung in,' he said, 'kung in.'

He showed me into a sumptuous drawing-room, not unlike one of the better Versailles nooks; it gleamed with old furniture, it glowed with fine painting. M. Gimpel strode briskly to a Louis XV side-table, discreetly signed by Jean Oeben, and unstoppered a crystal decanter.

'Grandy-and-soda?' he offered. He smiled. 'I know the English tickle.'

I, too, smiled.

'I am sure you do,' I said. 'Your English is remarkably good.'

'Thank you,' he said, handing me a glass and sitting down upon a watered-silk ottoman. 'I had a great gaster.'

'Ah, yes. Anthony——'

'Glunt. Exactly.'

'So his job here, all those years ago, was to teach you English?'

'Eggrything. English, nathenatics, scrikture, elocution.' He drained his glass. 'Gridge.'

'Gridge?'

'Ny hather, René Ginkel, hanted ne to learn all the English social attrigutes,' replied Jean Gimpel, by way of what could be dimly perceived as explanation. 'He hanted ne to go to Hinchester.'

'What is Hinchester?'

He looked up from his second glass, in obvious amazement.

'Hag you negger heard og Hinchester?' he cried. 'It is a great English gugglic school!' He sighed. 'Ny hather hanted ne to go there, gut Gernany narched into Goland, and...'

He spread his hands Gallicly.

'I see,' I said. I paused, wondering how to proceed politely. At last, I said: 'M'sieu, I can't help noticing your somewhat, how shall I put it, singular pronunciation. I was wondering—'

He stared at me.

'There is nothing singular agout ny gronunciation,' he said. 'As I told you, Nister Glunt hinsel taught ne elocution, the elocution og an English gentlenan. It nay ge—' and here he eyed my bicycle clips, 'it nay ge that you are not yoursel ganiliar hith the nodes and nanners og skeech og the Ukker Class.'

I nodded; any other reaction seemed pointless.

'It may be indeed,' I said. 'I am merely trying to fill in a little of the background of Professor Blunt's early teaching life. I see now he pursued elocution with that selfsame vigour he brought to, er, everything. I really find it very hard to understand, if you will forgive me, m'sieu, why your father refused to allow him to eat with you.'

My host shrugged.

'I glane the dungy,' he said.

'You blame the what?'

'The dungy.' He got up and poured us both another brandy. 'It's a gonklicated story,' he continued, above the siphon's hiss.

'Do go on,' I urged.

'Nister Glunt used to hag a dungy naned Guy. It used to sit on his knee. Now, you nay say that it is, how you say, gluddy odd hor a grown nan to hag a dungy sitting on his knee all the tine, gut—' and here M. Gimpel offered a wry little smile '—you and I are nen og the world, n'sieu, n'est-ce gas?...Nister Glunt nissed Canegridge and all the grilliant young goys he used to nix hith; Garis can ge a lonely glace. So he had this dungy; they hent eggryhere together. Gut ny daddy aggsolutely recused to hag the dungy sitting at the tagle at nealtines.'

In my head, the palest of grey dawns began to lighten the bizarre horizon.

117

'But in your classroom,' I said, 'the dummy was allowed to sit on Mr Blunt's knee?'

Once again, the pink hands were flung wide.

'No groglen!' he cried. 'On the contrary, the dungy constituted a nagnikicent teaching aid! No snorl goy could resist learning his lessons hron a dungy. Guy the dungy sat in his chair, I sat in nine, and Nister Glunt sat in a corner hith his suitcase and his headhones and his nicrohone.'

'I don't quite follow,' I said. 'How did it work?'

'Gerketly sinkle,' replied my host, in some irritation. 'Eggry gorning, the dungy said: 'Gonjour, Jean!' and I said: 'Gonjour, Guy!' and the dungy said: 'The lesson today is nathenatics. Here is a list og suns, you hag thirty ninutes. Grotractors nust not ge used. Do not write on goth sides og the gaker. *Gonne chance*!' Then I did ny suns, or Skanish, or gotany, and Nister Glunt sat in the corner nurnuring nessages into his nicrohone. Hron tine to tine, Guy the dungy asked ne questions, told ne to stog kicking ny nose or scratching ny gun, etcetera. Do you see? An ideal situation!'

As the final fragment slotted into place, I picked up my hat. M. Gimpel showed me to the door. As he opened it for me, I paused; the long hours spent before *Columbo* had not passed in vain.

'There's just one more small thing that puzzles me,' I said. 'Have you any idea what it was that Mr Blunt was transmitting during all those lessons, long ago?'

M. Gimpel tapped the side of his nose, and winked his eye, and shook his beaming head.

'Ny licks are sealed,' he said.

Castles in the Air

The oldest house yet found in England has been discovered on a Hampshire hilltop. It dates back 8,500 years, although very little recognisable remains. The house was an oval dwelling with fourteen main post holes and a view, on clear days, of the Isle of Wight. It incorporated 34 lesser stake holes, and several smaller round hutments stood nearby. A seven-year excavation has revealed a Middle Stone Age settlement. A hearth was found, along with piles of flints, hazelnut shells and carbonised seeds. —The Guardian

'VERY NICE,' said Guk, 'very peaceful.'

'It's a bit isolated, isn't it?' said Mrs Guk. 'We're miles from the nearest ditch.'

'We're having ditches put in,' said the developer. 'We've submitted the forms. They'll be taking a spur off the ditch up that settlement we passed in the cart. Yes, mains ditching is *definitely* on. Got the bloke coming down Friday week. From the Council. Absolutely no problem.'

'We could get by without a ditch,' said Guk.'My mum and dad never had a ditch. Look at that view!'

Mrs Guk tweaked her ratskin stole irritably.

'Your mum and dad never had a roof, either,' she snapped. 'If I'd wanted to be a hole-dweller, I'd never have left my first husband. Anyway, what view? I can't see no view.'

Guk shielded his eyes, pointed down the soft green slope.

'Where the fields go blue,' he said. 'That nice brown lump.'

'Fields go blue?' cried the developer. '*Fields go blue*? You don't get about much, do you? That's sea!'

'Never!' exclaimed Guk. 'I thought sea came to a point. Fancy! We could walk down to it, evenings.'

'It's a great amenity,' said the developer. 'People give their right arms to be near the sea, these days.'

'I can't think why, I'm sure,' said Mrs Guk. 'I've never liked blue.'

'Tell you a funny thing about sea,' said the developer. 'It goes in and out.'

'Gerroff!' cried Guk.

'Straight up,' said the developer. 'You could go down weekends and watch it. Wouldn't half impress visitors. If you want my opinion, it's all to do with that big brown lump in it.' He lowered his voice, glanced carefully to right and left. 'I reckon it's a god.'

Guk smiled triumphantly.

'What about *that*, mother?' he said. 'Having our own god within walking distance! If we built the kitchen facing downhill, you could look at him while you peeled the mice.'

His wife looked sharply at the developer.

'If it *is* a god,' she muttered heavily. 'We've only got his word. Personally, if *I* was a god, if *I* was in a position to pick and choose, I wouldn't stand in the middle of the sea. You'd get soaked.'

'Well, take it or leave it,' replied the developer. 'It's the only building plot on our books at the price. I can't muck about all day, there's a queue of people after this little number.'

'We'll take it!' cried Guk.

His wife sniffed.

'Tell me,' said Guk, 'can you recommend an architect?'

The developer beamed.'

'Can *I* recommend an architect?' he cried. 'You don't half fall on your feet, squire! Look, it so happens my wife's brother...'

'I see it as sort of, well, round,' explained Guk, 'with them smart little holes in for looking out the sides. So's you can see that god down there. It's a feature of the property, you know,' he added proudly.

The architect closed his eyes, visualising. He vibrated slightly.

'Also,' said Guk, 'we'd like the roof to slope. So's if anything fell on it, it'd roll off, know what I mean?'

'What he means,' interjected Mrs Guk bitterly, 'is we

120

appear to be dependent on rain dripping off the roof. We have been waiting six months for this ditch your brother-in-law was going on about.'

'Werl, councils,' and here the architect spread his hands, 'need I say more?'

'I have been down to our god,' said Guk, 'to pray for the Council getting their fingers out, but it doesn't seem to have done much good.'

'That,' snapped Mrs Guk, 'is on account of him not being a god at all. You have been praying to a lump.' She turned once more to the architect. 'Your brother-in-law seems to...'

'Hang about,' retorted the architect. 'He never said it was a god of *ditches*, did he?'

'He's got you there, mother,' said Guk.

'Shut your face!' barked his wife.

'Now, now,' said the architect. 'Right, let's sum up. You want a round dwelling with sloping roof. Personally, I wouldn't recommend it. It's neo-Paleolithic, that. Dead common. I mean, we've had a bloody recession of Pleistocene glaciers since then, haven't we?'

'Don't blind him with technical terms,' snapped Mrs Guk. 'He hasn't had all your advantages.'

'I've done all right,' grunted Guk. 'I bought this plot, didn't I?'

'Oh yes,' said Mrs Guk. 'Oh yes, you bought this plot, all right! Yes, it's generally agreed you bought this plot. There's no argument about that.'

'All I'm saying is,' said the architect, 'why not branch out a bit? Let yourselves go. I mean, it's a whole new era. Why not go for something,' and here he paused dramatically, 'Mesolithic?'

Guk glanced uncertainly at his wife.

'What's that like?' he enquired.

'Oval!' cried the architect ecstatically.

They stared at him. He selected a pointed stick from his quiver, and drew an oval in the dirt.

'Get away,' said Guk. 'It's not natural, that.'

'It's a whole new trend,' countered the architect. 'It's what the Middle Stone Age is going to be into.'

'It could very well upset the god,' murmured Guk, 'not being round.'

The architect glanced at Mrs Guk.

'It's going to be very fashionable,' he said quietly.

'It's been nearly a year!' cried Guk. 'You haven't even cleared the site.'

'Don't blame me,' replied the builder. 'It's your old lady wanted a bloody——what was it, Nerk?'

'Oval,' said his mate. 'Bloody oval.'

'Right,' said the builder. 'Takes working out, how much mud you need for an oval. If you'd wanted it round, you'd be sitting by the fire by now.'

'Why can't you just bring up a load of mud on the cart,' said Guk, 'use what you need, then take the rest back?'

'Did you hear that, Nerk?' said the builder.

'Got no idea,' said Nerk, 'has he?'

'Do you know what it costs to get the right mud, these days?' cried the builder. 'People been going mad since the last Ice Age, they're all into property, they reckon it's the end of the Glacial Era. Safe to invest in building, catch my drift? We can't just buy a load of mud and sit on it on the off chance, can we? It's working capital, mud. Anyway, you haven't got your ditch in yet. How we going to get the mud to the right consistency without water?'

'If the householder supplied the mud, of course,' said Nerk, 'we could do it on a cost-plus basis.'

Guk sighed.

'All right,' he said. 'You sure there are no snags?'

'*Snags*?' said the builder. 'Us, *snags*?'

'We been in this game a long time,' said Nerk.

''Course, it's bloody fallen down,' said the builder, 'what did you expect?'

'All them post holes,' said Nerk, surveying the very little recognisable remains. 'We *said* fourteen main post holes was too many. And as for thirty-four lesser stake holes...'

'Architects!' barked the builder. 'Haven't got the first idea, have they?'

'Ought to get their knees brown,' said Nerk.

'But all my mud,' wailed Guk, 'it's ruined! It's all over the place.'

'Yes, werl,' said the builder. 'Question of consistency. Can't say we never warned you.'

'If he'd had a ditch,' said Nerk, 'werl.'

'Oh, if he'd had a *ditch*,' said the builder, 'he'd be sitting by the fire by now.'

'We've been living in the open for two years,' said Mrs Guk, through gritted teeth. 'It's even worse than being a hole-dweller. I never thought I'd be involved in an evolutionary cul-de-sac when I married him.'

'I know what you mean,' said the builder. 'My wife's people are heath-dwellers. Very conservative. Wouldn't even crawl under a bush. You can hear their chests from ten miles away.'

'Tell you what we'll do,' said Nerk sympathetically. 'We could built you a hearth, as per specifications. Give you something to huddle round, wouldn't it?' He cracked a hazelnut, gobbled the kernel. 'Till the ditch comes in and you get the walls up.'

'Don't drop them nutshells all over my floor,' muttered Guk.

'Floor?' cried his wife, kicking a wormcast from what ought to have been her bedroom rug. '*Floor?*'

'Hurrah!' cried Guk. 'It's the ditch!'

He sprang up from the hearth and the smoking peat, and pointed. The builder and Nerk had returned, some eighteen months having elapsed, with four labourers, and begun digging a slit trench two hundred yards down the hill, between the Chez Guk site and the sea.

'Why are they digging it down there?' enquired Mrs Guk. 'It'll never flow uphill.'

Guk eased his arthritic joints down the slope, and lodged his enquiry.

'Not for you, this,' said the builder.

'Not for *us*?' shrieked Guk.

'Don't ask me,' said the builder. 'I only work here. Ask him.'

Guk turned, to see the developer emerging from the mist.

'What's this then?' shouted Guk.

'Building an estate,' said the developer. 'Several Smaller Executive Hutments. Bijou homes, know what I mean? For the discerning Mesolith.'

'*I'm* the discerning bloody Mesolith!' cried Guk. 'I been here six years, waiting for my fashionable oval home. If you put your development up down here, I won't even have anything to bloody discern! It's going to be between me and the god.'

The developer sighed.

'If it's any consolation,' he said. 'I don't reckon it's a god, after all. We've had it surveyed on behalf of a client who wants to put up a holiday camp, and the report does not indicate any sign of divinity.'

'Whatever it is,' shouted Guk, 'I want to be able to look at it.'

'Wish I could help,' said the developer, 'I really do. But I'm afraid the estate takes priority. It's a feature of the property, that view.'

'But what about *my* property? What am *I* going to be looking at?'

'Better ask my brother-in-law,' said the developer.

'Hallo,' said the architect, appearing from behind the cart. 'Long time, no see.'

'Never mind all that,' muttered Guk. 'Just tell me what's going up here.'

'Very nice little neo-Paleolithic estate,' said the architect. 'Thirty-two bijou round homes, plus patios.'

'*Round*?' shouted Guk. 'Bloody common old-fashioned working class round? In *our* neighbourhood? If I'd had round, I could've been sitting...what happened to oval?'

The architect shrugged.

'Never caught on, oval,' he said.

A Dingley Dell Situation

A good-humoured Christmas Chapter, containing an account of the ongoing marital involvements of the Pickwickians with some remarks about the reliability of the new Saab, a view of the yuletide economy with reference to the good offices of Mrs Margaret Thatcher, a disquisition upon such seasonal benisons as the quality of independent television and the scandal of welfare handouts to Trotskyite malingerers, together with some notes upon the sexual predispositions of Her Majesty's servants, the ubiquitousness of arabs, the inadequacy of daily help, the tide of blasphemous filth that threatens to engulf us all, and the gratifying buoyancy of the property market.

SHALL WE ALLOW OURSELVES the authorial licence of remarking that there was a particular spring to the step of Mr Winkle as he leapt from the tasteful leopardette driving seat of his Yule-buffed Peugeot and addressed himself to the wrought-iron intricacies of the Wardle gate?

Certainly, his spirit did not go unobserved by his good lady!

'Why do you not open my door for me, you bastard?' enquired Mrs Winkle. 'Can you not wait to get your hands upon the Wardles' au pair?'

'Shut your face, my dear!' cried Mr Winkle, doubtless distressed that his new executive kar-koat had snagged upon the Wardles' latch, leaving tufts of simulated beaver hanging from the elegant curlicues. 'And as to Miss Elke Lundqvist, let us remember that she is far from home this Christmas and doubtless in need of a little good cheer beneath the traditional mistletoe, or indeed anywhere else. Always provided,' and here the good fellow barked a short laugh that echoed ringingly across the Dingley Dell Development of Homes for the Discriminating Executive, 'she does not have a headache!'

He pressed the doorbell of Los Wardlos, and hardly had the

sonorous notes of *Volare* died than the rubicund countenance of Mr Wardle himself appeared, his bright-veined eyes twinkling in the light of the twin carriage-lamps, like very maraschinos.

'Huzzah!' cried Mr Wardle, a punch-clove flying from his shining lip and fixing itself upon Mrs Winkle's cheek like a commando's grapnel. 'Merry Christmas!' He swung wide the neo-Edwardian door. 'It is Kevin and Arabella Winkle, everyone!'

'Aha!' bellowed a cheery and familiar voice from within. 'Surgical stocking and friend!'

How they all laughed at Mr Pickwick's deft quip (for it was, of course, none but he), and clapped their hands, and nudged, and winked! Somehow, Mr Pickwick was always the cynosure of such jocund assemblies, Mr Pickwick with his gravel pits, his elegant Romford casinos, his discreet loan companies, his renowned nationwide Jolly Jiblet takeaway emporia, above all his cheery escort agencies from the august portals of which no Pickwickian had ever been turned away without a sloe-eyed mulatto or big Turk, at practically cost.

The Winkles having by now crossed the threshold, Mrs Wardle herself leapt graciously from the comfortable lap of Mr Tupman, with whom she had been commiserating upon the unfortunate inability of Mrs Tupman to comprehend the manifold pressures exerted upon a man doing his utmost to manufacture chiming dangle-dollies in direct competition with cheap South Korean labour, and advanced upon them, rebuttoning the bodice of her seemly lurex jump-suit as she went.

'Will you take a glass of punch?' she offered, her clear bell-like voice making the Scotcade chandelier tinkle and twinkle in the warm electric firelight. 'It is made from a special recipe Mr Wardle and I brought back from our recent travels in Ibiza.'

'Thank you so much, dear Mrs Wardle,' replied Mr Winkle. 'Mine is a large one.'

'That,' cried a beaming Mr Pickwick, 'is not what I hear!'

How the happy company roared! The welkin rang with a multitude of cries to the effect that Mr Pickwick was a caution, that he would be the death of them, that it was easy to see how he had revolutionised the fast food industry, and so forth; and, indeed, they might have been chuckling still, had Mrs Winkle

126

not chosen to change the subject by declaring her deep sympathy for Mr Pickwick at the tragic news that his dear wife had gone off with a teenage Carib bouncer from one of Mr Pickwick's own fashionable bingo establishments.

But hardly had this intelligence imparted itself upon the rapt company—how news of dear ones flies thick and fast when friends who have not met these twelve months past conjoin around the festive tree—than there came a great clatter-my-batter, a loud fulmunderdiddle, a roaring thunnerkin-bunnerkin from beyond the doors, as of a mountain of tin cans crashing down into the echoing valley beneath, and Mr Alfred Jingle, his auburn wig a-wry and his lipstick smeared, burst into their midst!

'New Volvo—missed gate—sharp turn—icy patch—bloody Peugeot—written off!' he exclaimed.

What a tumult ensued! What a rush to the door! And what a joyous relief flooded all their hearts upon their perception that it was not *their* Peugeot which had been reduced to scrap by Mr Jingle's untimely buffet! All hearts, that is, save the one pounding within the breast of the hapless Mr Winkle as that worthy stared, mute, at the pile of dismembered tin which had so lately, and so bravely, borne him thither.

'It is my opinion,' offered Mr Tupman, by way of consolation, 'that you had been better advised to have purchased a Saab. There is in their reinforced body shell a security afforded by none other of my acquaintance.' Here he indicated the outlines of the item in question, just perceptible through the frosty gloaming. 'Not, of course, that I am proud of my selection of a foreign product, but which of us in the wisdom of his years would now purchase the offerings of British Leyland?'

'How everything degenerates about us!' exclaimed Mrs Trundle, dashing a tear from her young and pretty eye with a Wedgwood-pattern Kleenex.

'So true,' nodded her husband. 'Personally, I blame the blackamoors, do I not?'

'Well said, dear Mr Trundle!' cried Mr Tupman warmly. 'I do not, naturally, have anything to reproach them with personally, and there is no gainsaying the appeal of their piccaninnies, but, surely, to take men so recently descended

127

from the colonial trees and place them in positions of responsibility within our great manufacturing industries is flying in the very face of nature?'

'And furthermore,' declaimed Mr Pickwick, who had joined the outside party with a shrewd view to valuing Mr Winkle's Peugeot for scrap, 'my long and if I may say so successful entrepreneurial career leads me to believe that if the good Lord had wished men to form themselves into unions, He would have placed chimney pots on their heads!' As several of the company applauded this wisdom, he turned to his dimpling neighbour. 'What say you to that, dear Mrs Tupman?'

Mrs Tupman lowered her eyes demurely.

'What I have never been able to understand,' she murmured, 'is how people capable of putting a man on the Moon seem totally unable to stop rice from sticking together.'

It was at this point, as all stood nodding sagely, that the door of Mr Jingle's Volvo opened, and a Fat Boy emerged. Mr Pickwick, by way of enquiry, turned to Mr Jingle, and raised a quizzical eyebrow.

'Reason I bought Volvo,' explained Mr Jingle. 'Saw advertisement—man driving Volvo—late at night—deserted countryside—flagged down by comely young fellow—fellow climbs in—talk about antiques—frightfully cosy—turns out young fellow attracted by Volvo—ideal car for me—rushed out—cash on nail—here we are!'

'Won't you please introduce us?' enquired Mr Wardle.

'Ullo,' said the Fat Boy.

'Few words,' explained Mr Jingle. 'Hairdresser—MI5—nice manners.' He adjusted his hairpiece. 'Promised him trip to France.'

Mr Wardle cleared his throat.

'Shall we go in to dinner?' he said.

And so they did. And what a feast was there! Such avocado soup, such taramasalata, such poppadums, such deliciously thawed ratatouille, and—goes it not without saying?—such poultry! No mundane turkey or downmarket duck at this groaning board, but fashionable goose, the mounds of white fat steaming and quivering on each eager plate, or elegant pigeon, a generous gift from Mr Pickwick's new shoot (acquired by him upon the takeover of an ailing massage-parlour empire), each little bird so well accounted for by the guns of Mr Pickwick's parliamentary acquaintances that the Yuletide dining-room echoed with the crunch of bridgework and the patter of pellets in the finger-bowls!

And the conversation! How the witty perceptions flew hither and yon upon such divers topics as hysterectomy and central heating, the relaxation of exchange controls and the brilliance of Miss Penelope Keith, and with what oohings and aahings and claspings of hands did each of that company greet the news of the other, anent the almost embarrassingly ridiculous prices that the houses of all of them could now command.

Yet what was all this but the joyous gustatory prolegomenon to the entry of the Pudding? The lights went out, the Fat Boy squealed, Mr Pickwick sprang cheerily on Mrs Tupman, and then, her radiant features lit tantalisingly from beneath by the glow of incinerating Spanish brandy, Miss Elke Lundqvist bore in that giant ebon sphere, that stone-ground low-calory pesticide-free masterpiece, that Sunday Times Club miracle offer *pudding*!

How thunderous the aplause! How eagerly the nearest men grasped their hostess's plump thigh in gratitude! How maliciously glinted the fair eyes of the ladies in the flickering pudding-light!

But what is this! The ravishing Miss Elke Lundqvist, her thoughts perhaps not there but in that far fjord to which the worthy Mrs Wardle would not let her return this Christmas and where her young friends may even at this moment be rolling ecstatically around their Yuletide sauna, the ravishing but preoccupied Miss Elke Lundqvist has *slipped*!

The pudding flew! The flaming liquor spilled upon the remarkable embonpoint of Miss Elke Lundqvist! And, true to the traditional gallantry of his English stock, the selfless Mr Winkle, until then morosely quiet with his thoughts of broken cars and yet more broken teeth, leapt from his chair and hurled himself upon her, beating with his bare hands the flames which threatened to engulf her bust!

What confusion! What tumultuous cries! What threshings in the dark!

The lights snapped on, and there, supine upon the Casa Pupo rug, smouldering, yes, but otherwise unharmed, Miss

Elke Lundqvist lay, muttering those Nordic imprecations, reader, over which both decorousness and monolinguality require us to draw a blessed veil. And beside her, oddly bent, the unnervingly inert form of the evening's hero, Mr Kevin Winkle.

With Mrs Winkle's pastry-fork protruding from his throat.

NEXT WEEK: A further good-humoured chapter in which Sergeant Buzfuz knocks a confession out of Mrs Arabella Winkle.

How Now! A Rat?

EVER SINCE OUR CAT was run over by an Austin Cambridge in the autumn of 1969, I have looked under cars.

The cat, I should like you to know—for no better reason than if your face is plunged into a sopping handkerchief you will be disinclined to read further—survived. Its tail, however, did not, and was duly disposed of by a tidy vet along with the rest of the day's bleak loppings. The cat came home, a somewhat bewildered amputee, and for some months thereafter sat on our front wall, staring bitterly at the Austin in the drive next door, and, whenever the remorse-torn owner appeared, swishing its stump.

It was not my neighbour's fault. Prior to the accident, our cat slept under cars, ignoring one of life's prime tenets; which is that if your hobby is snuggling up against radials, it pays to be a light sleeper.

So for ten years the cat has slept on the sideboard, and I have looked under my car before igniting. Thus it was that yesterday morning, outside the College for Distributive Trades in Leicester Square, I saw the rat.

Now, hitherto, I had known one thing about the rat (which is one thing more than I know about the College for Distributive Trades), and that was that a rat is more scared of you than you are of it. It is the one thing I know about all animals, and I tend to proceed as if I believe it, trusting that it is also the one thing that animals know about people. If I ever meet an alligator, I'll let you know who screams first. Anyway, there was this rat, looking out from behind my rear tyre rather winsomely, as if hoping that Beatrix Potter might stroll past and put it in the big money.

I kicked the tyre.

The rat began rooting in its ear.

I opened the car door, and slammed it.

131

The rat shut it eyes.

You don't have too many choices open, with a rat under your rear wheel. Either you drive off, singing to yourself to drown the crunch and possibly wondering what there is in the tool kit that will prise rat bones from your tread; or else you look ostentatiously at your watch, note that 7.50 am is no bad time to take a stroll, and trudge off into the sleet.

In the square itself, on its pitiful smear of khaki grass, the rubbish towered; twenty feet high, perhaps. And very sinister: not, as it were, honest rubbish, haphazardly scattered, jamjars, boxes, sardine cans, bones, old bedsprings, not *visible* rubbish; but those appalling giant maggots of grey plastic bags, guts filled with *hidden* rubbish. Poke them, they move and settle; they squelch; they shine in the drizzle, as if with diseased sweat; they look poised to bloat and split, spilling their rotting innards. They are *live* rubbish.

They are also Soho rubbish; it does not pay to speculate too far on this.

There was a sign up, a weird piece of cosmetic jargon, a bureaucratic placebo, cobbled by some official finger after, I have little doubt, much inter-departmental winging of yellow bumf: the sign said TEMPORARY REFUSE RECEPTION CENTRE. Oh, really? As if the maggots had crawled here, like boat-people, like battered wives, to be fed Horlicks and Jaffa cakes by cheery WRVS Minivers in lisle stockings, before being bussed out to more permanent encampments in, say, Dorking or Hereford, where the smaller maggots could romp and flourish, and forget.

Over the rim of this repulsive tip, Shakespeare is just visible. Not, perhaps, my favourite impression of him; the marble digit lies along his cheek, there is a cheap quizzical ripple to his lip; it is a poet from a Goldwyn bio-pic, it is The Bard Having A Bit Of A Think, it is The Swan Of Avon Conceiving Sonnet IX.

Nevertheless, ill-chiselled or not, it is the best of England stood among the worst.

From his four stone mates that gaze upon his feet from the four corners of the square, assorted other ironies vibrate. Here is John Hunter, anatomist, surgeon, giant of British medicine, whose riveting *Treatise On The Natural History of Human Teeth*, though written in 1778, is still a watchword wherever thinking dentists foregather, and whose monumental *Treatise On Venereal Disease* is still ignored in a thousand upstairs rooms not fifty yards from where his stone eyes gaze. How does this great engineer of health feel now, with mouldy muck about his pedestal?

Or Joshua Reynolds? To immortalise beauty, to freeze grace, to permanentise an age of elegance, to end up gazing at a fungus-frosted bean tin with a fish-head in it?

And Isaac Newton, that great but self-effacing genius, who dreamed of the refining revelations yet to come? 'I seem to have been only a boy playing on the sea-shore, and diverting myself in now and then finding a smoother pebble or a prettier shell than ordinary, whilst the great ocean of truth lay all undiscovered before me.' Well, the great ocean of truth lies before you now, old cock. Uncovered. Crusted Kleenex and half-eaten trashburgers and torn porn pix and old dog-ends, is where we would appear to have come.

Only the fourth bust yawns. Hogarth has seen it all before. That it has actually grown worse since Gin Alley is probably no surprise, either.

Partly because the present festering detritus is only the foreground to the more permanent rot behind. Let us line up our cheap ironic foresight between these two convenient hills of rotting industrial action: how neat it is that The Sex Shop should lie a dozen yards beyond! Next to that, Peep Show, it says, Free Admission, and next to that, Models Required, Apply Within. Last night's drained addicts stumble around the pedestrian precinct, waiting for the amusement arcades to open, waiting to turn a trick to feed the habit: *Scouting For Boys* has become a rather different book.

The AA flanks the west side of the square, another institution up the spout: change and decay, friends, decline and fall, buy my *Big Girl's Book Of Free Tyre Gauges*, go on the Treasure Trail, win an AA lollypop.

Thinking of tyres, I returned slowly to my rat.

An interesting little bastard, the rat. Cornerstone of literary symbolism. Just what you need in Leicester Square, Albert Camus in his grave these eighteen years, and still Algiers FC can't find a decent new goalkeeper. They broke the mould: Pat Jennings is all very well, but he's all fingers and thumbs when it comes to plague. Not me, though: there's still a lot of literary juice to be wrung out of *Rattus rattus*.

133

We have consistently failed to learn the true lesson of Skinner's box: when Burrhus Frederic Skinner first popped a rat into his patent box, thereby ensuring that behavioural psychology would never again be a subject you could discuss over dinner, his intention was merely to demonstrate simple conditioning: the rat would bang a lever with its conk and receive a Smartie, it would push another lever with its paw and receive a poke in the eye. Thus taught, it remembered.

All rats do.

However—and this is the lesson to be hammered home to the dim biped—if you put a *man* in Skinner's box, he keeps getting poked in the eye. Thus taught, he never remembers. The poke in the eye, of course, takes various forms: war, backing second favourites for a place, buying used cars from little old ladies, going to Benidorm, picking up big blondes with hollow legs, striking for a forty per cent increase—whatever man happens to keep on doing, he keeps getting poked in the eye, and he keeps jumping back into the box and thumping the lever.

In this way, Smarties have been all but eliminated from human society, and if you look round Leicester Square today, you will see the result. It is a festering little microcosm of greed, lust, disease, violence, and general decay.

That the rat under my tyre was fully aware of all this—he may possibly have missed the reference to Pat Jennings, but that's about all—I have no doubt whatever. That is why he did not choose to move; in me, he instinctively recognised a man who had come, grudgingly, to respect the rat, and who would not, therefore, emboss him to the tarmac.

For the rats now know what Skinnerians do not choose to recognise: that it is not the human being which is a complex analogue of the rat, but the rat which is a simple analogue of the human being, and that it is through its clear simplicity that the rat will survive, and through his befogged complexity that the man will go under. In Leicester Square, the marbled remembrances of that complexity in its rare clarity are piled around and hidden by the detritus of rotted intelligence.

The rats will win.

'How now! A rat? Dead, for a ducat, dead!'

But behind the arras, it was a man that got it, in the confusion.

134

Red Handed

Bulgaria, through the Bulgarian Telegraph Agency, offered yesterday to co-operate fully with Scotland Yard in clearing up the cause of death of two Bulgarian émigrés in London. It is suspected that a poison-tipped umbrella was the murder weapon.—The Guardian

BENEATH THE HEATHROW *ARRIVALS* sign, Detective Inspector Clench leafed through *Penthouse*. Whenever he grunted, trembled ash floated down from his Whiff; and as it did, he moved, by reflex, his shimmering toecaps from the line of flight.

'Look at that,' he muttered. 'You plug it in the mains. Diabolical.'

Detective Constable Filbert did not look up from his *New Society*.

'Ah,' he murmured. 'Sir.'

'Ban the lot,' said Clench. 'Root 'em out, burn the stock, throw the key away. Come down like a wolf pack. Mob handed.' A light flared in his hard little eyes. 'In the small hours,' he said. The light faded. 'If I had my way,' he said.

Filbert pencilled a note in the margin of an article about the rehabilitation of stranglers, and closed his paper.

'I think a case might be made out for the therapeutic value of such, er...'

'Oh!' cried Detective Inspector Clench, holding the gatefold up before him and addressing himself to her from a distance of some six inches. 'Oh, he thinks a case might be made out for the therapeutic value of such, er! Oh, well he would, wouldn't he, Sharon? He will have delved deep into all such matters up at the Varsity, what? There is little what slips past the beadies of Detective Constable Filbert BA. He is a good bloke to have in your corner when the chips is down, Sharon, my word he is! Any villains pull their shooters on Professor Clench or anything, Sharon, he'd slap 'em silly with his diploma, wouldn't you, son?'

Filbert swallowed; polished his glasses, vigorously; waited.

'I'm afraid I don't know a great deal about Bulgaria, sir,' he said, after a while. 'Do you?'

'Yes,' replied Clench. 'I looked it up, didn't I? The word *bugger* comes from it, according to the dictionary. Also, its capital is called Sofia.'

'Is that all?' said Filbert.

'All?' replied Clench. 'More than enough, if you ask me. Put two and two together,' and here he put one huge hand on his hip, fluttered his lashless eyes, and pursed his thin lips, 'follow my meaning?'

'Ah,' said Filbert.

'Yes, I should think our little colleague will be mincing his way through Customs any minute now,' said Clench. 'Watch out for a bloke in regulation boots and a handbag.'

'It'll be jolly interesting working with someone from an entirely different, as it were, juridical culture, won't it, sir?' said Filbert.

Clench stared at him for a while.

'I think I'll call him Vanessa,' he said, at last.

Filbert's neck coloured.

'As a Socialist,' he murmured, 'I think it only fair to...'

'Give child molesters a new packet of boiled sweets?' suggested Clench heavily. 'Sentence muggers to six months at Claridges? Elevate George Davis to the peerage, possibly?' He folded his magazine, slipped it into his coat-pocket, glanced at his watch. 'Well, you and Vanessa are going to have a lot in common, son, I can see that. Doubtless you and him will while away many a happy evening up your diggings, discussing *Das Kapital* over the instant, painting placards, collecting signatures for Chilean tearaways. Yes, very nice, I'm sure you'll get on very well with this foreigner. Pity he's not black, really.'

'I'm sorry?'

''Course you are, 'course you are,' said Clench, getting his bulk upright. 'Still, he's probably swarthy. Probably looks very nice in his pearls.'

He turned; and stopped, because his way was blocked.

136

'Insbegtor Glench?'

The man was of Clench's height, but perhaps half as broad again. The head set in the astrakhan collar seemed to have been finished on a lathe: the nose buffed flat against the face, the tiny ears hardly breaking the line of the close-cropped head.

'That's me,' said Clench.

Expressionless, the Bulgarian detective clasped Clench to him, and hugged.

Released, Clench glanced across at Filbert.

'There you are,' he said. 'What did I tell you?'

But the words were gasped rather than spoken, and when the other two turned to go, Clench touched his rib-cage secretly and gingerly, just to make sure.

They had reached the escalator opposite W.H. Smith, when the Bulgarian suddenly, pointer-like, stiffened. Then he sprang; and a young man poised to pocket an unpurchased ball-point found himself dangling a foot above the ground. But only briefly. Having examined him dispassionately for a moment or two, the Bulgarian let go with a short right hook. The young man fell to the floor in a faint patter of teeth. As he lay there, the Bulgarian booted him, twice. Then he trod on his fingers. Then, with remarkable delicacy, he picked up the fallen pen and handed it back to the cashier.

'Oh, God!' muttered Detective Constable Filbert to the Bulgarian. 'Did you caution him, sir?'

The Bulgarian screwed up his eyes. He turned to Clench.

'Woddy mean?' he said.

'He means,' said Clench, gleefully, 'did you advise the little bleeder of his rights?'

'Wod rights?' asked the Bulgarian. 'Issa griminal. Issa willain.'

'Point taken,' said Clench. 'Clean up here, will you, Filbert? Me and Boris are going off for a drink.'

And Clench, humming, led the Bulgarian away.

Later that afternoon, Clench and Filbert were sitting in Clench's office. Clench was bitterly typing out warrant applications in octuplicate; Filbert was reading *Andreas Baader:*

The Restless Spirit, a tear occasionally glistening behind his bi-focals.

'Got to clear this up soon,' muttered Clench, 'umbrellas, diplomats, MI5, foreigners, corpses, autopsies—we could be here over bloody Christmas!'

'It's an extraordinarily sensitive area, sir,' said Filbert.

The door opened.

The Bulgarian detective came in. He had a small balding man under one arm.

'Hallo, Boris,' said Clench, not without warmth. 'We was wondering what had happened to you. I've just got another eighty or ninety forms to fill in, then we'll get under way. Who's that?'

'Is killer,' said the Bulgarian. He dropped the man to the floor.

'A suspect?' cried Filbert. 'So soon?'

'Woddy mean susbegt?' said the Bulgarian. 'Is killer.'

'You mean he's admitted it?' cried Clench.

'Nod yed,' said the Bulgarian. 'I only just pinchim. Is known willain. I geddim from files.'

The prisoner recovered his breath, and staggered to his feet.

'It's a fit-up, Mr Clench!' he cried.

'Stone me!' exclaimed Clench. 'It's Foxy Collinson! Well, well, well! I have spent much of my working life trying to put Foxy away, Boris. Only thing is, there was always eighty-seven people willing to swear they was having a fish supper with him in Melbourne at the time.'

'I got a lot of friends, Mr Clench,' said Foxy.

The Bulgarian hit him with an electric typewriter.

'Poor fellow,' said Filbert, kneeling down swiftly beside him, 'he went to a secondary modern, you know. Good heavens, what's this shoved inside the lining of his coat?'

'Is umbrella,' said Boris. 'I geddim bang to rights. Also in bockets is 9mm Luger and four Mills bombs.'

'Funny,' said Clench, 'for a forger.'

Filbert had stood up, and was staring at the regulation hat-stand.

'I'd been wondering what happened to my brolly,' he murmured. 'I don't like to mention—'

The Bulgarian picked up the typewriter again. Clench laid a soothing hand on his arm.

'I wonder if you'd mind leaving us for a moment, Filbert,' he said.

The constable went out, snatching up his unfinished yoghurt furiously.

'We mop up now, yes?' enquired the Bulgarian. 'I arrange identity parade. Come!'

He picked up Foxy Collinson, and walked through the door into the next room, where three squat men in crumpled brown suits stood fingering their homburgs.

'Is men from Embassy,' explained the Bulgarian. 'Is widnesses.'

'DET IS KILLER!' cried the men from the Embassy, pointing. They shuffled out.

Detective Inspector Clench lit a Whiff. The match-flame shivered as he fought to suppress elation; memories whirled in his head, fetched up against problems. He paced the room, heavy-booted.

'Boris,' he began. He stopped. He looked at the inert villain. 'Boris, while my respect, no, my admiration, knows no—what I mean is—'

'I know wod you mean,' said the Bulgarian. 'You god funny system here. You worrying about gedding conwiction, yes?'

'Lawyers,' muttered Clench. He turned, walked across to the coffee machine, punched a button savagely.

Behind him, glass exploded. He spun around.

There was no window, now. Nor was there a Collinson.

'We god conwiction,' said Boris.

'This note,' said the Detective Chief Superintendent, 'puzzles me, Filbert. Inspector Clench says he has flown to Sofia to join the Bulgarian Police Force. Is it some sort of code? Perhaps some sort of joke?'

'No, sir,' said Filbert. It's straight up. He has gorn orf with that Commie poof, hasn't he?'

The Chief Superintendent looked up from the note.

'I say, Filbert,' he said, 'are you feeling all right?'

'I'll survive,' said Filbert.

Talkin' Wid de Lord

THE PROBLEM, as I see it, is not theological at all, but social: when, that is, the Almighty shakes whatever it is I have for a hand (a wing? a flipper? an ectoplasmic pod?), informs me that He is pleased to meet me, and offers me a plate of little sausages on sticks, do I reply: 'I will give thanks unto Thee, for I am fearfully and wonderfully made' or 'I see QPR played another blinder, then?'

If, of course, He would ever say He was pleased to meet me. Leaving aside such metaphysical imponderabilia as whether He already knows me even as I am known, how do we begin to make sensible guesses about divine etiquette? After all, what class is God? Is He a toff? Lower middle? Senior executive? Working? Not—marginally possible—English at all, but someone who will simply click his heels and snap 'Entzückt!' or (shaking His Rastifarian locks) cry 'Gimme some skin!'?

Perhaps He doesn't shake hands at all. Many foreigners (if He will forgive me, and there is every reason to believe that He will, this being a trespass of minor proportions) embrace; Eskimoes rub noses; some Melanesians, according to Margaret Mead, pull one another's ears on meeting. It is possible He does all of these, and more.

Though, on balance of probability, not. With a million people dying every week, there would never be time for anything but the most cursory of greetings: three people every two seconds pouring into Reception from geriatric wards, DC-10's, Cambodian bunkers, fogbound motorways, imploded tankers, KKK rallies, inept barbershops, East End casinos, potholes, scaffolds, free fall parachute displays—many of them, too, still somewhat bewildered and in no shape to have their ears pulled by the Almighty.

Unless time is different There, mind. A thousand ages in His sight are, as I understand it, like an evening gone: Crossing

Over may well be like going into Italy and suddenly finding small change with 1,000 written on it. You may get anything up to six eternal months to the hour sterling, Over There.

It's a complicated business, eternity.

I shouldn't have got myself enmeshed in its boggling coils at all, had it not been for Glenda Jackson, Willie Whitelaw, Flora Robson and, of course, Richard Baker. They, and 596 like them, are why I am standing here today, just inside the pearly gates, wondering if I ought to be wearing a dinner jacket. For those six hundred eminences have just presented a petition to the General Synod of the Church of England, asking for the restoration to normal worship of the Book of Common Prayer and the Authorised Version of the Bible, and have thus set a cat among the liturgical pigeons more than likely, as such things traditionally do, to leave the loft full of bloodstained feathers and beak-torn fur.

Now, I must point out immediately (since I have no wish to spend whatever mortal time I have left writing mollifying letters to millions of apoplectic readers whose temple veins begin to throb like lugworms whenever they feel that the Litany is under the cosh) that I care not a whit how people worship, or, indeed, whether they worship at all. With the gas-boiler on the blink and the lawn full of moss and a phone-bill just in that makes the National Debt look like Bob Cratchit's take-home pay after stoppages, I have scant inclination to worry about other people's immortal souls; and in fact should have paid no attention to my own, had it not been for a remark passed on this morning's *Today* programme, while I was shaving, by a hired torpedo sent along by the General Synod to stick up for his employers' desperate tinkerings. 'It's all about,' he murmured, 'finding a comfortable way of talking to God.'

Which, as it was bound to do, left me for some minutes staring, motionless, at that soap-girt face which in the fullness of time, or (who knows?) its shallowness, may, if the General Synod, Richard Baker, and numerous other unimpeachable authorities are to be credited, be staring at its Maker and murmuring rubbish about how nice it is to be here.

Because how *will* one talk to Him?

The manner will be the least of one's worries. Personally, though I risk offending against Glenda Jackson and incurring the wrath of Willie Whitelaw, I shall probably stick to the vernacular, since I should feel a fool, upon shaking hands/rubbing noses, if I were to say: 'O God our heavenly Father, who by Thy gracious providence dost cause the former and the latter rain to fall upon the earth, that it may bring forth fruit in the use of man, we give Thee humble thanks that it hath pleased Thee...' and so on. I do not talk like that, and should anyway have a job sustaining it when the conversation turned to whether He had enjoyed *Annie Hall*.

Which is where we approach the nub: for while the Synod and the Chartists currently lock horns on how God is to be addressed, I am chiefly exercised over the fraught business of what we shall actually talk *about*. What, in short, is He interested in?

I am assuming that He and I will not have a great deal of time together, but at the same time assuming that He will try to get around and have a word with everyone, since He is not called the Lord of Hosts for nothing. I suppose I see the occasion as a sort of huge Divine Garden Party, with the newly dead pouring in constantly through one gate, having a drink and a bridge-roll and a quick chat, and then pouring out again through another, towards some further destination as yet unspecified. We shall all thus have only a very few minutes to make an impression; and if that seems a somewhat worldly and ignoble ambition, I have to say in my defence that that is part of my nature and I do not wish to be fobbed off with a nod and a smile and promptly forgotten by the Almighty. I shall, after all, have waited a long time (the longer, if He will once again forgive me, the better) for this chance, I shall have to have popped my very clogs for the opportunity, and I have no intention of being no more than a brief fuzzed face in the crowd, instantly shoved out of sight again as a mob comes in from the latest Kurdish uprising.

I had, as a matter of fact, a sort of dress rehearsal for it, once, and I do not intend to let the like happen again. I was at a Royal wedding reception, almost certainly through a misaddressed envelope, when HM the Q, such were the peristaltic convulsions of the huge crowd, suddenly appeared in front of me, as in some bizarre Paul Jones. She smiled (radiantly, I believe the word is), and I glanced down deferentially, frantically framing some extraordinarily clever epigram about its being remarkably warm for the time of year, and when I looked up again, she had turned into Bernard Levin. I watched her smile being borne away through the mob with an expression on my own stricken face which led the solicitous Bernard to clutch my forearm and enquire whether I wanted a glass of water.

I have no intention of letting that happen Over There. Much as I should enjoy Bernard's scintillating company for (if Einstein will forgive me this time) the duration, I do not plan to move from the celestial spot until God and I have chewed the fat for an adequate spell.

But how to go about it?

Normal cocktail-party opening gambits are, of course, quite useless. 'Have you ever noticed...?' or 'Has it ever struck you as peculiar that...?' or 'I bet you didn't realise that...?' are quite obviously out of the question. Indeed, omniscience itself could well prove to be an unclearable hurdle, since it would patently come as no surprise to the Almighty that Clement Freud once held the record of 105 omelettes in half an hour or that the male rabbit, if startled, will eat its own children. Facts are the one thing calculated to make the divine eye glaze and wander.

Likewise, jokes. Bizarre though it may be to ponder it, God has heard something like eighteen million jokes, including over two hundred about a man who went into a chemist's shop. Worse than that, and still more bizarre, is that—omnipotency being the thing it is—He also tells them better than anybody else.

We may well be on safer ground with opinions. Assuming that theologians have got it right in framing the concept of Free Will and weren't just cobbling any old thing together to make some sort of logical sense out of life's contradictory lunacies, I think we may take it that our opinions are our own and have not all been previously covered by God. He may, that is to say, be fascinated by our view that the new Lancia reminds us of the old Fiat, intrigued by our suggestion that it is better, when trying to get to Maidenhead from Barnes, to avoid the M4 altogether, and surprised to learn that we felt *Tinker, Tailor, Soldier, Spy* to be incomprehensible cobblers (enabling us, perhaps, to get in some snappy riposte, such as 'It's all right for you, Almighty, you knew who the mole was all the time, har-har-har!')

Not, mind, that there might not be dire pitfalls even here. We do not, for example, know whether the Almighty Himself holds views; is there any point in having opinions when You are in a position to alter the conditions under which You hold them (if there are any Jesuits out there, my number is ex-directory)? Indeed, especially for those who do not cleave to the Free Will dogma, it may be that the facts *are* God's opinions, i.e., He feels that the tallest mountain in the world should be exactly 29,002 feet high and that Elton John should go bald, which means that you could be on very unsteady ground if you were to use your precious minutes over the elysial Babycham in saying that, in your opinion, the First World War was a bad thing. He might have enjoyed the Somme enormously, the supernal equivalent of blow-football, and meet your small talk with a very stony eye indeed.

Which, now I come to think further upon it, may well be the reason that Willie and Glenda and Richard and all the rest are in favour of sticking to the frequently unfathomable 1662 version; because when all is said, done, and tastefully interred, would it not be better, at that great encounter in the sky, for me to grasp my Maker firmly by the hand, look unwaveringly into His welcoming eye, and cry, with Psalm 147: 'HE HATH NO PLEASURE IN THE STRENGTH OF AN HORSE: NEITHER DELIGHTETH HE IN ANY MAN'S LEGS?'

Which will not only resonate wonderfully over the surrounding hubbub, but also baffle even Him so effectively that He will still be wondering what it was that clever little soul meant long after I have passed through the further gate, and gone.

No Quarter!

A Thrilling Serial Story of the Afghan War

The story so far: It is the winter of '79-'80, and devilish doings are afoot from Cairo to the Khyber! The Bharmi of Persia has been whipping the dusky heathens into a frenzy, Johnny Turk's niffy kinsmen are chopping one another into catsmeat for the sheer jolly fun of it, as these chaps will, the swarthy Gyppos are as restless as ever (particularly as their suspicions grow that the crafty Hebrew is plotting something typically devious against them), while, in Afghanistan, the powder keg lying athwart the British lion's overland route to India awaits the imminent sparking of the dreadful fuse!

There is no question but that the sooty hordes are giving our tail a severe tweak, and even Uncle Sam's bald eagle is looking askance at his bedraggled feathers! Can all this be mere coincidence? Not a bit of it! Behind this massed pottiness of the ragged infidels lies our old adversary, the Russian bear, grown once more restless in that cage of tempered steel in which the Empire has confined him; straining yet again to burst out and gain that foothold on the Indian Ocean which will ensure his domination (or so he thinks!) of our trade routes to the East, Ivan has marched on Kabul. There are skirmishes at Kandahar! There are clashes at Jalalabad! There is the crackling of musketry along the Khyber! And, as the old names ring out once more, and the old ghosts stir above the thin red line of ancient graves below the snow-capped Kush, all the world wonders. Will Old Albion bestir herself from her sleepy shires? Will the lion roar anew? Will the bright bugles of Aldershot echo again across the distant fastnesses of the turbulent East?

*Need one ask! Even now, a British Expeditionary Force is disembarking from its Dan-Air Britannia, not twenty miles from the seething Afghan capital...*NOW READ ON

'God, it's devilish hot!' exclaimed Snotty Mouse-Fondling, as

145

his Doc Martens touched the Afghan tarmac with a hiss of decomposing rubber. He whipped his topee from his Adidas bonk-bag, and jammed it on.

'I say!' cried Buffy. 'What a wizard tile!'

'Yes,' said Snotty, setting his fine jaw and gazing at the simmering horizon, 'it belonged to my father.'

Buffy followed his chum's stare.

'Is he—' he faltered, '—is he buried out there somewhere?'

'No,' said Snotty, 'he has a stall in Portobello Road. He's knocking these out at £3.95. They're made in Korea.'

Buffy nodded sagely.

'Yes,' he muttered, 'he's a clever swine, your yellow milliner.'

'Not really,' said Snotty. 'The pater's picking 'em up for two quid apiece.' He laughed his easy, indolent laugh. 'Almost a hundred per cent retail mark-up, what?'

Buffy smote his thigh with his riding-crop!

'By heaven!' he cried. 'And they say old England's finished!'

Snotty turned his stern blue eyes upon his tubby friend.

'Who does?' he barked.

'Sorry, old chap,' murmured Buffy. 'Just an expression. I say, who's this fellow?'

Approaching them across the dusty airstrip was a short naked man, entirely painted green; on his head he wore a bowler hat, affixed to which was a hand-lettered sign bearing the legend INGLISH TWITT and a downward-pointing arrow. He extended his hand.

'Witherspoon,' he said, 'British vice-consul.'

Snotty shook his hand.

'Jolly good camouflage, old man,' he said. 'I took you for a tree, except for the hat. I think that's probably a mistake.'

'It isn't that,' said Witherspoon. 'This was the only way the students would let me out of the Embassy compound.'

The men of the BEF reeled! They gnashed their teeth! They shook their mighty fists!

'Heathen scum!' thundered Buffy.

'And not, I suspect, students at all,' muttered Snotty, tapping the side of his aquiline beak. 'Anyone with a degree would know there was an e on *twitte*, what? I shouldn't think there's a manjack among them who's spired a potty in his life! Red-infested rebels, more like.'

Two white runnels chased suddenly down Witherspoon's verdant cheeks.

'Thank God you're here!' he choked.

'Steady, old fruit,' muttered Snotty, smiting the vice-consul on the shoulder and staring with characteristically taciturn courage at his emerald palm, 'no need for blubbing now! Lead us towards the sound of the guns!'

'When are the rest arriving?' enquired Witherspoon.

'Rest? Good God, man, are twelve stout Englishmen and true not enough? Did you not see *Zulu!*?'

Witherspoon shook his head.

'They smashed our projector,' he said. 'They burned our films.' He blinked, twice. 'The consul himself perished trying to save *Big Ones*.'

Despite the broiling sun, Snotty's blood ran cold! A vein began to twitch in his left temple! He snatched up his duty-free carrier!

'I think it's time,' he said, between clenched teeth, 'that we had a little chat with Mister Marx!'

Snotty and Buffy lay on their tummies, scrutinising the brown Kabul plain from a convenient foothill through their powerful Woolco binoculars. Behind them, the men had dug in, in trusty Cockney fashion, and were biding their time in traditional manner with cheery games of Binatone squash on their portable Sonys. The waiting was always the worst part.

'I make it,' said Buffy quietly, 'two thousand T-62s, sixteen SAM batteries, four hundred APCs, and ten gunship squadrons.'

Snotty gripped his plump chum's bicep.

'Good counting, old man,' he said quietly. He turned his head, and shouted: 'Trotter!'

'Sar!'

'Loudhailer, Trotter!'

'Loudhailer, sar!' barked the honest Trotter, weaving deftly through the scrub at the doubled crouch. He handed the gleaming instrument to his young leader. 'Good thinking, sar, begging your pardon. 'E cannot bear the taste of cold megaphone, your Ivan, sar!'

'Thank you, Trotter. How's the missus, old chap?'

'She's a clapped-out old ratbag, thank you, sar!' barked Trotter.

'Splendid, Trotter!' cried Snotty.

'God,' said Buffy, as the two pals inched forward towards the enemy lines, 'you're wonderful with the men, Snotters!'

'A knack,' shrugged Snotty. He got to his knees. 'Ready, old man?'

As one subaltern, they sprang upright, the loudhailer snapping to Snotty's firm-set lips.

'I SAY DOWN THERE!' thundered Snotty. 'DOES ANY OF YOU SPEAK ENGLISH?'

From the serried turrets, two thousand tank commanders looked up, as the hot hills sent Snotty's message echoing bravely back. After a minute or two, a figure clambered down from the leading tank and began walking slowly towards the British position. Snotty and Buffy strode smartly out to meet him. The three saluted. The Russian pointed at his chest.

'Is reading all kinds of English,' he announced. '*Blick House, Olive Twist*, you name it.'

'Jolly good,' said Buffy.

'I'm only going to say this once,' said Snotty, fixing the Red beast's eye. 'I am empowered by Her Majesty's Government—'

'Great white queen across water,' said Buffy, pointing.

'—to say that we do not intend to stand idly by while you engage upon acts of flagrant belligerency in Afghanistan. If your forces are not withdrawn immediately, then the British Olympic Committee will have no option but to—'

'Ayeee!' screamed the Russian colonel, his cowardly eyes rolling. 'You would not pull—'

'—have no option, I repeat, but to withdraw from the women's relay!'

The cringing foreigner dropped, moaning, to his knees.

'Pull yourself together, man!' snapped Buffy.

The Russian stood up again, slowly, his fists knotted.

'English devils!' he said.

'Never mind that,' barked Snotty. 'Just nip back and put

our ultimatum to your masters, chop-chop! You have fifteen minutes.'

They watched him go.

'Do you think it'll work?' asked Buffy.

'I hope so, old chap, for all our sakes,' replied Snotty. 'If not, I shall have no other course open but to pull out of the pole vault.'

Buffy's pink chops paled! He bit his lip!

'Look, Snotty,' he said, in a strange voice. 'You wouldn't think me a frightful wet if I, well, sort of prayed? As it were. I mean, well, I wouldn't call myself a regular churchgoer, but—'

Snotty put a friendly arm around the younger fellow's shoulders.

'There are no atheists in foxholes, Buffers,' he murmured.

Whereupon the grateful Buffy sank carefully to his knees and put his hands together. But hardly had he done so when a stirring cry rang out, away to their left!

'No need for that, chums!'

Buffy sprang erect! Snotty spun on his heel! A tall willowy figure was striding towards them through the thornbushes, steering an adroit path so as not to snag his crushed-velvet coat, nor dislodge his yellow felt fedora. A handkerchief danced in his sleeve, like a trapped swallowtail.

'Good heavens!' shouted Snotty. 'It's Vivian Carew, from the British Council in Nepal!'

'It is, it is!' cried Buffy. 'He was known as Mary Lou, to the poofs at Katmandu, he was better than they felt inclined to tell! But for all his—'

'Oh, do put a sock in it, Buffy!' snapped Snotty. He shook Carew warmly by the hand, as that worthy winced ambiguously, and cried: 'What on earth are *you* doing here?'

'I was dropped on the Russkies' west flank early this morning,' replied Vivian. He took off his hat, and mopped his brow. 'Have you ever parachuted? It's absolutely thrilling, all that wind rushing up, all that silk billowing out above, a sort of wild hungry tugging at shoulder and groin, it's better than *The Gang Show*, I can't wait to—'

'But why on earth did they send *you* in?' urged the baffled Snotty.

'It's what I believe is called a pincer movement,' said

Vivian. He giggled. 'I have dealt Ivan the most fearful body blow, it's *so* exciting! Have you any notion what I was doing while you were threatening his silly old Olympics?'

The two chums shook their heads.

'*I*,' declared Vivian proudly, '*I* was informing them that unless they cleared off *immediately*, the British Council would be forced to cancel next summer's projected Soviet tour of *Rookery Nook*!'

'Good God!' cried Buffy. 'No wonder our Russian chappie caved in so quickly. He must have known all along that—'

'Quite,' interrupted Snotty. He stroked his jutted chin. 'You know, chums, it seems almost unfair, somehow, blasting Ivan with both barrels like that. Doesn't it?'

They looked at him, as, below them, two thousand tank engines started up, and two thousand gearboxes crunched grudgingly into reverse.

'Not to me, old man,' replied Buffy. 'This isn't a game, you know.'

Snotty slipped his field-glasses back into their case, and shut it.

'I suppose you're right,' he said.

Near Myth

Russian scientists have photographed what they believe are the remains of Atlantis. The Soviet Academy's Institute of Oceanography said that analysis of photographs taken deep in the Atlantic showed what appeared to be the remains of giant stairways and walls midway between Portugal and Madeira. —Daily Telegraph

'IF THAT KID DROWNS,' said Peleus darkly, looking up from his poolside recliner, 'it'll bloody ruin my holiday. We are not insured against you dunking him.'

Thetis tugged Achilles from the hotel pool, by his heel.

'It'll toughen him up,' she said. 'You don't half go on, sometimes.'

'As King of the Myrmidons,' said her husband, 'I am paid to go on. I got responsibilities. These include making sure there's a next King of the Myrmidons. You do not help matters by chucking my sole heir in the deep end every morning.'

'It'll make him arrowproof,' said Thetis. 'About time we had an arrowproof monarch. It said in the brochure that the Hotel Atlantis offered, and I quote, an Olympic-sized pool guaranteed to render our esteemed guests invulnerable. I wouldn't have come otherwise. I've always avoided Madeira. It's full of mortals this time of year. Common as dirt.'

'You don't want to believe everything you read in brochures,' said Peleus. 'It said this was a family hotel. There's a woman in the suite next door who's come here with a swan. They're not even married. I don't call that a family hotel. I didn't know where to look this morning when he was pecking his cornflakes and touching her up with his wing under the table.'

'He was a shower of gold when he signed in,' said his wife. 'I complained to the manager about the swan business, and he

151

showed me the register. Mr and Mrs Shower Of Gold. He said it wasn't up to him to check credentials. Go and swim in the sea,' she called to Achilles, who was sniffing a waiter who had just turned himself into an asphodel rather than catch a nearby guest's eye, 'it'll tone up your muscles.'

Peleus watched his son toddle off towards the beach.

'There's narwhals out there,' he said, shading his eyes against the Atlantic glint. 'Tritons, sirens, you name it. Half of bloody Loch Ness comes down here for the summer. I hope he'll be all right.'

'Watch it,' snapped Thetis. 'I was a fish once.'

'Don't remind me,' said Peleus bitterly. 'That was the same year you were a flame, a giant crab, and, if my memory serves me right, a small pond. I married a Nereid. That was the deal. If I'd known I was going to end up married to a bloody pond, I'd have gone off with that big Indian bird.'

'I wish you had,' said Thetis. 'It would've served you right. She's been a tortoise for the past ten years.'

'Nothing wrong with tortoises. Bit of lettuce now and again. No trouble.'

A scarlet dragon in the deckchair beside them leaned across.

'It might interest you to know,' said one of its heads, 'that the world rests on the back of a tortoise.'

'Rubbish!' cried Peleus.

'What did he say?' said the dragon's other head.

'He said rubbish.'

'Bloody sauce!' said the second head.

The dragon got up and stomped off, its breath shimmering the seascape.

'What did I tell you?' said Thetis. 'They'll let anyone in here. Chinese, anyone.'

'It's the Teutons I can't stand,' said Peleus. 'I swear they get up two hours early just to grab the best deckchairs. *And* they've brought their own tree.'

'It's called Yggdrasil,' said his wife. 'I saw the label when it came off the roof of their chara.'

'I don't care what it's called,' snapped Peleus, 'they got no business planting it outside our window. I went on the balcony this morning, there was a horse looking at me.'

'It belongs to Odin,' said his wife. 'It roots in the foliage.'

'Very nice,' snorted Peleus heavily. 'Tree with a horse in it, that's what I call a sophisticated religion!'

'I heard that!'

Across the pool, a huge Teuton had risen to his feet. He raised an enormous arm.

'See this hammer?' said Thor.

Peleus looked away.

'If you were half a man,' said Thetis, 'you'd...'

'I *am* half a man,' said Peleus. 'One of the troubles, being half god, half mortal. Suppose he thumps the mortal half? I could spend the rest of eternity walking about half-corpse. Ever thought of that?'

Thor sat down again. The Teuton party began to laugh, and throw rocks about: some turned into minor Azores, one or two became Vikings, a small pebble metamorphosed as a fountain and began reciting eddas.

'Flash buggers!' muttered Peleus. 'Sometimes I wonder who won the war.'

'Hallo!' cried Thetis. 'What's up with Achilles?'

The little boy was running up the beach screaming. Peleus leapt to his feet, and ran to gather him up.

'What's happened?' he shouted.

'I saw the whole thing,' said a jellyfish, as a wave deposited him at their feet. 'Chuhinaga, by the way; I handle war, weather and after-sales service in the Solomons. I always come here August. Anyway, I was out there having a bit of a float when suddenly this bloke comes whistling out of the sky, nearly fell on your kid.'

'Icarus,' said a centaur who had been playing French cricket with a group of corn-dollies. 'They're a funny family. His old man's still up there. Blooming nuisance, the pair of 'em. I was at the Club Méditerranée in Crete last year, they fell on my hut.'

'Come on, son,' said Peleus, wiping the boy's tears. 'Let's go and have an early lunch.'

The three Greeks were stopped at the dining-room doors by a short, liveried sphinx.

'Table near the window,' said Peleus.

'What's a Grecian urn?' asked the sphinx, nudging him.

'I've no idea,' said Peleus stonily, 'kindly show us to...'

There was a faint pop.

'Hallo,' said Thetis, 'you're a stoat.'

Achilles picked his father up and shook him.

'Dad-dad!' he cried gleefully, 'Dad-dad!'

'What's happened?' squeaked Peleus.

'You don't muck about with me, mate,' said the sphinx sternly. 'I ask a riddle, I expect a bloody answer, chop-chop.'

It snapped a claw grudgingly, and Peleus re-appeared. The trio made their way into the restaurant, found their own table; a leprechaun in a wing collar appeared with menus.

'Nearly everything's off,' said the leprechaun, 'begob.'

'Off?' cried Peleus. 'It's only quarter-past twelve.'

'Don't blame me,' said the leprechaun. 'We had a party of hydras in for the first sitting. Begorrah. Business convention. There was only the dozen of 'em, but sure and wasn't there a hundred and eight heads they was after having on 'em? Bedad.'

Peleus sprang to his feet.

'Don't give me that!' he shouted. 'I am sick to death of this rat-hole! You cannot get in the bloody pool for Wop mermaids, you cannot get a decent chair for all them lousy Norse layabouts, not to mention a balcony with outstanding horse views and people banging anvils half the bloody night, you cannot go in the sea without loonies falling on you, you cannot even close your eyes for a second without immigrant dragons buttonholing you with their half-baked heathen ideas, your so-called highly trained staff far from attending my every whim as per brochure prefer to turn guests into stoats at the drop of a handkerchief, the swan next door is never, pardon my French, off the nest so's you can't hear yourself think in our room for the rattling of the furniture, the sauna's been full of griffons singing rugby songs ever since we got here, and now you have the gall to tell me that a party of commercial monsters has come in and eaten everybody's dinner! Let *me* tell *you*, sunshine, I happen to be a demigod with friends in very high places, and I shall not hesitate to...'

'Leave it out,' said a heavy voice. 'I've told you once.'

Peleus turned.

Thor was towering beside him.

'I don't talk to navvies,' said Peleus.

154

Thor sighed, and hit him with his hammer.

Whereupon the swan, who had just come into the restaurant, immediately changed, on seeing a fellow-Greek in trouble, into a large bull. It walked across to Thor, put its huge head down, and tossed him through the wall.

Things screamed.

Thunderbolts began to fly.

A few upper floors collapsed into the garden, causing a number of hysterical bushes to burst into flame and start running about, spreading yet further disorder and destruction, and by the time Thetis and Achilles had dragged the unconscious Peleus out of the disintegrating restaurant, the New Wing (which contained a party of vampires who had been hanging quietly in the wardrobes waiting for nightfall) had begun to burn quite vigorously.

And they only just had time to gain the mountainside behind it before the whole collapsing, blazing, shrieking edifice of the five-star Atlantis began to slide slowly down the hill and into the waiting sea.

The hiss awoke the battered Peleus. He touched his bump. He winced. He gazed at the boiling surface of the sea. He sucked his loosened teeth. He shook his head.

'It's the last time I come here,' he muttered.

Spring Fever

AWAKE, PARTLY, from nightmare of dismemberment, Torquemada unscrewing head; find ear in small son's hand, ear still on (just), son shrieking hysterically into occupied ear:

'They're doing it! They're doing it!'

Spring from bed, instinctive spring, all Blitz children got this spring, still able to get from bed into Morrison shelter in two secs flat, if we had one; stumble through bedroom door, down corridor, into son's room, snap on light, gerbils freeze, like defendant and co-respondent caught in Regent Palace tryst by wife's gumshoe (*see Exhibit A above, flash, Tri-X, f 5.6, explanation follows*).

Gerbils have stopped doing it.

Bend over cage, blow on gerbils (as recommended in standard work, *Your Gerbil*), gerbils unfreeze, whizz round cage like fur bullets, vanish into pile of chewed bedding; go still.

Eyes ungum, focus on son.

'Doing what, exactly?'

Son shrug.

'Same as yesterday. Doing it and rolling about. They woke me up.'

'They'll be all right now,' I say, with resonant authority of man for whom no gerbil mystery remains veiled, probably brought up by same when abandoned in Gobi; Tarzan of the Gerbils. 'You go to sleep.'

Turn off light, lurch out. Small daughter now in corridor.

'Do worms have babies?'

'Shut up.'

156

Four o'clock in morning. Do worms have babies. Ask Tarzan of the Bloody Worms.

Slide back into bed, gingerly, daren't wake wife, wife is raving rodentophobe, covers eyes during *Tom and Jerry*, still gets shakes at realisation that gerbils are actually in house, *under roof*, may gnaw way out any day, murder family in beds.

Stare at ceiling.

Should have listened to wife ten weeks ago. Son put gerbils on Christmas list, father put gerbils by son's bed, wife put father in hospital, nearly. Wife finally gave in (son scream most of Boxing Day), provided gerbils incarcerated to wife's satisfaction. Spend Boxing Day Plus One building thing in garage, building thing *from* garage, planks, wire, steel sheeting, thing finally resembles Durham E. Wing, needs four people to carry it up to son's room, no way out for gerbils unless gerbils able to contact someone prepared to do low-level daylight bombing run, parachute commandos in, lay on oxy-acetylene.

Ensconce gerbils. Gerbils two weeks old, small as pocket fluff.

Shop assured me both gerbils female. Must have two females. Males fight. Anyone with two males ends up with two corpses. Anyone with mixed pair ends up with nine million gerbils.

Worry about girl in shop. First week, keep holding gerbils up and peering closely while *Your Gerbil* propped on table at *Chapter Two: Sexing*. Immaculate drawing of gerbil procreative kit, small, yes, but definite. Stare at own gerbils. Own gerbils not got kit. Just fur. Stare back at book. Male (i) Female (ii). Stare back at own gerbils.

Nothing.

Could be Duff Lot (iii?), born inadequate.

Himmler

Has got some simmler,

But poor old gerbils...

Weeks pass, get through January without deaths or pregnancies, gerbils clearly female pair after all, son and I relax, gerbils get on with Life's Work. Shredding. Shred everything. See *Chambers Encyclopaedia*, 'cheek-teeth are fundamentally biserially cuspidate, upper incisors grooved'. In lay language, this means gerbils born to shred as sparks fly upward. Put anything in cage, gone in ten seconds: bog-rolls, cardboard boxes, feeding bowls, little ladders, fingers. All end up in pile of sawdust. By end of January, come to conclusion gerbils not gerbils at all, hence lack of correspondence with *Chapter Two: Sexing*. What we have is pair of mutant death-watch beetles.

Son wants gerbils to *do* things. Fetch, beg, roll over, track, pen sheep. Son buys exercise wheel on way home from school, exercise wheel a good start in training.

Exercise wheel shredded in 9.3 seconds.

Wife turning out to be right. If gerbils ever escape, will shred house. Would come home from work, find gerbils polishing off last reinforced steel joist, burp, start on house next door.

But never shred each other. Relationship entirely amicable; occasionally hurl one another aside in crazed dash if something shreddable dropped in cage, otherwise no problems.

Except, of course, for cat.

Cat been uneasy ever since gerbils on premises. Cat has lived out of tins for sixteen years, suddenly on Christmas Day walking lunch is delivered. Cat go barmy. Cat obviously feels Christmas present wrongly addressed, cat probably had gerbils at top of *own* list. Living lunch now behind son's door, inside tiny Spandau; cat's brain falling apart in rage, cat hurling itself constantly against son's door until worn out. Try to tug cat away from door, cat digs claws in carpet like Chris Bonington going up Eiger.

But cat finally accept lot, grudgingly, cats philosophical animals. Major difference between cats and wives. All plain sailing from then on, gerbils fall into happy daily routine, eat, shred, pee, shred, eat, etc.

Until two days ago.

Putting on tie when son burst into bedroom, yelling.

Return with son to Gerbil Scrubs. Gerbils have jaws locked together. One gerbil is on back of other gerbil. Grab *Your Gerbil*, flick through pages, find place; blow on gerbils. Gerbils fly apart like exploding muff; begin shredding things.

'Were they fighting,' says son, 'or mating?'

'Impossible!' cries Lord Greystoke. 'Females neither mate nor fight.'

If, of course, females. Wonder about holding gerbils up

again, but gerbils now considerably bigger, could shred whole hand in three seconds.

Son go to school, gleefully, evilly. You'll never guess what my gerbils were doing...

Drink coffee, read *Your Gerbil* twice. Lot of stuff about grooming, housing, *exhibiting* for God's sake. Nothing about what they look like when they're actually...

If they are.

Go upstairs, to *Chambers*. All that stuff about teeth. Also, 'skull has enlarged bullae and brain-case, weak zygoma, rostrum and mandible'. Sound like libel lawyers, Zygoma, Rostrum & Mandible, but what are bullae? Take down SOD. *Bulla:* A vesicle containing watery humour. Ah. Know how it feels, most days.

But nothing about mating postures.

Now nine o'clock. Ring Regent Pet Stores. Girl's voice.

'Er, I bought two female gerbils, I *thought* they were females, ten weeks ago, and now they're, er, when gerbils mate, what does it, as it were, look like?'

'The male mounts the female. Was there anything else?'

'They seemed to be savaging one another at the same time.'

'Oh. Are you sure they're females?'

'Not really.'

'You should hold them up and see if one is further apart than the other.'

'One what?'

'I got a shop full of people here.'

'You mean their, er...'

'Look, they're all laughing. Give over laughing.'

'I tried that weeks ago. I couldn't see anything. They've been all right up till now.'

'Well, they would. They mature at ten weeks. That's when things start. You'll have to separate them if they're males.'

'How could they be males if they're mating?'

'Oh, they try it, if there's no female about, shut up, you, sorry, sir, not you, shut *up* laughing...'

Ring off, after normal pleasantries. Not normal gerbils, though? All I need, couple of bent rodents, take your partners for the Gay Gerbils.

Look at gerbils again. Shredding.

Go to work.

Come through door, eight hours later.

'They're doing it again!'

Spring, that's where the trouble is. To everything there is a season.

Dash upstairs, grab camera, take Exhibit A, will get ten prints, send off to *Living World, Any Answers, Horizon,* David Attenborough, Esther Rantzen, *Does The Team Think?*

Dear Marjorie Proops, would you look carefully at the enclosed...

As flashgun pops, gerbils leap apart. Probably impossible to capture gerbils *in flagrante delicto,* otherwise *Your Gerbil* team would doubtless have been on it like a shot, just the thing for private circulation among Genuine Gerbil Collectors Only, should have thought of that before.

Thirty hours on, lying awake, ear cocked for sound of whatever it is they're doing. Is this contact love or hate? Will it result in birth or death?

Is it bit of both?

Are gerbils, in short, like us, give or take a little shredding?

What is going on in that enlarged brain-case?

Peculiar time, Spring.

GELECEK BİTTİ...

ANLAMSIZLIK ÜÇLEMESİ - 1

ERSİN TOKGÖZ

Akasya Kitap : 50
Edebiyat – Roman : 1

GELECEK BİTTİ

Anlamsızlık üçlemesi - 1

ERSİN TOKGÖZ

Yayın Yönetmeni : Fatih BASUT
Hazırlayan: Fatih BASUT
Derleyen: Ersin TOKGÖZ

Dizgi ve Sayfa Düzeni:
Gözde Dizgi 0312.433 17 83

Kapak Tasarım: Fatih BASUT
Montaj & Kapak Baskı : TDV Matbaası
İç Baskı : TDV Matbaası

GENEL DAĞITIM VE PAZARLAMA

0 (212) 248 08 39

ISBN : 978-975-8916-50-4

Eylül 2007

AKASYA KİTAP
Tuna Cad. Bulvar Pasajı 3/10 Kızılay / ANKARA
Tel-Faks: 0312 431 51 42
www.akasyakitap.net
e-mail:akasyakitap@gmail.com

SUNUŞ

Neo-Marksist filozof Luis Althusser, eşine masaj yaparken boğazını sıkıp öldürmesinin acısını ve suçluluk duygusunu, ne belli bir süre kaldığı hapishanede ne de uzun süre tedavi gördüğü akıl hastanesinde atamaz üstünden. O duygu peşini özgürlüğünü aldıktan sonra da bırakmayacaktır. Onun için kaleme sarılır ve "Gelecek Uzun Sürer"i yazar. Anlattıkları, baştan sona o duygudan kurtulma çırpınışıdır, ki kitabına bulduğu isim, kurtulamasa bile o umudunun çok güçlü olduğunu gösterir. Öyle ya, umutsuz bir gelecek hayal edebilmek, hele hele bunun "uzun"luğunu göze almak, olanaksız...

Neden Althusser'den bahsediyoruz? Çünkü bir anlamda Althusser'e ters bir nazire Ersin Tokgöz'ün Anlamsızlık Üçleme serisinin ilk kitabı "Gelecek Bitti."

"...Çok uzun süren bir gelecekti Althusser'in dediği gibi.. Ama bitti işte... Artık her şey sonsuza dek aynıyla baki..." diye bitiyor Gelecek Bitti'nin girişi.

Evet, gelecek uzun sürebilirdi belki. Ama bitmişti. Ve her şey bittikten sonra başlıyor.

***

"Antikahraman olamayacak kadar kahraman, kahraman olamayacak kadar silik, normal olamayacak kadar naif, üstte yada altta izole olamayacak kadar normal, bitiremeyecek kadar yaşama bağlı, sürdüremeyecek kadar isteksiz ve nefret dolu..." diye tanımaya başladığımızı düşünsek de kitapta hiçbir zaman vücuda gelmeyen kahramanı, bu ilk "tanımlanamaz tanım" daha sonra çokça karşılaşacağımız cevapsız soruların ilk hazırlayıcıları olarak çıkıyor karşımıza. Çünkü bu "her şeye açık kapı bırakan tanımlama girişimi" yine boşlukta bırakarak son bulur: "Bu mudur?" Cevap açık: Hayır!

Neden hayır? Hayır bu kadar netse, "evet" ne? İşte bu "evet"i bulmaya çalışmanın anti-romanı "Gelecek Bitti." Çünkü yazar hayırın olmazlığından sıyrılıp evet cevabını ısrarla arasa da, o cevaba ulaşamayacağının bilincinde; "Sorulan sorular... Cevap arayarak yada öylesine. Alınan cevaplar, soruyla ilgili yada öylesine. Aslında ne cevap verenin soruyla ilgisi vardır nede soranın cevaba ihtiyacı. Yaşamın ise hiçbirine... Olmayanlar etrafında kazara örülmüş ve devam eden, öylesine süregelen bir döngü... Soru var mı? Neyle ilgili? Ya cevap...?"

Yoktur... Ama yine de tam bir nedir arayışıdır "Gelecek Bitti."

***

Bir yüzüyle hüzünlü bir aşk anlatısı... Hikaye, kahramanımızın, kişiliksizleştireceğini düşündüğü için reddettiği aşktan tüm karşı koymalarına rağmen kaçamaması, kendisini uzak tutamaması, daha sonra başta düşündüğü ve hep dışında yer almaya çalıştığı "kişiliksiz oluş'un" her haline girmesi, yaşadığı iç savaş ve en sonunda aşkını kaybetmesinin hikayesi. Hiçbir zaman vücuda gelmeyen, bir anlatıcısı ve bir de O. olan iki kahramandan oluşan bir anti-roman. Ne dış mekan betimlemesi, ne anlatıcının yada O.'nun neye benzediği ne de başka kişiler, hak getire, göremiyoruz. Özellikle betimlenecek bölümlerin alelacele geçilmesi, olay başlıyor derken iki cümleyle kapatılması dikkati dağıtmamak için bir manevra sanki.

Ama dediğimiz gibi bu sadece bir yüzü. Ve en basit yüzü. İyi okuyucu daha çok şununla ilgilenecek: Nietzsche'den Kant'a kafa tutan felsefi diyalektler, bir sanrının ürünü gibi görünen sürrealist akıl yürütmeler, "Toplumsal varoluş," "Duygusal Varoluş" yada "Varolanların Dünyası" gibi tanımlama girişimleriyle anlamsız oluşu sorgulamalar, anlamsızlığın karşısında illa var olmak için debelenen insan doğasının zavallılığına ilişkin çözümlemeler ve hepsi altı çizilecek aforizmalar...

Peki tüm bunlardan geriye ne kalıyor? Şu; "...Tanrısal kusursuzluğu kurmaya çalışırken zihnimde, bunun için yükselmeye çalışırken varolanların dünyasının gerekliliklerinin hepsinden, bu yükselişin önünde gördüğüm en büyük engel olan karşı cinse duyulan aşkla tahayyül sınırımın bile üstünde düşmüştüm aşağılara. Aldığım mesafeyi düşününce, bunun bir süreç sorunu olmadığını anlıyordum. Milat yoktu. Milat yoksa, tamamlanmış da olamazdı. O zaman beni sarmalayan bu duygunun anlamı neydi? Diğer tarafta; toprak ne kadar çekiyorsa, sıcaklığa karşı özlemim de o boyuttaydı. Sanırım çok yakında her şey bitecek. Toprağa çekilişim, içinde yer almakla; sıcaklığa özlemim, ateşle son bulacak. Mutlak karanlık, toprak ve ateş. Bekliyorum..."

Yada şu; "...İçimden çıkararak yaktığım ışığın aydınlığıyla görülebilecek her şeyi gördüm... Artık ışığım sadece hüznü ve derin kaybedişlerimi gösteriyor bana. E, o zaman neden kapatmıyorum ışığı? Klik sesiyle birlikte bana gösteremeyeceği tüm o "şey"lerden neden kurtulmuyorum? Mutlak karanlıktan neden hâlâ kaçıyorum? Umut mu hâlâ arsızca? Gelecek bitti oysa. Hadi, biraz cesaret. Görülebilecek iyi bir şey kalmadıysa artık..."

Evet, geriye sadece biten bir gelecekle ilgili yığınla soru ve asla tatmin etmeyen cevaplar kalıyor. Belki gelecek başlamadan ortaya çıkan sorular... Ve belki de o yüzden "Gelecek Bitti..."

Gelecek sürdü ve bitti... Uzun mu... Dahi ölümlülerin ölümleriyle, trajik varoluşların -ki ne kadar çokturlar, gözünüzü herhangi birinden kaçırmanız olanaksızdır- birbirinden habersiz solup gitmesiyle, gelecek uzun sürdü ve bitti...

Pazarlık yaparken gerilen ağızların şiddetinde, otobüs kuyruklarında, şu üstümüzü değiştirirken kan ter içinde kaldığımız kabinlerin tuhaf ter kokusunda, karşı taraftan gelen iki dişinin "O bana böyle dedi, ben de ona dedim ki" şeklinde kulağınıza yapışıveren yarı cümlelerinde tanık olursunuz trajik varoluşlara... Sıradan, alışılmış, çoğunluğun farkındalığını zorlamayacak cinsten yaşantılardı bunlar.

Yüceltilmiş trajediye gelince... Daha fazla ağlamakla arınabilseydik keşke... Anlamsız seslere, görüntülere, birbirini izleyen benzer günlere farklı duruşumuz olabilseydi, hepimiz çok iyi yazsaydık, çok güzel aşık olsaydık her defasında... Ölümüne aşık... Değersiz canlarımızın ortaya konulduğu yeminler ve yakarışlar olmasaydı mesela... Dolaysızca çıksaydı her söz... Benliğimizden kopup gelseydi... Acıdan bir yerlerimizi kesip kanatsaydık ve duvar diplerinde mevzilenseydik olası bir taarruza karşı... Yücelterek yukarılara değil; en dibe, hep daha dibe çekseydik varlığımızı...

Bunu da yapanlar oldu elbette... Öz'ün farklı ifadesinden başka bir şey değildi ortaya çıkan. İntihar ederken; kendini ve yapıtını olumlamaya çalışan yazarla, kelimelerin yerlerini "sanatsal" olsun kaygısıyla öyle değil de böyle değiştiren bir amatör arasındaki fark, birinin hâlâ nefes alıyor olmasından da öteye geçemedi... Geçemezdi... Yüceltme yöntemleri... Aşağıya ve yukarıya doğru... Belki daha az insan anladı onları... Daha karmaşık çözümlemeler yapıldı üzerlerinde... Karşılaştırmalar da hep belli kriterler üzerineydi.. Kadındı, aykırıydı, kalabalıklar içinde yalnızdı, karşı koyuşun ete kemiğe bürünmüş halleri falan vardı onlarda... Anlaşılırdı işte... Üzerlerine yeni kitaplar yazılıp raflara özenle dizilebilirdi mesela... Belirlenen sınırlar içinde enine boyuna çekiştirilerek, daha birkaç nesil için "ışık tutacak" yorumlar bu yüzden yapıldı tüm klasikler üzerine.. Bir süre daha idare edelim diye...

Trajedi… Normale denk düşmeyen her yaşam alanını trajedi olarak adlandırıp, acımak… Belki de bu biçimde, trajik olana duyulan özlemi, kini, vicdan azabını ve korkuyu (o çok istenen ama hiçbir zaman ortalamanın duyumsamaya cesaret edemeyeceği korkuyu) yok saymaya yönelik tanımlama trajedi..

Karıştırıyor olabilirsiniz… Tekrar gözden geçirmenizi öneremeyeceğim çünkü her defasında aynı algılayış biçimini, size ait olan ve o sımsıkı sarıldığınız yorumlama yeteneğini, aciz farkındalığınızı değiştirmek zaman problemi değil… Gelecekte belki diyebilirdim. Ama uzun zaman bekledik… Çok uzun süren bir gelecekti Althusser'in dediği gibi.. Ama bitti işte…

Artık her şey sonsuza dek aynıyla baki…

BİRİNCİ BÖLÜM

I.

Karaydı, kapkara... Baktığım her yer mi, yoksa gözlerimdeki tek renk mi? Bilmiyorum henüz... Ne zaman bu kadar karardı her şey diye bakıyorum, önceye yada sonraya ilişkin bir veri bulamıyorum. Miladım yok...

Fildişi kulemin yıkılması ne zamana rastlıyor? Yada kurulması... Yıkıldığına göre kurulmuş olmalı.

Düşünüyorum...

Uzun soluklu kısa bir hayat... Solukların hepsi, alıp verirken, tırpan gibi keskin. Mutsuzluğuma ilişkin bir şey bilmememe rağmen, mutsuzum hep. Ne sevgi dolu bir aile, ne sorunsuz bir yaşam, ne daha sonra hızla azalacak etrafımdaki onca insan... Hiç anlamadıklarını düşündüm hiç anlamadığım beni. Neden mutsuzum?

Düşünüyorum...

Düşüyorum, düşünüyorum...

Genler mi..? Kalıtsal özelliklerimi taşıyanlar benim gibi değil ama. Biricik değilim kesinlikle. O zaman neyim ben? Niye?

Antikahraman olamayacak kadar kahraman, kahraman olamayacak kadar silik, normal olamayacak kadar naif, üstte yada altta izole olamayacak kadar normal, bitiremeyecek kadar yaşama bağlı, sürdüremeyecek kadar isteksiz ve nefret dolu.

Bu mudur?

Hayır...

Bu, gereksiz bir yaşam öyküsüdür...

II.

Güneşle üzerindekileri çıkaran ve ayazla tekrar giyinen. Güneşin yada ayazın karşısında herhangi bir değere sahip değilsin. Neden üzerine alınıyorsun?

Duvarlar yarılıyor. Üzerime basarak geçiyor kimsenin görmediği kişiler. Bu, yeni değil. Nerede başlamıştı?

Askeri okulda iki savaş pilotu, iki sevgili. Sorunsuz hayatları, bir film yıldızının, çekeceği yeni filmde canlandıracağı savaş pilotu karakterini özümsemek üzere gerçek savaş pilotlarıyla birlikte olmak için birliğe gelmesiyle, değişir. Fazlasıyla popüler ve yakışıklı aktör, kadından hoşlanacak, kadın; geçici bir süreliğine de olsa sevgilisi ile aktör arasında kalacaktır. Sevgilisine olan bağlılığı ve aşkı(!), aktörün popülaritesi karşısında mevzisiz kalacak ve "hayır, yapmamalıyım, ama...." iç çekişmelerine rağmen sevgilisini aldatacaktır. Tabii aktör, eğitimini tamamlayıp gidecek ve her şey kaldığı yerden devam edecektir...

Milat bu değil kesinlikle. Ama bir otel odasında izlediğim üçüncü sınıf bir filmden arta kalan bu kareler, toy düşüncelerim için baş belirleyici olacaktı o zaman. Evet, kesinlikle sadakat diye bir şey söz konusu değildi. Eylem olsun olmasın, herkesin bir yerlerde sana tercih edebileceği ikame birileri mutlaka olacaktı. Belki ulaşılmaz idoller, belki yanı başındaki birisi... Detaydı gerisi ve ben detayları önemsemiyordum. Değil mi ki önemli olan kapının açık olup olmamasıydı. O kapının aralık yada sonuna kadar açık olmasının, birilerinin girip girmemesinin önemi neydi? Ve not düşecek, kenara çekilecektim: *1-Yerine koyabileceğini bulduğun anda değiştirdiğin her şey. 2-İkamesi bulunanların bitişe yazgılı oluşu. 3-Oluşun her şeyi ikameleriyle var etmesi. 4-Ve bu yazgıyı değiştirmek için geliştirdiğin tutunma metotları. 5- Toplumsal varoluş.*

Hiçbir zaman kendimi genele ait hissetmeyişim, her zaman toplumsal olana, genel kabullere karşı oluşum, bu enstantaneyle –tabii ki koskoca bütünü karşılamaktan çok uzak ama ne gam- kendine yeni bir kılıf bulmuştu. Çocukluğumdaki aşırı saldırganlığım, ilk gençliğimdeki hırçınlığım, daha sonra ailemin dehşetle izlediği kitaplara kapanışım, üniversitenin ilk yıllarındaki yurt odasından çıkmayan hayatım, bulduğu kılıfı çok sevecek, tek yatağım ve kitaplarımdan başka bir şey olmayan izbe evimden sadece zorunlu ihtiyaçlarımı karşılamak için çıktığım yeni bir dönem başlatacaktı. Günlerce eve kapanıp okuyor, benliğimin her zaman çok büyük bölümünü kapladığını düşündüğüm, beni amansız zorlayan libidomla baş edebilmek için kendimi hırpalarcasına mastürbasyon yapıyor, kasıklarımı değil beynimi rahatlatmaya çalışıyordum. Notre-Dame'ın Başdiyakozu'nun verdiği mücadeleden daha zorlu bir mücadele içindeydim. (Ah Hugo! Tanısaydın beni, Başdiyakoz'unun azabının sönüklüğü karşısında ne kadar bedbaht olurdun...) Ne okul, ne sınavlar, ne hepsi birkaç kişiden oluşan arkadaşlar, ne de başka bir şey... Evden çıkışım yoktu. Evden çıkmam demek, kabul edemediğim, bir türlü içinde yer alamadığım ve "toplumsal varoluş" olarak nitelediğim şeyin (Adını bilmiyorum ama ona "toplumsal varoluş" diyorum[1(1)]) bir şekilde içinde yer almak demekti ki hele yeni formum, bunu yıkım olarak kabul edecekti.

Günler, günler, günler... İnkar, ısrar, sıkıntı. Kibir, aymazlık, arsızlık... Günler, günler, günler...

Nefretimi yada sevgimi, kılıfım oluşturuyordu. O dönemdeki tek evrenimi okumalarım belirliyor, o evren ise hep bu kılıf çerçevesinde anlam kazanıyordu. Auguste Comte'un ikiye ayrılan sosyolojik tahlillerinden 1845'e kadar olan birinci bölümünü sübjektif bir şekilde kabul ediyor, bu dönemden sonraki bakışını –*İlke olarak aşk, temel olarak düzen, amaç olarak ilerleme*- Clotilde de Vaux'nun, en nihayetinde bir kadının, etkisi altında kalışı nedeniyle yumuşatmasından dolayı reddediyor, sisteminde sevdiği kadını ölümüz kılmak, kutsal-

---

1   (1) Lao Tse'nin Tao'yu açıklamak için "Adını bilmiyorum ama ona Tao diyorum" sözüne eğretileme...

laştırmak için çırpınmasından dolayı Comte'u bağışlamıyordum. Kafka'ya Milena'ya yazdığı mektuplara kadar duyduğum yakınlık, mektupları okuduğum zaman nefrete dönüşüyor, zorlasa da Kant felsefesi, sırf Kant'ın hayatına kadın sokmayışından dolayı eksenim oluyordu. Tabii bunların, düşüncelerin özü ile birebir ilişkisi yada bütünü anlatmada vazgeçilmez şeyler olması gibi bir anlamı yoktu. Sadece; kılıfım kendini tarihe referans ediyor, rahatlıyordu. Nietzsche'nin neden "üstüninsan" yaratamadığının kendimce çözümünü buluyor, eril ve dişil iki karşıtın düzen oluşturup temel belirleyici olduğu bir evrende, üstün insan yaratma çabalarının bir ham hayal, bir kandırmacadan öte olmadığına karar veriyor ve Nietzsche'nin şahsında bu çabalarla ilgili de son noktayı koyuyordum: *Ni(ç)e insan üstün insanı yaratmayı denedi. Formüller... Neye yaradı? Metodoloji hatası... Hastalıklı varoluş... Sıkıntı...*

Evet, formüller bir işe yaramayacaktı. Kılıfım, en nihayetinde, kılıftı. Ne kitaplara tekrar dalışım, ne zihnimi libidomdan ve kalbimden uzaklaştırmak için mastürbasyon ve şapla geliştirmeye çalıştığım çözümler, ne uyuşturucuya ve onun sanrılar dünyasına sığınışım... Kılıfımın daha güçlenmesini sağlamayacak, zamana da yavaş yavaş teslim olan yeni formum, ilk gediklerini vermeye başlayacaktı. Bir kadın kokusu, bir kadın sesi, bir kadın teni, kapandığım ve hepsini yok saymaya çalıştığım dünyamda, aradığım ve özlediğim tek şeye dönüşmüştü. Bulaşmadan kurtulmak için bir kadına sahip olmanın en kaba yolunu seçecek, kendimden sadece para vererek alacağım bu "*şeyler*" sonunda, tekrar kendime, o tek gerçek sandığım yada olmasını istediğim kılıfıma dönecektim (Ah, ne büyük yanılgı!). Ama kutsal kabul edilen bir ayın kutsal saatinde giriştiğim bu eylemden son anda Sartre benzeri bir bulantıyla hızla, korkarcasına uzaklaşacak, tekrar başladığım yere dönecektim. Sisifos'un çilesi[2][(1)] tekrar başlıyordu.

───

2 [(1)] Söylenceye göre, Tanrılar tarafından cezalandırılan Sisifos, büyük bir kayayı bir tepenin zirvesine çıkarmakla cezalandırılır. Kaya, tam tepeye konmuşken kendi ağırlığı ile geri yuvarlanır ve Sisifos kayayı tekrar tepeye doğru itmeye başlar. Ve bu çile, sürer gider...

III.

Hazırlıklarını tamamladın varsayalım. Ama dursana. Kalkış yok. İznin var mı?

Hazırlıklarımın hepsi tamamdı. Kalkış yapıp kendi korunağımda tüm tarihe inat, verilenlerin hepsine nazire yaparcasına, Tanrıyla dalaşırcasına adeta, idealize ettiğim gibi yaşayacaktım. Yaşayacak, gösterecektim.

Kime?

Neyi?

Ah kibir! Söylencelerin hepsini üreten, o söylencelere, karşı söylenceleri de beraberinde getiren kibir...

İlk gediklerini veren kılıfım, artık tamamen tarumar olmak için hazırdı. Ve Tanrı'nın kusursuz dünyası, kusursuz dünyanın kusursuz zamanlaması, tam da bu anda çıkardı O.'yu karşıma. Yatmaya hazırlanırken çıkagelen zamansız misafir gibi. Kovamazdım... Kovamadım.

Aynı sınıfta olmamıza rağmen birbirimizi neredeyse tanımıyor olmamız; benim tamamen kendi yaratımım olan, O.'nun ise yığınla somut sorunlardan kaynaklanan dönem kaybı ile tüm dersleri birlikte alt sınıflarla almamızla sona ermiş, son zamanlarda her ortalama arkadaş gibi görüşmeye başlamıştık. Derse girdiğimde beni görüp hiç beklemediğim bir şekilde çağırmış, yanına oturmamı istemişti. Sürekli okumaktan kir içinde bıraktığım Üçleme'nin kirlerini akıtan ıslak elimin izlerini özenle silmiş, kitaba gösterdiği özeni yarı tebessümle izlerken sanki bakışlarımdan anlamış gibi Beckett'i anlamadığını ve hiç haz etmediğini söyleyerek aynı özeni yazarından esirgemek istercesine dudak bükmüştü. Anlamamasına şaşırmamıştım. Ama yine de anlatmaya çalıştım Beckett'i:

"Hayatın sürekli yinelemeler, aynı yinelemeler, aynı gibi gözüken farklı yinelemeler, tamamen farklı yinelemeler, farkı gözden kaçsa da küçük bir ayrılık ile ortaya tamamen yeni bir durumun çıktığı, aslında aynı yinelemelerden oluştuğunu görüyorsun Beckett'ta. Aslında açık olmasına rağmen kavranamaz bir içeriğe sahip gibi gözüken olaylarda en önemli ile en önemsizin aynı değerde olması, 'değer'lerin birbirinden farklı olmaması, en nihayetinde bir yaratım olan 'değer'in en önemli ile en önemsiz arasındaki aynılığı, hayata bakıştaki kavramsal trajedi ve onulmaz yalnızlığı ve onulmaz acıyı işaret ediyor bir bakıma. Örneğin; Watt'ın sevmediği iki şeyden birisinin ay diğerinin güneş olması ve yine Watt'ı tiksindiren iki şey varsa onların da toprak ve gökyüzü olması, Beckett'ta; ne yerde ne gökte yer almamayı, ne topraktan ne gökyüzünden beslenmemeyi verirken, hepsini olumlayan ve hiçbirini kabul etmeyen bir 'Araf' içinde yer almanın sonsal bir şaşkınlığına denk düşüyor. Şaşkınlık, anlamamaktan değil, tam tersi, anlaşılan karşısında umudun ve çıkışın olmamasından kaynaklanıyor. 'Aynı anda hem karanlıkta hem aydınlıktaysak, açıklanamaz olanla da karşı karşıyayız demektir' diyen Beckett, açıklanamaz olanın açıklamasını sezerek, söz'le kenara çekiliyor."

Açıklamaya çalışırken açıklamak istediğim şey gibi karıştırdığımın farkındaydım.

"Belki. Ama yine de üslubu çok kasıntı geliyor bana. Sanki anlaşılmamayı marifet sayan bir hali var. Özellikle, 'Ben böyle yazayım, anlamasın kimse ve ben var olayım' der gibi. Yada çirkinliğini yüceltiyor, kim bilir?"

Acaba olmadı mı kaygısıyla espri ile bitirdiği sözlerini gülümseyerek karşıladım. Olmamıştı. Olması gerekiyor muydu? Açıklamaya çalıştım:

"İki tarafı var bunun. Birincisi; biz bu Araf halini anlamıyoruz. Kültürümüzde yok bir kere Araf olgusu. Toplumsal bilinç altımız 'ya cennet ya cehennem' der bize. Bunu başka kavramlara da uygulayabilirsin. Düzenli iki uç. Şematik bir hayat anlayışı. Kontrolü daha kolay. Kafa karışıklığı daha az. Cehennemi de düşlesen Araf'ın boşluk sancısından uzaksındır. İkincisi dille; bizim, metinleri yorumlayışımızla ilgili. Düşün; asla ne öğretildiğini anlayamadığım okullarımızda edebi metin 'giriş-gelişme-sonuç' akışı ekseninde öğretilmedi mi hep? Girişle sonucun aynı hacimde olmaması öğrencilerin kompozisyon derslerinde kırık not almalarının başlıca sebebi oldu. Ve bu sistematik, bize metnin girişini aratu. Gelişme bölümü neresi, ya sonuç ne ki ruh haliyle okuttu kitapları. İlla olay olacak, illa sonuç olacak, hele hele ana fikirsiz, asla. Şimdi tabii Beckett sadece çirkinliğinden böyle yazmış, anlaşılmamak için zorlamış kendini diyecek okuyucu. Tüm bunların yanında bırak alıştığımız gibi kahramanlar bulmayı, neredeyse var olmayan Beckett'in anti kahramanlarının anlaşılmaması, kabul edilmemesi ve kenara bırakılması çok anlaşılır."

Böyle mi olurdu ilk konuşmalar? Haddini bildirir bir halim vardı. Niye ki? Ah, ne aptaldım! Ne düşündüğünü anlayamadan, tekrar görüşmek üzere ayrıldık.

IV.

Belirleyenin izin verdiği ölçüde belirlemeye çalış-
mak. Kısmi yaratıcılık. Bunu bilmeden. Yanılgı. Ve
yaratıcılık da bitti...

"Gel hadi, konuşalım..."

Her şeyin başlangıcı... Arkadaşları ile otururken aslında çok uzaklarda olduğunu sezip daha önce yapmadığım şeyi yapıp yanına yaklaşarak çağırmıştım.

Hakkında ne biliyordum ki?

Ne yaptığı, nasıl yaşadığı yada kiminle birlikte olduğu hakkında hiçbir fikrim yoktu. Ama bir sorun vardı. Benim teklifsizce "gel" dememe neden olan sezişim, zaten susta olan kılıfımın parçalanmasına yönelik en somut adımdı tekrar fakülteye dönüşümden sonra.

Tanrım, nasıl bir hayat, nasıl bir çocukluk, nasıl bir genç kızlık ve nasıl bir aile! Ayrı ebeveynler, destek olmak bir yana, ortada olmayan bir baba, ne yaptığı belli olmayan bir anne, koskoca bir şehirde yapayalnız bırakılan bir insan. Ne kadar da yabancıydı bana tüm bunlar. O. anlatıyor, ben hayretle ama şaşırmadan dinliyordum. Tek şey diyebildim O. anlattıkça:

"Her şey çok kötü..."

Her şey çok kötüydü. Kendisiyle sorununu çözememiş olan, anlamdan anlama koşan, bulamayan, kılıf üstüne kılıf ören, her şeyin gerçekten çok kötü olduğunu perdelemek için halden hale giren ben, başka ne diyebilirdim? Her ne kadar onun sıkıntılarını yaşamamış olsam da aslında temelde ortak bir noktada buluştuğumuzu göstermek istercesine her şeyin neden zaten "kötü" olduğunu, kendi sıkıntılarının da bu kötü tasarım içinde yer aldığını O.'ya anlatıp rahatlatmaya çalışıyordum;

"Aslında hayat zordur. Hele bazıları için daha da zor. Eğer bazı şeylerin kodlarını kıyısından çözmeye başladıysan, ki ancak kıyısından çözebilirsin, daha da zordur her şey. Bak, biz şu anda bahçede oturuyoruz. Görüş açımız, bulunduğumuz yer itibariyle son derece sınırlı. Yukarıya bak. Yukarıdan bakan öğrencinin yerine koy kendini. Şu karşıdakinin diğerine bakışının evreni, yandakinin kendi içindeki hali... Yukarıdaki, burada olan her şeye hakim. Eğer görmeyi biliyorsa... Belirleyici olan gördükleriyse onun ruh hali ile şu karşımızda oturanınki nasıl aynı olabilir. İşte, çözdüğün her kod da buna götürür seni. Yükselir, yükselirsin. Yükseldikçe kopar bağın, gördüklerin fazlalaşır. Daha önce gördüklerinin anlamsızlığını duyumsarsın ve daha sonra görebileceklerinin şu an gördüklerini anlamsızlaştıracağını bilir paniğe kapılır, kapıldıkça yükselir, yükseldikçe paniklersin. Bir yandan sana tanınan zamanın en tepeye çıkmana yetmeyeceğini bilir umutsuzluğa düşersin, bir yandan da bu umutsuzluk yukarıya daha süratle çıkmak için iter seni. Böyle bir kısır döngü bu."

Sözlerimin O.'nun sıkıntıları ile ne ilgisi vardı? O., bana kanıyla canıyla yaşadığı somut şeylerden bahsediyordu oysa. Yalnız bırakılmışlığı, ailesi tarafından terk edilmişliği, maddi sorunları...

Kibir...

Retorik gevezeliğimin kusma istemi yaratmak yerine hayranlıkla dinlendiğini görmek devam etmemi zorunlu kılıyordu, ettim:

"Ve açmaz şu; Kusur her taraf. Anda var olan, belki zorlama, belki tezi geçerli kılma oluş nedeniyle olan, 'iyi' diye adlandırılan genel kabuller nereye kadar taşıyabiliyor bizi? Yaradılış anlatılarında geçmese de; vakit başka vakitken Tanrı'nın kusursuz dünyası hüküm sürüyordu. Zıtlıkların aynı anda yaşanmasından doğan acılar ve başka acıların olmadığı bu zamandan Tanrı sıkıldı ve kusursuzluğun idesini geride bırakıp her şeyi çekip aldı. Bilgileri saklı tutup dengeyi çekti. İşte sancı da o andan itibaren başladı. Bunun için körüz ama en güzeli görmeyi düşleriz, bunun için sağırız ama o billur sesten başkası kesmez kimseyi, bunun için en ağır kütleyiz ama yerçekiminin hıncını kuşlardan çıkarırız. Kusura bakan tarafımızın baskın olduğunu bilsek de, kusursuzluk döneminden aktarılan o belli belirsiz bilgi yüzünden bu kadar arsızız. İşte, bin yıllar boyu sadece kusursuzluğun idesinin genler kanalıyla aktarılıp imgelemimize yerleşmesine rağmen bir türlü pratiğe geçirilememesi, insan oğlunun onulmaz azabını oluşturuyor. Şimdi, her taraf bu kadar azap doluyken 'iyi' nasıl gerçekten var olabilir? Mümkün mü bu? Bunun içindir ki her şey kötü. Çok kötü..."

"Peki, şu anki durumdan memnun mu Tanrı?" Sordu belli belirsiz... Aynı şekilde cevap verdim:

"Sormak lazım." Ve ekledim:

"Bu kadar kötü bir tasarımın içinde her şey hüzne gebe doğal olarak. Orgazm ol hüzün yaşa, olamazsan da... Bilirsin termodinamik yasasını. Ve bilirsin ki mutluysan, birinin mutsuzluğunu mutluluk olarak kullanırsın. İşte, mutluluğunun bir yerlerde mutsuzluğa neden olduğunu bil ve hüznünü devam ettir. Senden dünyaya, dünyadan sana ne? Öl."

O. yokmuş gibi konuşuyordum. Bu kadar mı unutmuştum insanlarla konuşmayı? Kuramsal bir kitapta geçen düşünceler değildik, yaşayanların dünyasındaki iki insan olarak karşı karşıyaydık oysa. Hala kendi zihnimde yaşar, o kapanma günlerimde binlercesini yaptığım bitimsiz uslamlamaları sese dönüştürür bir halim vardı. Neden bu kadar uzaktan konuşmaktan alamıyordum kendimi?

Ama anlıyordu. Hayretler içindeydim... Zihnimdeki kadın formuma uymuyordu bakışlarındaki anlam. Anlamamalıydı. Anlamamalıydı ki haklı çıkayım. Eve daha bir nefretle gideyim, o siyah duvarların arasına daha sıkı gömüleyim ve köşeye büzülüp kendi garabetimi yok sayıp kılıfıma tekrar daha bir güçlü sarılayım. "Busunuz hepiniz işte. Bakın, sizin için kaç büyük beyin kendini telef etti. Kahrolsun hepsi ve kahrolsun bu zayıf yaradılış" demeliyim.

Demeliydim. Diyemedim.

Bakışlarındaki anlamdan sıyrılıp O.'yu da kadın geneli içine yerleştiriyor ve geneli, en bayağı demagojileri bile hayranlıkla izleyen zayıf yaratıklar olarak düşünüp hâlâ kılıfıma sığınmaya çalışıyordum. Ama sarmal kırılmıştı. Kaçmak boşunaydı. Anladı, yüzüme baktı ve aşık oldum.

Neydi aşk tasarımım? Hangi aşk masalları büyütmüştü beni? Hangi gerçekler büyüyü bozmuştu. Düşünüyorum...

V.

Varlığınla ilişkilendirdiğin ama varlığınla ona bir şey ifade etmediğin dış gerçeklik... Seni, eninde sonunda yok sayacaktır. Hazır mısın?

Düşlerime sığınmamın anlamı yoktu. Küçükken annemden dinlediğim masallardaki mutlu sonlara ve katıksız sadakate pay biçip "Belki de her şey sandığım kadar kötü değil" diye ikna etmeye çalışıyordum kendimi. Peki; ya kılıfım? Tanrısal kusursuzluğa hazırlanırken ben, Tanrısal kusursuzluğun önündeki en büyük engeli somut aşk olarak görüp uzak durmaya, kendimi kılıfıma hapsetmeye çalışırken başta bu engel olmak üzere tüm engellerden korunmak için... Olacak şey miydi şimdi bu. Ama dış gerçeklik beni yok sayıyordu. Oysaki merkez bendim, değil mi? Yoksa yanılıyor muydum?

Hazır olmasam da zaman, asla körelmeyen kutsal bir törpü gibi kendinden emin bir şekilde ilmekleri teker teker öğütüyordu. Artık eskisi gibi okumuyor, daha önce kanatlarıyla yükselip geri kalan her şeye dudak bükebilmek için beklediğim gece, bir an önce bitmesi gereken bir kayıp zamana dönüşüyor, geceyi yalnızca sabaha kapı açsın ki gidip O.'yu göreyim diye bekliyordum.

Bu kadar çabuk mu dağılacaktı binam. En sağlam malzemelerden inşa ettiğimi düşündüğüm yapım, korunağım, kartondan bir korunak kadar da mı mukavemet göstermeyecekti? Göstermiyordu. Ama bu heyecan da anlamlı olmalıydı. Tanrım...

Metroda, sanki onun da onca sefer ve onca saat arasında benim olduğum vagona bineceğini biliyor gibi bekliyordum. Sözleşmemiştik ama onca sefer, onca vagon, onca kapı varken benim bulunduğum vagona, benim karşısında bulunduğum kapıdan, giriverdi. Kıyafetine kadar; mavi kot pantolonu, yakası açık mavi gömleği, çizmeleri, her şeyine kadar tam da beklediğim gibi karşımdaydı... Şaşırmadım. Daha sonraları da defalarca hiçbir iz olmamasına rağmen hissettiğim gibi O.'yu her şeyiyle hissetmiştim.

"Nasılsın?" dedim bahçede otururken.

"Daha iyi!"

Neden daha iyi? Kendime bile itiraf etmediğim ona akışımın onun da bana akışı ihtimali karşısında önlenemez şeylere gebe oluşu, ürpertmişti beni. Başka bir şey olsundu ve iyi olmasının benimle ilgisi olmasındı. Anlamlardan kaçıyordum. Neden daha iyi? Sormadım...

Ama O. sessizlik istemiyordu. Daha önceden hazırladığı belli kağıtları uzattı bana. Şiir yazıyormuş, bakabilir miymişim, nasılmış acaba.

Ben miydim onay makamı? Nedendi bu hazırlık? Budalaca ukalalığımı bildiğim için daha sonra kırılmasın diye daha okumadan temize çıkarmaya çalıştım kendimi;

"Şiirden pek anlamam. Okuduğum da söylenemez. Ama bakayım."

Önce baktım, sonra tekrar okudum ve bir kez daha... Beklemediğim bir durumdu. Çırpındıkça daha derine çeken bataklık gibi ne yana dönsem daha da batıyordum. Kadınlar, sadece üreten erkekleri esrikleştirip sığlaştıran yaratıklardan başka neydi? Bir elin parmaklarını geçmeyen kadın yazar, filozof, şair kayda bile değmeyecek bir toplam tutmuyor muydu? Yada ben mi yanılıyordum? Yoksa benim apriori cinsiyet ayrımcılığım mı sınanıyordu. Oysa ki, kendimi evrenin merkezi gibi görme yanılsamasından kurtaralı epey zaman geçmişti. Değil mi ki oluşun benimle uğraşma zorunluluğu kalmamıştı. Ama darbe üstüne darbe alıyordu yapay binam. Evet şimdi de şiirleriyle çıkmıştı karşıma ve gör diyordu.

"Çok güzel" diyebildim sadece. Ekledim;

"Beklemezdim senden."

Kabalaştığımın farkında değildim. Öylesine döküldü dudaklarımdan.

Şaşırmıştı. Açıklamaya çalıştım;

"Sen derken kişiselleştirmiyorum kesinlikle, yanlış anlama. Ben biraz sorunluyum bu konuda. Kadınların durduğu yer, evrendeki görevi, var olma nedeni hakkında."

Merakla sordu;

"Nasıl yani?"

İzah etmeye çalıştım;

"Tanrı, insana kusursuzluğunu gösterip, mükemmeli amaçlatır. Bu, çok Tanrısal bir kaygı insan için. Ve mükemmele yaklaşabilecek beyinler de vermiştir insana, özellikle erkeklere. Bu kusursuzluk özlemini aşk olarak nitelersek, aşk nesnesine ulaşmayı amaçlayan insanın önüne başka bir aşk türü de koyar aşılmaz bir engel olarak. Ki bu da kadınlara duyulan aşktır."

Deli saçması... Karşı çıktı;

"Sadece kadınlar mı engel buna. Diyelim ki doğru... Yine de aynı şey tersten de okunamaz mı?"

İtirazını kabul ettim;

"Olabilir tabii. Ama olabilir derken bu olabilire fazla şans verdiğimi söyleyemeyeceğim. Bu, benim ön yargım. Önyargıların yanılgı payını saklı tutarak, önyargımda diretiyorum."

"Neden?" dedi. Anlamak istiyor gibiydi.

"Çünkü öyle olmalı. Çünkü insanoğlu bin yıllardır Tanrı'nın kusursuz yüzüne hasret. Ulaşmaya çalışıyor. Ama yine bin yıllardır başladığı yerden bir adım ileri gidebilmiş değil. Hâlâ aile, hâlâ kadın, hâlâ ilişkiler. Cinsiyetin var oluşu evrenin devamının teminatı sanki. Belki Tanrı özellikle böyle dizayn etti, kim bilir. Düşünsene; Tanrısal kusursuzluğa yaklaşan bir insan topluluğunu. Tanrı neye tutunacak artık? Bu, kahır belki. Ve ben bu kahrı kadınların üstüne atıyorum. Kayırıyorum belki cinsimi. Bilirsin; Nietzsche birçok yol dener üstüninsan formunu yakalayabilmek için. Bana göre tek bir şey yapmalıydı Nietzsche; cinsleri ayrıştırmalıydı ve kadınlara dair hiçbir kaygısı olmayan taraf üzerine yapmalıydı çalışmasını. O zaman olabilecek bir hamur varsa olurdu ancak. Ama neye yarar? Zaman geçiyor, hepimiz ölüyoruz. Ve herkes aldığı yerden devam ediyor bir yere kadar. Ama bir yerde işte, o onulmaz acıya, libidosuna, hislerine yani insaniliğine izin verdi mi; bin yılların üst üste konulan taşlarının aslında sadece yatay dizildiğini görüyorsun. E, yatay yükselti de olmayacağına göre, bu kısır döngü bitmiyor. Tanrı'nın kusursuz yüzü özlemden, boşa çırpınışlardan ve en nihayetinde acıdan öteye geçmiyor ve ben suçluyorum. Oluşun sorumlusu Tanrı'ya gücüm yetmediğinden, yetmeyeceğinden, bir anlamda hıncımı kadınlardan çıkarıyorum. Daha doğrusu kadınları sembolleştirip kendime yöneltiyorum şiddetimi. Belki ileride tanırsan, daha iyi anlarsın benim bu açmazımı."

Acımasızlığım, kutsala saldırışım, anlaşılmaz öfkem şaşırtmıştı. Sanırım, kendi sonumu hazırlıyordum. Biliyordum ki anlaşılmaz olan, anlaşılır duygular yaratır. Belki anlaşılmazlığın tehlikeli sınırlarının anlaşılıra çekilme diyalektiğiydi bu. Hayran bakışlardan ürkmüştüm. Önlem almam gerekiyordu. Damdan düşercesine dedim;

"Anlamadığın bir dilde konuşuyor olmamdan dolayı duyduğun ilgi... Bilinmeyene karşı olan merak. Yok etmek için kazanmaya çalışmak. Alıp verme diyalektiği....Sıkıntılısın. Sıkıntını geçirecek her şeyi ben biliyorum. Sıkıntının sende, bilginin bende oluşu tesadüf mü?"

Ne anlatmaya çalışıyordum? Nereden gelip çıkmıştı bu sayıklama hali. İğrendim kendimden. Özür diledim, kalktım, gittim...

VI.

Ebesin. Sobelediğin her oyuncu sensin. Biliyorsun.
Ama bilmen bir şey değiştirmiyor. Sobeliyorsun.

Kendimi yakalamış olmanın verdiği kızgınlık ve suçluluk duygusuyla belli bir süre görüşmedim O. ile. Aramalarına sessiz kaldım, her zaman bir bahane bulup uzaklaştım. Hala ısrar ediyor, hala gerçekleri inkar ediyordum.

"Yarın İstanbul'a gideceğim. Gitmeden önce görmek isterdim seni."

Telesekretere mesaj bırakmış. Tamam, gitmeden göreyim... Ama görmüyorum.

"Döndüm. Ankara'dayım."

İyi. Geçen zamanda ne çok mücadele etmiştim kendimle. Zorlayarak tekrar tutunmaya çalışmıştım kılıfıma. Parçaları toplayıp teker teker dikmiştim dağılan tüm parçaları. Ama iplik çürük olmalıydı. Yoksa burada olması neden hemen O.'yu görme isteğine dünüşsündü ki bende amansız.

"Tamam, hemen geliyorum."

Gittim. Okulun kantininde arkadaşlarıyla oturuyor, fakültede birinci olan kampanyalarının İstanbul elemelerinde nasıl yarıştığını tartışıyorlardı şevkle. Zoraki, kıyısından iliştim topluluğa.

"Bak, bunlar da orada çektirdiğimiz fotoğraflar." diyerek bir demet fotoğrafı uzattı. Özenle yapılmış saçlar, üzerinde sadece özel günler için ayrılmış kıyafetler, suratlarda birbirinin aynı yarış atı ifadeleri, yüzlere yapışık zoraki kasıntı gülümsemeler. Yakıştıramadım O.'ya. İğrendim. Kibar değildim;

"Bunları bana neden gösteriyorsun? Ben olsam bu fotoğraflara bakar, kendimden nefret ederdim. Sen, bir marifetmiş gibi bana gösteriyorsun."

Şok!

"Kalk dışarı çıkalım."

Çıktık. Ortada bir suç olduğunu sezen ama kendi suçunu bilmeyen çocuklar gibi mahcup, söylendi;

"Neden kızdığını anlamadım..."

Fotoğrafları tekrar gösterdim, arkadaşlarıyla yaptıkları başarı konuşmalarını anımsattım.

Açıklamaya çalıştı;

"Biliyorsun. Biz burada öğrenciyiz. Ve yapmakla yükümlü olduğumuz bazı şeyler var. Bu kampanya çalışması da bunlardan birisi. Ne olmuş yani yaptığımız bir işin başarısını kutluyorsak.?"

Ve tavsiyede bulundu;

"Uçlarını bu kadar sivriltmemelisin."

Belki.

Ancak ben de aynı okulda öğrenciydim. Aynı yükümlülükler benim için de geçerli olmalıydı. Ama değildi. Demek ki bu sözün genel geçer bir doğruluğu yoktu. Hala kabaydım;

"Özür dilerim ama benim böylesi aptal gerekliliklerle işim olmaz. Herkes istediği gibi devam etsin. Ama ben ait değilim. Dön istersen arkadaşlarının yanına."

"Hayır, senin yanında olmayı tercih ederim."

Tercih etti ve benimle kaldı. Uzaklaştık oradan. İlk tahakküm. Hep düşünmüştüm yokluğunda şiirlerini okurken; bu şiirlerin yazarı sevebilir mi beni? Böylesi şiirlerin konusu olabilir miyim bir şekilde? Halbuki edebiyatla mastürbasyon yapmaya ne kadar da karşıydım. Başlangıcı ve sonu kendinde olan bir süreç değil miydi yazın? Nasıl bir nedene bağlanabilir, nasıl o nedenden hareketle bir sonuç beklentisine girilirdi. Giriyordum ama. Egom, kendime inat, aşkımı bu beklentiyle paralel götürüyordu. Sanki böyle bir sonuç cılız yaradılışımın zaferi olacaktı. Nerede kalmıştı edebiyatın olaylar dahil her şeyden bağımsız olabileceğine, olması gerektiğine ilişkin demagojilerim. Ne farkı vardı şimdi; en ufak bir duygu kıpırtısını, sahip olduğu küçücük dağarcığıyla kelimelere döken amatörden duygularımın? Hani ben en farklıydım? Ama yine de o şiirlerin yazarının benim için yazacağını sezerek, kendime inat bıyık altından gülüyordum. Ah, neyin peşindeydim ki.

"Özledim seni çok."

"Tahmin edemezsin benim özlemimi…"

Ne zaman birleşmişti ellerimiz, nasıl başlamıştı her şey bir anda. Neyle esrikleşmiştik bu kadar? Cevap veremiyor, tedirgin bir mutlulukla an'ın tadını çıkarıyordum. Kayıplarımı göz ardı edip kazancıma yönlendiriyordum kendimi. Sorulardan uzak duruyordum büyüyü bozmamak için. Ama uyarı şarttı;

"Bak, sana anlaşılmaz gelebilirim. Beni farklı olarak da yorumlayabilirsin. Bu, başlangıçta ilgi nedenidir karşı taraf için. Her tarafın aynılıkla dolduğu bir evrende, farklı olan her şey çözülmesi gerekli bir giz olarak görülür ve bu da doğal olarak ilgiyi getirir. Ama paradoksal bir şekilde, başlangıçta belki seni bana çeken şey, daha sonra benden uzaklaşmana da neden olacak. Zaman, aynı tutumları farklı yorumlamanı sağlayacak. Yani, benim başlangıç nedenim sonuç nedenimi de oluşturacak sende. Düşünmen lazım bunu. Kafası karışık insan, hele erkek, bir yere kadar çekicidir. Daha sonra bu erkeğin kafasını toparlaması, muhtemel eşini, muhtemel çocuğunu, muhtemel yuvasını duru bir kafayla hayata karşı, her şeye karşı koruması beklenir. Benimse toparlayacak bir kafam yok."

Yatıştırmaya çalıştı;

"Saçmalama. Aşkımı nedenlerle ifade etmiyorum ben. İçimdesin. Bu, öncesiz ve sonrasız bir aşk. Rahat ol."

Rahat değil ama hâlâ esrik bir haldeydim. Başladığım yer neresiydi? Şimdi nerede yer alıyordum? Zorlama bilgeliklerime ne olmuştu? Aşık olmak, aşık olduğun kişiyle hayal kurmak, hayatı birlikte programlamak şimdi ne kadar da doğal görünüyordu bana. Düşündüm çok değil daha bir hafta önce el ele tutuşup eşya bakan çifti beynimde nasıl mahkûm ettiğimi. Onlar seçmeye çalışırken eşyalarını, ben kafalarının üzerine çizdiğim balonların içine muhtemel konuşmalarını yerleştiriyor, alışverişten sonra içinde yer alacakları diğer ritüelleri resmediyor, bu küçük burjuva tavırlarını lanetleyip uzaklaşıyordum. Peki şimdi? Bu kadar hızla değişen neydi ki tüm o sahneler sevimli gelmeye başlamıştı? Bir yandan öncemi koruma telaşıyla değişikliği yadsımaya çalışırken, bir yandan da içinde bulunduğum anın büyüsünü bozmamak için düşüncelerimden uzaklaşmayı deniyordum.

Bu düşüncelerimden onun sorusuyla uzaklaştım. Şiirlerini nasıl bulduğumu merak ediyordu. İstanbul'a gitmeden önce bana bırakmış, hepsini okumamı istemişti. Tekrar tekrar okumuş, "evet bu" demiştim. İlgisiz olmadığımı göstermeliydim. Detay verdim:

"Her kadın bir şaire aşıktır diyorsun şiirlerinin birinde. Gerçekten aşık mıdır her kadın bir şaire?" diye sordum.

"Kesin değil tabii. Olabilir ama."

Tabii ki kesin değildi, tabii ki olabilirdi. Veya olup olmasının önemi neydi. Şiirdi sonuçta ve imgeydi bu. Neden illa bir gerçeğe dayamaya çalışıyordum ki bu imgeyi? Anlamsızca atıldım;

"Hayır kesin bence!"

Benim olmayan bir düşünce üstüne böyle kesin konuşmam dayanılır gibi değildi. Neden O.'ya bilgelik taslamakta ısrar ediyordum her zaman? Hangi kompleksimi yada hangi korkumu bastırmaya çalışıyordum bilgiç tavırlarımla yada neden kaçıyordum? Ama o hastalık yine tutmuştu. Sıksam da kendimi biliyordum ki yine başlayacağım.

Ve başladım:

"Yazmak yada yaşamak. Hayatın iki ucu olarak kabul et bunu. Yaşayanlar yada yazanlar olarak da sınıflayabiliriz insanları. Yazanlar gerçekte yaşayamayanlardır ama neyin ne olduğunu hiçbir zaman bilemeyen ve asla bilemeyecek olan kadınlar aslında bu adamların yaşam kısırı olduğunun farkına varmadan aşık oluverirler şairlere."

Kendi havamda, konuşuyordum. Tırnaklarımı geçirebilir miydim hâlâ? Kendimi tasarladığım yönün aksine bir akışta bulmam nedeniyle kendime duyduğum hıncı ondan çıkarmam için bir fırsattı işte. Değerlendirmeye çalıştım ve devam ettim;

"Ah, ne kadar da güzel kullanmış imgeleri! Ah, bu ne duyarlılık! Ah, böyle yazabiliyorsa duygularını, nasıl yaşar kim bilir! Hangi kadının o zavallı beynini sarmadı ki bu düşünceler? Hangi kadının kalbi çarpmadı edebi madrabazları görünce? Hangi kadın kapılıp gitmedi?"

Saçmaladığımı düşünüyor olmalıydı.

"Abartıyorsun..." diye itiraz etti. Vazgeçmiyordum;

"Belki... Ama bir şeyi tüm hücreleriyle yaşayan adamın duygularını yüceltip yazmayacağını düşünüyorum. Yaşadığı şeyin büyüsünü kim bozmak ister kelimelere indirgeyerek? Kelimelere indirgenecek kadar elle tutulabilecekse zaten duyguları, onun yaşanmasından ne çıkar? Ortalamalar zaten söz konusu değil. Ben, iki uçtan bahsediyorum. İki uçta da sadece birisi olabilir. Ancak..."

"............"

"Kahramanlık öykülerini kahramanların kendisi mi armağan etti tarihe? Atilla'yı kahramanlık notlarını tutarken gören var mı? Büyük İskender elinde kalemle mi koşturdu kıtadan kıtaya? Mecnun kağıtları değil kendini tüketti. Pavese'i düşün. Eğer evlilik tekliflerinden birisi kabul edilmiş olsaydı, bulsaydı aradığı ilişkiyi, okuyabilir miydin o satırları? Bukoswki, Boudleare'den daha iyi aşık değil mi gerçek hayatta. İşte, bunun için kesin diyorum, çünkü kadınlar bu kadar ileri götüremezler uslamlamalarını."

Aferin bana... Nasıl da vermiştim ağzının payını! Göstermiştim ne kadar zayıf bir cinse ait olduğunu. Önümde diz çökebilirdi artık. Ah, hâlâ kurtarmaya çalışıyordum kendimi. Lanet.

Evrenin merkezi olmaktan çoktan çıkmış, tüm verilenlere karşı açtığım bayrağı indirmiş, kaçmaya çalıştığım, içine düşmemek için şekilden şekle girdiğim anaforun ortasında bulmuştum kendimi. Düşünce arası katmanlarda değil, aşkın hallerinin elle tutulur dalgalanmaları arasında gidip geliyordum. Rahatsız kişiliğim yine bırakmıyordu peşimi ama kaygılarım artık daha ele avuca gelir haldeydi. Diğer yanda; bir anlamda tensel temastan uzak seyreden aşkımız, hızla o yöne doğru akıyordu. Bu ne ironi!

Orgazm sonrası hüzün; ne büyük korku. Hâlâ içinde bulunduğum durumun en basit beşeri gereklilik olduğunu idrak edemiyor, hâlâ bir yerlerde kutsala pay biçiyor, kendimde, O.'nun yüzünde, ortak evrenimizde hâlâ kutsalı yaşatmaya çalışıyordum. Ve bu kutsalı bozabileceğini düşündüğüm, aşkımıza konduramadığım cinsellik, korkularımı tetikliyordu. Cinselliği, birbirine akan ruhların bedenler aracılığıyla birleşmesi olarak değil, insanın hayvaniliğe en çok yaklaştığı, pespayelik durumu olarak yoruyordum. Yakalayıp içeri tıktığı suçluların arasına düşen polisi resmeden Amerikan filmlerindeki adamın durumuna benziyordu halim. Değil mi ki ben, aşkı (hadi aşkı kutsala refere ettim diyelim...), cinselliği mahkum etmiş, bu konuda ne çok infaz yapmıştım. Şimdi ya kutsal bozulursa? Her orgazm hüzne gebe değil miydi? Her hüzün bitişi işaret etmiyor muydu? Her korkunun kaynağı bitişle ilgili değil miydi?

Uzak durmaya çalışıyordum. Ama artık eve gitmek gerekiyordu. Merak ediyordu yaşadığım yeri. Ah evim! Tek başıma her şeye karşı durabileceğim yanılsamasını gerçeğe dönüştürüp olmaz hayaller kurduğum, içinde tüm korkularımdan arındığım, tüm çırpınışlarımın tek tanığı evim. Kaçacak yerim kalmamıştı. Olası sonuçlara hazırlamaya çalıştım O.'yu;

"Seninle eve gitmekten korkuyorum. Birlikteliğimizin, aşkımızın dokunulmazlığını parçalayacağı düşüncesi ur gibi içimde, kemirip duruyor beni."

Kaçamamıştım...

Yanılmıştım. Her orgazm hüzün değilmiş demek. Aşkımı konumlandırdığım yer, cinsel orgazmın ulaştırdığı doyumun ulaşamayacağı bir yerdeymiş meğer. Başlamasını hiç istemediğim bu aşkın bitişinden çok korkmuştum. Ama görüyordum ki çok tali kalıyordu tüm bunlar. Nasıl da dokunamamıştı cinsellik aşkımıza. Bir yerlerde yanılıyor muydum yoksa? Başka ne diyebilirdim ki;

"Teşekkür ederim."

"Ben teşekkür ederim."

VII.

*Tesadüfe bırakamayacak kadar değer veriyorsun ya-
şama. Sana rağmen olana katlanamıyorsun. Her şey,
senden önce, sana rağmen başlamış, devam etmiyor-
muş gibi... Değer yanılsaması.*

Evlenmiştik...

Ne ailelerin karşı çıkması, ne ikimizin de işsiz oluşu, ne evlilikle ilgili düşüncelerimizin evlilik olgusuyla ilgisizliği... Tek kaygımız vardı;
birbirimizden ayrı kalamazdık. Kalmamalıydık. Başlangıçta birlikte
yaşamayı denemiş, şartların zorlayıcılığı mutlak birlikteliğimizi tek
kanala hapsetmişti: Evlilik. Değiştiremediğimiz için seçip evlendik.
Tüm evlilik ritüellerinden uzak (Değil mi ki ben bu kadarını artık
kaldıramazdım. Hele sevdiğim insanın bu ritüelleri bir şekilde iste-
yebileceğini hiç düşünemezdim. Her ne kadar ısrarla yok saydığım
ve "toplumsal varoluş" diye nitelediğim şeyin evlilikle en orta yerine
girsem de, hâlâ kendimle mücadele ediyor, artık duruşumla değil
kavramlar üzerinden götürüyordum mücadelemi.). Olmayan maddi
gücümüze oranla şatafatlı –Ki bu şatafat, ödünç takım elbiseler ve
borç parayla yenen yemekten öte değildi- ve tüm davetlilerin iki
nikah şahidinden oluştuğu bir törendi hepsi.

"Biz evlilik için değil, evlilik bizim için bir araç. Birlikteliğimiz için..."

Rahatlatmaya çalışıyordum. Buruktu. Nerelerden geçerek gelmiştim
bu aşamaya. Nelerden vazgeçerek... En nihayetinde bir imza töre-
ninden öte anlam taşımayan bu gereklilik durumunun sefaleti, bundan sonra her zaman birlikte olacak olmamızdan daha mı önem-

liydi? Neden buruktu ki? Yoksa her şey bir yana O. bile herkesin yaptığı gibi mi olmasını istemişti de ben anlamamıştım? Evet... anlayamamış ama ilk işareti almıştım. Haklı mıydım yoksa? Neredeydi o mısraların aşkın yazarı? Neredeydi "Evet, bir kadın olacaksa ancak bu olabilir" dedirten, varolanların dünyasının tüm gereklilikleri yok sayan O.? Yoksa her kadın en nihayetinde bir kadın mıydı? Sanırım her kadın en nihayetinde bir kadındı.

Alışmaya çalıştım.

Artık evde daha fazla toz alınıyor, hepsi birkaç parçadan oluşan eşyalarımız daha özenle düzenleniyor, daha önce muzip bir söylenmeyle karşıladığı dağınıklığım soruna dönüşüyor, kitaplarımız; üzerinde konuştuğumuz, incelediğimiz, tartışıp araladığımız kapılardan zevkle el ele yükseldiğimiz hareket noktamız olmak yerine sadece raflara evimizin en gösterişli eşyaları olarak özenle diziliyor, bizi bir araya getiren o aşkın dünyanın sıkıntıları aşılması gereken, belli bir zaman aralığının konuları olarak kalıyordu. Sorunlarımı çözememiştim oysa, sorularımı cevaplayamamıştım. Hatta kendimi ters yüz ederek daha bir zorlaştırmıştım her şeyi kendim için.

Ve... Daha önce beni anlayacağını düşündüğüm tek insan; artık büyümem gerektiğini yineleyen, ne zamana kadar bu şekilde gideceğini soran, normalleştirme meleği gibi etrafımda omuzlarıma binip adam gibi bir adam olmaya yönlendiren 'eş'e dönüşmüştü.

Suçlamıyordum. Çocukluğundan itibaren ailesinde yaşadığı ayrılıklar, bir türlü düzene girmeyen hayatı, yerinde ve zamanında yaşanmayan duyguları ve çekebileceğinden çok yüklendiği sorumlulukları duru bir hayat isteğini suçlanılır kılmıyordu.

Ama bu arada ben, neysem oydum. Uyum sağlamaya çalıştım.

İkimizin de işe girmesi maddi durumumuzu görece düzeltmiş, birbirimizi evlenmeden önce daha fazla görüyorduysak da bu gerçek, sorun olarak sadece duygu yoğunlaşmalarında karşımıza çıkıyordu. Sırf daha fazla birlikte olabilmek için evlenmemiş miydik? Başlangıç noktamızdan ne kadar da uzaklaşmıştık. Bizi birleştiren o aslı nasıl da kaybetmiştik. Ama artık daha fazla para kazanıyorduk. Sorun olmamalıydı...

Artık şiir yazmıyordu. Bir şeyler karalıyor ama önceden hayranlıkla karşıladığı eleştirilerime tahammül edemediği için bana göstermiyordu. Ne yazdığını merak ediyor ama daha önce yaptığı gibi kendisi getirip bakmamı istesin diye beklediğim için ne soruyor ne de o yokken bakmak istiyordum. Bunun geride kalan bir hayal olduğunu anlayınca ısrar ettim. Artık öykü yazıyormuş, bitirmemiş ama yine de madem istemişim... Uzattı sonunda. Kendinden emin bekliyor onaylamam için.

"Bence enerjini şiir için harca." dedim kıracağımı bilerek. Duyguları incinen her insan gibi tartışmak yerine suçladı;

"Böylesin zaten. Hiçbir şeyi beğenmezsin. Yazdığın ne var peki? Sen kendini ne sanıyorsun ki?" diyerek elimdeki kağıtları yırtarcasına aldı. Sakindim, cevapladım;

"Ne sanabilirim ki? Fikrimi söyledim. Hepsi bu."

En dayanamadığı şey, kızgın olduğu anlarda benim sakin olmam, ses tonumda hiçbir oynama olmamasıydı. Benim de bağırmam, sesimi yükseltmem gerekiyordu sanırım. Ancak elimden ne gelirdi ki.

Mücadele edecek hali yoktu. Alçalttı sesini, yakındı sadece;

"Zaten artık benim hiçbir şeyimi beğenmiyorsun. Çok değiştin. Ne olur bu kadar katı olmasan." dedi yarı yalvarır, yarı suçlar bakışlarla.

"İlgisi yok. Katı olabilirim ama hep katıydım. Anımsa; kantinde bana uzattığın fotoğraflardan sonra gösterdiğim tepkiden daha katı değil tepkim şu an. Ama şartlar değişti ve sen aynı ben'i farklı yorumlamaya başladın." Aptalca bir tekrar içindeydim.

Devam ettim;

"Bilirsin, şiirlerini çok beğenirim. Ama neden illa başka şeyler de yazacağım kasıntısı içindesin, anlamıyorum. Bir şey yazıp yazmamanın kendi gerekliliğini tartışmıyorum. Madem yazıyorsun, yazıyorsundur. Ama bu yazını beğenmedim."

Açıklamamı tatmin edici bulmamıştı. Hâlâ aynı soruyu soran gözleri üzerime kilitlenmiş, "lütfen" der gibi bakıyordu. Tatmin etmeliydim; "Şiirlerinde imgeler çok güçlü. Olması gerektiği gibi. Vurup kaçıyor. Bir anlamda böyle bir şeydir şiir. Nokta atışlar. Aynı şeyi bu öykünde de yapmaya çalışmışsın. Yer yer bütünü göz ardı ettirecek güçlü bir imge, daha sonra bu imgenin ağırlığı altında ezilen, sanki tek varoluş nedeni bu imgeye bir şekilde yamanmak, yanında küçük düşmemek yada imgeyi anlaşılır kılmak olan uzun açıklamalar. Bırak imgen olduğu gibi kalsın, açıklamaya çalışıp ona ihanet etme."

"Anladım..." dedi uslu uslu. Ama kesmek istemiyordu bu kadarla, incinmesi geçmemişti. Bu kadar kırmış mıydım?

Gücünü toplamış, saldırdı. Sesi gene yükselmişti;

"Kesintisiz okuyorsun. Eve bak, kayda değer tek eşyamız kitaplar. Hem okumaya, kitaplara bu kadar öncelik veriyor, hem de benim şiirlerimi lütfen överken 'yazmanın kendi gerekliliğini tartışmıyorum' diyerek 'dua et susuyorum' şeklinde bir anlamda göz dağı veriyorsun. Bu ne çelişki?"

Açıklamaya çalıştım yine sinir bozucu bir sakinlikle çelişkimi kabul ettim;

"Olabilir tabii.."

Bu kabulün aslında onu yatıştırmak için bir manevra olduğunu, olabilir derken öyle düşünmediğimi bilecek kadar tanıyordu beni. Açıklamam için sessizce bekledi. Hayal kırıklığına uğratmadım ve yine üst perdeden girdim;

"Sanat adı verilen farklılık çabaları. Dokunulmazlık zırhıyla örtülürken özgür ifadenin sözcüsü olma girişimi. Beğenmediği, farklılaşmaya çalıştığı yığının özgürlüğüne ihtiyacı olan sanat. Ve sanat yapıcılar. Rahatsız küçük varoluşlar. Küçücük... Bu çelişkilerden daha mı derin benimkisi?"

Sadece retorik bir soruydu. Cevap vermedi. Devam ettim;

"Düşünsene; sanat yapıcılar tarafından sanat öyle kutsanır, öyle bir yere konur ki, neredeyse kimse ulaşamaz, öyle bir yerdedir sözde yaratımları. Hadi öyle olduğunu kabul edelim. Madem sanat yapıcılar biz normal insanların ulaşamayacağı bir yerdeler, bizim gibi normal insanlardan beğenilme, takdir görme, onanma gibi beklentileri neden olsun? Bir şekilde bizimle ilgili ne varsa, tüm 'biz zavallı insanların' halleri ile ilgili olmamaları gerekir değil mi? Ama bir yandan bizden özgürleşmeye çalışırken yaratım süreci için, bir yandan da bize ihtiyaç duyuyor kendini olumlamak adına. İşte bunun için rahatsız küçük oluşlar diyorum onlara ben. Yığından tek farkları taşıdıkları rahatsızlık. Hepsi hepsi bu. Kaldır at, bir şey kaybetmezsin. Çünkü sana gerçekten kazandıracak olanlar, bir kenara kaldırılıp atılamayacak olanlar, ironik bir şekilde ya yazamayacak kadar iyidirler, ya hayatta kalamayacak kadar problemli. Öyle sizin sanat yapıcılar gibi, küçücük rahatsız varoluşlarla, kırıtarak, fularlarla arz-ı endam etmezler. Kendilerine fazla olan varlıklarını bir de başkalarına yük edemezler."

'Yazamayacak kadar iyi' sözü O.'nun benim yazmamı istediği zamanlar yazmamama karşın söylediği 'Çünkü yazamayacak kadar iyisin' sözünü anımsatmış olacak ki kendime pay biçtiğimi sanıp tekrar saldırıya geçti;

"Ne yani, sizler sadece varsınız. Yaşar gidersiniz. Tarih, bizim gibi yazan ve dolayısıyla yaşayan ortalamaların devamıdır, öyle mi?"

"Tarihin, en azından bilgimize dahil olan tarihin, ortalamalardan ibaret olması başka konu. Yalnız şu var; Var olanların bilindiği bir dünyada olmayanların değerinin verilmesi elbette mümkün değil. Ancak bu, onun gerçekte olmadığı anlamına gelir mi? Yada bildiklerimizin salt gerçekliği oluşturduğu ne kadar geçerlidir? Olup da bilgimize dahil yok mu sayacağız?"

Anlamsızca baktı yüzüme. Sığlık yormuştu, inledim;

"Ah ağırlığa hiç de dayanıklı olmayan yaşamsal yüzey... Derinliğine neler gömdün?"

Hala aynı bakış... Anlamaması umurumda değildi. Sayıklar gibi söylendim;

"Yüzeyin taşıyabilme kapasitesinden fazla özgül ağırlığı olan için gömülmek kader olabilir. Yüzeyin taşıyamaması da... Ama bu döngü..."

"Yani?" dedi daha bir anlaşılmaz bir ifadeye bürünüp. Gücümü toplayıp daha basitleştirerek anlatmaya çalıştım;

"Yani şu; İki çizgi düşün. Çizginin birisi seviye olarak en altı, diğeri ulaşılabilecek en üst noktayı işaret etsin. İki uç nokta varsay ve alttan üste doğru sırala. Birinci basamağa zincirin en zayıf halkası İclal Aydın'ı, son basamağa da en güçlü olarak Dostoyevski'yi yerleştir mesela. Aralarındaki tek fark sıralamadaki yerleri. Yerleri ne olursa olsun aynı kümedeler ama. E, o zaman? Bu örneği istediğine uygula. Aklına ne gelirse işte. Peki, bu insanların ortaya çıkardıklarını salt gerçeklik kabul edebilecek misin? Diojen hakkında ne biliyoruz? İzin verdiği kadarını değil mi: "Gölge etme..." Örneğin, bu sözü de söylememiş olsaydı, Diojen'i hiç olmamış mı kabul edecektik? Yani bilgelik yarışındaki insanlar, insanlıklarıyla bilgeliğin neresindeler? İnsan olmak – bilge olmak - var olmak...Nasıl bir düzlem? Mümkün mü?"

Kılıcını kınına sokmuş, cevabı benim vermemi istiyordu;

"Öyleyse, ne olacak, ne olmalı?" dedi yatışmış bir halde.

"Bilmiyorum. Sadece çoğu şeyin problemli olduğunu biliyorum. Yanlış bir oyunu doğru oynayamazsın derler. Bu da onun gibi bir şey. Metodoloji yanlış, yaratılış metodolojisi. Yada yaratılışta sıkıntı yok da işte Tanrı'nın kusursuzluktan canının sıkıldığı, o, bilgileri saklı tutup dengeyi altımızdan çekme anından sonra bozuldu her şey. O zamandan sonra Tanrı'nın kusursuz dünyası bizim için ham hayal olarak kalırken, kusur tasarımının içinde tarih de yerini aldı. Zamanlar, sistemler, değer yargıları, inanışlar... Aynı can sıkıntısının farklı dışavurumları. Ve bu sıkıntılı oluşun peşinden koşan tarih. Aldananaldatan diyalektiği. Her iki taraf da bilinçli bir şekilde sürdürürken bu diyalekti, ben nasıl verebilirim 'ne olacak' yada 'ne olmalı'nın cevabını? Kazananların yazdığı tarihte kaybedenleri kaybederken, yok olanın aslında tarih olduğu açık değil mi? Kaybedenlerin kayıplarına ilişkin düşülen notlar, neler kazandı(rdı)klarının dökümü değil ki. Sonuç; kaybeden tarih yada tarihin kaybolması. Başlangıcı ne, sonu ne? Yanlış bir tarih kaybedilmiş de değil midir sence? İşte, tarihin sonunun geleceğine ilişkin tüm kehanetler de bu çıkışsızlığın, yanlışlığın derin bir duyumsamasının dışa vurumu. Peki tarihin (kaybeden) sonunun geleceğine dair kehanetler, başlangıcına ilişkin ne söyleyebiliyor? Olmayan üzerine söylenen, olan üzerine söylenmeyen kadar."

Konudan uzaklaşmış, fırtına dinmiş, O. yatışmıştı. Ben?

VIII.

Uzamı yitirip katı nesnelerin ortasından geçerken, kaçmaya çalıştığın tüm cisimlerin ortasında aldın yerini. Onları yok sayıp -yok belki- bütünleştiğinde, alamadığın hazların toplamını acı olarak verirken başkalarına, başkalarının orada olmamasına seviniyordun. Yine de o duygularla –duygusal varoluş- tanımladın TAANSAŞ'ı.[3](1) Sen, hainsin.

Aramalar, bulamamalar, bulduklarını 'aradığım şey işte' diye anlamlandırmalar, yaratılan anlamlardan kaçmalar, kaçılan anlamlara sığınmalar...

O., anlamdı her şeyden önce benim için. Belki O.'da olmayan bir anlam. O.'ya değil yarattığım anlama aşık olmuştum ihtimal, bu yeni anlama yüklediğim değerle geri kalan anlamlarımı göz ardı etmiştim. Ama öncekiler gibi bu da parçalanıyordu. Bu kaçıncı parçalanma? Artık parçaların izleri bile her şeyi karmakarışık etmeye yeterli.

Tekrar seçmeye başlamıştım sanrılar dünyasını. Önceden, yalnızken, katlanılamaz gelince her şey, ki ne çok olurdu, ölümü seçmeyi denerdim. Ama intiharın birçok yolu vardı. Hem kalanlar için daha az azap verici yollar. Yada her zamanki gibi kendimi bu düşüncelerle kandırıp kolayına kaçıyordum. İşte, ben de bağlarımı tamamen koparmak yerine sanrılar dünyasını seçerek belli bir zaman aralığında zaman ve mekanla aramdaki ilişkiyi kesiyor, bir bakıma kopardığım

---

3   (1) TAANSAŞ'ın süper market Tansaş'la ilgisi yoktur. Sadece başkişinin boyutu başka zihin dünyasını ifade eder...

bu bağlarla sağlıyordum devamımı. Ve tutunamayınca yeni yaratımıma, tekrar seçmeye başladım, gizli gizli.

TAANSAŞ'taki dostlarım, aralarına tekrar dönüşüm şerefine en eşsiz sanrıları sunuyorlardı bana. Zaman, mekan, hareketi sınırlayan fizik kuralları, her şeyi kurulu saate çeviren neden-sonuç ilişkisi, 'toplumsal varoluş' ve 'duygusal varoluş'a dair ne varsa, hepsinden uzaktım TAANSAŞ'ta. Daha sık seçer olmuştum. O., biliyordu benim TAANSAŞ'ımı. Ne çok korkar, nasıl da tedirgin olurdu. Bu sefer söyleyemiyordum. Olanın farklı yorumlamasını kabul edemezken, algılanmayan etrafında oluşturduğum bir evreni nasıl anlatabilirdim.

Anlatamazdım.

Anlatamadım. Ama O., kopuşun farkındaydı. Beni, varolanların dünyasına çekmeye çalışıyordu;

"Özel değilsin kesinlikle. Özel değiliz. Herkes kadar sıradan, herkes kadar sıra dışı. Sahte değerler yaratma boşuna."

Biliyordum özel olmadığımı. Biliyordum özel olsam bile bir şeyin değişmeyeceğini. Sızlandım;

"Sadece rahatsızım, her şeyden."

Yatıştırmaya çalıştı;

"Yaşama duyduğun eleştirel yakınlık ile yığından ayrıldığını sanıyorsun. Sırtın dönük, yalnızsın. Bu; zevkti senin için, bu acı, bu, oluşun... Tek başına. Ama biliyorsun. Tek başına değilsin artık. İçindeki boşluğu anlamıyor değilim. Ama bir yerden sonra yenmen gerekir, hiç olmazsa yok sayman. "

"Haklısın, hadi gidip normal olalım. Yok sayalım" demem gerekirdi. Ne kadar isterdim demeyi. Diyemedim;

"Yarattığım değerler sahte olabilir. Ve haklı olduğunu kabul edip bu değerlerin hepsini atabilirim de. Ama sorun bu değerlerin atılmasında yada atılmamasında değil. Sahte olmayan ne? Onu bulamıyorum. Sonuna değin götürebilecek kadar yüzde yüz doğru olan... Yada illa bir şeyin götürmesi gerekiyor mu onu da bilmiyorum. Veya gitmek gerekiyor mu? Bir şeyin yerine başka bir şeyi ikame etmek değil mesele. O, işin en basit kısmı. Bir şey olmalı. Öyle bir şey ki, tüm sancılarından kurtaracak, beyninin içindeki karıncalanmaları tamamen söküp atacak bir şey. Gerekliliklerden öte, hesap kitaptan öte, korkulardan öte, ödülden, cezadan öte. Bilmiyor muyum benzer sıkıntıların bin yıllardır sayısız kişi tarafından yaşandığını. Özel değilim tabii. Ama Araf'tan kurtaramıyorum kendimi yine de."

Beklediği cevap değildi.

"Ama ben, ama biz..." diye fısıldadı.

"Biliyorum her şeyi aslında. Yavrusunu kesesinde taşıyan kangurular gibiyiz. Olması gereken ne varsa, kesemizde. Zamanı gelince başlarını çıkarıp hatırlatıyorlar kendilerini. Oluş, bunu böyle ayarlıyor. Yapılması gereken, tez canlılık edip elimizi keseye sokup karıştırmamak. Ama işte, kesenin içindekileri bildiğim için onları görmeden rahat edemiyorum. Zamanlamadaki hatam, içeridekilerin formunu değiştiriyor. Kendini gösterme zamanı gelmemiş mutluluğu alarak vaktinden önce, mutsuzluğa çeviriyorum. Yada bana verilen her şeyi aynı sona uğratıyorum. Sıralamayı bozuyor, içerdeki her şeyin formunu deformasyona uğratarak bir gulyabaniye dönüştürüyorum. Farkındayım bunun ama elime koluma hakim olamıyorum."

Korkmuştu.

"Yapmamalısın."

"Yapmamalıyım."

Yapıyordum.

Hâlâ "...Ama biz" der gibi bakıyordu. Teskin etmeye çalıştım;

"Evet sen, evet biz. Senden aldığım güçle her şeye karşı durdum. Sana tutundum Araf'tan uzaklaşmak için. Başlangıçta çok güçlüydü bağ. Her şeye yetebilecek kadar güçlü. Ama özel olmalıydık birlikte farklı bir yerde olmak için. Fakat senin söylediğin gibi, özel değiliz. Farklı olamıyoruz. Geçen her günde, duygularımız gibi biz de sıradanlaşıyoruz, sanırım zaman sorunu, henüz kabul edemiyorum 'olağan'ın 'belirsiz' bir parçası olmayı."

İlk kopuşlar... Başlangıçta da uyardığım gibi, O.'yu bana çeken nedenler, artık aramıza giren mesafenin nedenlerine dönüşmüştü. Kafam karmakarışıktı. Tüm kafa karışıklığıma ve hayal kırıklıklarıma rağmen, ki ne kadar da çoktular, ruhum hâlâ ona doğru kesintisiz akıyor, ancak çoğu zaman karşılığını bulamıyordu. O.'nun da kafası karışıktı. Olan, olması gerektiği gibi değildi. Benden farklı olarak, kafa karışıklığını daha bir yöneliş olarak göstermiyor, hızla uzaklaşıyordu.

"Artık eskisi gibi değiliz. Ayrılığı düşünmeliyiz."

Söylemek için uzun provalardan geçtiği belli. Ne diyeceğimi merak ederek gözlerime bakıyor. Kalakalıyorum.

"Ayrılık?"

Neden sonra anlamlandırıyorum duyduğum kelimeyi.

"Sence mümkün mü? Olabilir mi bu?" diye direnmeye çalışıyorum.

Acaba neden bahsettiğini biliyor muydu?

Sanırım biliyor. Sadece bilmekle kalmıyor, bildiğini normal kabul ediyor olmalıydı.

"Neden olmasın? Her ilişki bitebilir. Belki her ilişki belli bir yerden sonra bitmeli. İlişkinin bağlamı olan aşk ortadan kalktıktan sonra devam etmek, ne kadar anlamlı ki?"

Demek bazı şeyleri ıskalamıştım. Ne zamandan beri birlikteliğimiz 'ilişki' olarak niteleniyordu? İlişkimizin bağlamı olan aşk, ne zaman ortadan kalkmıştı? Ayrılıkların olabileceğini bilebilecek kadar tecrübeliydim. Ama nasıl anlatabilirdim her şeye karşın genele uymayacak bir durum olduğunu, aşkım öncesiz ve sonrasız derken, bundan gerçekten de öncesiz ve sonrasızı anladığımı. Anlatamazdım. Anlatmadım;

"Görmedim. Ayrılık yoktur benim dünyamda. Ama bitmeli diyorsan, bitmelidir." diyebildim sadece anlamsız, avam bir jargonla.

Bitmişti. Evi terk etmiş, annesinin yanına taşınmıştı.

Neydi mutluluk tasarımım? Hangi katıksız mutluluk masalları büyütmüştü beni? Hangi gerçeklerle mutluluğun ham hayal olduğu çarpılmıştı yüzüme. Düşünüyorum...

IX.

Sorulan sorular... Cevap arayarak yada öylesine. Alınan cevaplar, soruyla ilgili yada öylesine. Aslında ne cevap verenin soruyla ilgisi vardır nede soranın cevaba ihtiyacı. Yaşamın ise hiçbirine... Olmayanlar etrafında kazara örülmüş ve devam eden, öylesine süregelen bir döngü... Soru var mı? Neyle ilgili? Ya cevap...?

Ne soru vardı ne cevap, yada ne çok soru ve ne çok cevap vardı. İçimdeki boşluk izin vermemişti hayatı diğerleri gibi yaşamama. Ayrılık sadece bana özgü değildi. Biliyordum, milyonlarca birliktelik gibi milyonlarca ayrılık da vardı. Ama yine de önce inkar ettiğim, kaçmak için debelenircesine mücadele ettiğim ancak başaramadığım, yenilgimi aşk kavramına ihale edip içinde yer aldığım bu şeyi korumak için yine benzer bir mücadele içine girdiğim yeni evrenimden de başarısızlıkla, yenilerek ayrılmayı kabul edemiyordum. Sevgilinin gitmesi değildi sorun. Her çabamın bir şekilde başarısızlığa dönüşmesiydi. Yaşamla ilgili tasavvurlarımda bir eksiklik olmalıydı. Ki ben, hep dokunulamayanı aramıştım. Her anlamda. Aşksa eğer, değil dış etkenlerin, tarafların bile dokunamayacağı aşklar; hayata karşı duruşsa; hayata dair ne varsa, hissedilenlerin yada hissedilmeyenlerin dünyasının dokunamayacağı bir duruş olmalıydı. Ve şimdi, kılıfımın parçalanmasının yüceltilmiş haline getirdiğim aşkım, aşkımın yöneldiği kaynak beni terk etmiş, sorulardan arındıramadığım zihnimin acabalarını daha çok yaşanılır olana/olması gerekene yönlendirmeye başlamıştım.

Nerede hata yapmıştım? Yada doğru yapmış mıydım? Ben dememiş miydim, "Benim başlangıç nedenim sonuç nedenimi de oluşturacak." Düşünmesini istememiş miydim bunu? Onun düşünmesini isterken, ben de biraz düşünemez miydim? Üst perdeden uyarı yaparken, bilmiyor muydum nelerle karşılaşacağımı? Neye karşı koruyabilmiştim O.'yu? Kurdurmuş muydum geleceğe ilişkin hayaller? Kurdurmalı mıydım?

Neye şaşırıyordum ki? Kabul etmeye yanaşmadığım neydi? Yoksa yaşadığım aşkı; "Hayır, ben herkes gibi olamam. Aşk realitesinin içinde, hem de taraflardan biri olarak nasıl bulunabilirim" diye reddeden egom, şimdi de aynı şekilde aşkla ilişkili bir ayrılık fotoğrafının içinde, taraflardan biri olarak bulunmamı mı kabul etmiyordu. Kendimi illa bir şekilde ifade etmeye çalışmam, ifade ettiğim her şeyin adını koymam, koyduğum adı, dünyanın bilmem kaçıncı harikası olarak nitelemem, nitelediğim her kavramın içine hapsolmam, tutsaklığımı, bir esaretten çok; "İşte, bak, yığın ta aşağılarda, sürünüyor. Bense, üstte izoleyim." yanılsaması ile yüceltmem, her yüceltmenin yapaylığı ve her yapay olanın kendi kendini zamanla yok etmesi nedeniyle çakılırcasına aşağıya, "sürünenler" diye dudak büktüklerim arasına düşmem ve her şeye tekrar sıfırdan başlamam, tutsak olduğum egomdan başka neyin ürünü olabilirdi. Tam tersini düşlerken, zulamda egoların en şişkinini barındırıyor olmalıydım. Hissedilen dünyayı her ayrıntısına uygun bir metaforla karşılayan, hissedilmeyeni de aynı metaforlarla yok sayan egom. Korunmak üzere oluşturduğun kozan seni ne zamana kadar saklayacak. Hem neden? Oluşunun korunmaya ihtiyacı mı var? Ah kibir! Ah insani zaaflar!

Kendimi neyle ifade ediyordum? Zorlama bilgelikler? Değer yanılsamaları? Paranoyak narsizm? Uysal baş eğmeler? Huzur-acı aşkları? Aşksız ilişkiler? İlişkisiz aşklar? …….? Örnekleri çoğaltmanın anlamı neydi? Zaman geçiyor, ben tükeniyordum ve yeniden yaratıyordum tekrar tüketmek için kendimi. Ve nitekim yeni durumlara uygun yeni formlarımı yaratacak, lanet varlığımı devam ettirecektim.

"Nefes alamıyorum sensiz. Dönmek istiyorum."

"Dön..."

Biliyordu beklediğimi. Biliyordu her zaman bekleyeceğimi. "Sana olan aşkım, her şeyi hoşgörecek kadar büyük." demiştim vaktiyle. Ne büyük bir hataydı bu söz, ne büyük bir hataydı bu bakış, ne büyük bir hataydı böylesi bir yöneliş. Oysa bir kötülük görememiştim böylesi bir yönelişte. Ve gerçekse bu, ki gerçekti, açıklanmasında. Yanılmıştım. Ne kadar da toydum, ne kadar da toy kalacaktım. Görecek, öğrenecek ama örendiklerimi davranış koduna çeviremeyecektim.

"Bırakıp giderken seni, karmakarışıktım. Gidebilecek kadar bitti sanmıştım aramızdaki bağ. Yanılmışım."

Ne diyebilirdim ki? Söyleyecek sözüm yoktu. Susmayı tercih ederdim ama konuşmam gerekiyordu. Anlamlı sözler yerine sadece kafasını karıştırdım;

"Sadece gidilemeyecek kadar mı kalmış. O zaman pek bir şey kalmamıştır sanırım. Tüm dünyayı yok sayacak kadar büyükken başta, eğer sadece gidilemeyecek kadara gerilemişse, yakında gitmeni engelleyecek kadar da kalmaz..."

Polemik kapılarının açıldığını ve benim buna hazır olduğumu sezdi. Göze alamadı. Sadece;

"Öyle demek istemedim. Sensiz nefes alamadım. Affet." dedi.

Affettim.

Ama ayrılık realitesi yerleşmişti birlikteliğimize. Artık böyle bir şeyin olabilirliği vardı bizim için. Sarmal kırılmıştı. Birincisini az bir hasarla atlamış olsak da (Az mı?), başlangıçta düşünülmesi bile imkansız olan bu kavramı olabilir bir şey olarak zihnimize sokmuş olması, ilk ayrılığın bıraktığı en belirgin mirastı.

"TAANSAŞ'la aran nasıl?"

Sordu korkarak. Duymak istemeyeceği bir konuya girdiğinin farkında. Söyledim;

"Ne olmasını bekliyorsun. Koptukça elimdekiler, tutunmaya çalışıyorum. İçimdeki boşluktan gelen hava akımı üşüttükçe, ısınmak için boşluğu doldurmaya çalışıyorum olmadık şeylerle. En olabiliri sendin ve sen..." devam etmedim. Gerek yoktu.

"Üzgünüm."

Üzgün olmalıydı, sanırım.

"Hayır, üzülmen için yada sitem olarak söylemedim. Gerçekten de, varsa eğer bu boşluğun ikamesi, sendin. İkame; sadece başlangıçta. Şimdi boşluğumun bile senin ikamen olamayacağından korkuyorum. Boşluğuma yerleştirirken seni, sığdırmam için daha çok yer açmam gerekti. Çıkınca sen, yada daha sonra çıkarsan, ne yapacağımı bilemez hale geliyorum. Hava akımı artık çok daha güçlü. Ve bu akımda neyle, nereye, nasıl tutunurum, bilmiyorum."

Sevinmesi mi üzülmesi mi gerektiğini bilmiyordu.

Sarıldı...

Dil olmasaydı keşke. Kelimeler olmasaydı. Susmak yetseydi. Sadece susmak gerekseydi.

Sarıldık.

Sustuk ve kaldık.

X.

Düşüyorsun aniden kalkıyorsun çarçabuk. "Düştüğümü gören var mı?" Düşürdüklerin umurunda değil. Toparlan ve bir şey yokmuşçasına yoluna devam et. Gitmek istiyorsun. Gidiyorsun. Nereye?

Üstümüzü başımızı iyice silkmiş, tozlardan arındırmış, bir şey yokmuşçasına yola koyulmuştuk tekrar. "Onlara bakmaktan vazgeçti, onlar da varolmamaya başladılar" diyordu yazar(1). Bakmaktan vazgeçişimizin, olmasını istemediğimiz ne varsa, karşılaşmaktan korktuğumuz her ne ise, ortadan kaldıracağını düşündük. Hiçbir şey olmamış gibi davranıyor, ilk başlarda "Ne?" "Neden oldu" sorularının cevabını bulduk sayarak kendimizi, tekrar yaşamın gereklerine ayak uydurmaya çalışıyorduk. Evden taşınmış, yeni evimizde hiçbir şeyin bize dokunamayacağı yeni bir hayat başlatmaya karar vermiştik. Uçlarımın sivriliklerini almaya çalışıyor, başka olabilirliklere de olanak tanıyor, yapabildiğim kadar normalleşmeye çalışıyordum. Adam nasıl olunur bilmiyordum ama adam olmaya karar vermiştim. Tarihten biliyordum ki; devam etmek için güçlü olmak yerine uyum sağlamak şart. Ama nasıl uyum sağlayacaktım? Neye? Ne için? Soruların önemi yoktu.

Adam olabilir miydim? Evini, işini düşünen, iyice aptallaşmamak için ara sıra okuyan, ailelere, arkadaşlara, akrabalara zaman ayıran, yani herkes gibi yaşayıp ölümü bekleyen biri olabilir miydim? Yetecek miydi bunu istemem? Her şeyi aceleye getirmekten vazgeçecek, kesemdekilerin zamanında çıkmasını bekleyebilecek miydim? Yaşam değildi adam olanların gündemi. Hiçbir kitle iletişim aracı ile ilgisi olmayan bir magazinel hayattan ibaretti, kurgulanan ve kurulanın ardından geriye kalan kuru gürültüydü her şey ve benim de kuru gürültü içinde yer almam gerekiyordu adam olmam için. Yaşamı, yaşamla ilgili olan oluşu gündemimden çıkarmam, hissedilenlerin dünyasının içinde yer almam... Becerebilecek miydim? Bunu mu istiyordu? Böyle olmadığım için sevmemiş miydi beni? Böyle olmadığım için sevmesinden dolayı çekmemiş miydi beni kendine?

Uzak durmaya çalışsam da kaçamadım yine. Sordum anlamsız;

"Başladığımız yerden ne kadar mesafedeyiz şimdi?"

Neden sormuştum, durduk yerde. Dilimin altında ne vardı gene. Anlamadı doğal olarak, sordu;

"Nasıl yani?"

"Basbayağı. Dört yıldır debelenip duruyoruz. Adına aşk diyip karşı koymadığımız şey kalmadı. Neresinden alırsan al, aldığımız mesafe ne?"

"Aşağı yukarı herkes aynı."

"Herkesin aynı olması değil problemli olan. Problem, mesafe alınamayacağının bilinmemesi. Yada bizim bunu bildiğimiz halde arzsızca mesafe almaya çalışmamız."

Mesafe

Yuvarlak, kocaman bir tepsi düşün. Al, karıncaları koy onun içine. Yapacakları en radikal şey, tepsinin kenarlarına kadar gelip dolaşmaları olacak. Kenardan taşmak isteyen düşecek dibe, kaybolup gidecek. Her varlık gibi onlar da kaybolmaya karşı geliştirecekleri içgüdüsel direnme ile o tepsiyi tek evrenleri olarak kabul edecek, tüm yaşamlarını, yaşam diyebilirsek buna, burada devam ettirecekler. Sen bu tepsinin içindeki her şeye müdahale edebilirsin. Yani bir anlamda bağışlayabilir yada hepsini suyun altına tutup boğabilir, parmağınla ezebilirsin. Bir acıma yada bir kahkahaya neden olur en fazla onların o zavallı mücadeleleri, gidip gelmeleri, tüm devinimleri. İşte, debelenip dursun karıncalar istedikleri kadar, gidecekleri yer belli. Yapabilecekleri hamleler de. Onlar attıkları her adımın dünyayı değiştirmeye atılmış adım olduğunu düşünseler de sen buna mesafe alıyorlar diyebilir misin?"

Yine ne diyorsun der gibi payladı;

"Saçmalıyorsun."

Saçmalıyorduysam da devam ediyordum;

"İşte biz de, biliyorsun, farklı değiliz. Binlerce tepsi var. Biz sadece binlerce tepsinin birinin içindeki binlerce kişiden biriyiz. Adını aşk koyup, adını iş koyup, adını daha binlerce şey koyup mesafe almak için boyumuzdan büyük enerjiyle boyuna debeleniyoruz. Ve tepsiyi elinde tutan da bakıp vakit geçiriyor bizimle. Bu yanılgının, birisinin oynadığı oyunun figüranı olduğunun bilinciyle gözlerimi parlatıyorum alttan, gururumu incitiyor bakıp bakıp gülmesi ama o kadar küçüğüz ki ona karşı ve o kadar kalabalığız ki, kızgınlıktan kan çanağına dönen gözlerimi, çatılan kaşlarımı, gerilen suratımı, titreyen elimi ayağımı görmüyor. Ve ben bu duyguların bıraktığı marazi ruh yapısıyla, kalakalıyorum."

Eğer birisi saçmalıyorsa ona öğüt vermelisiniz. Verdi;

"Sen de herkes gibi yap. Bakma yukarıya. Görülemeyecek kadar küçük olduğunu biliyorsan, küçüklüğüne yaraşır şekilde yaşa o zaman."

Kabul ederek karşı koydum;

"Mutlaka. Ama işte, mesafe sorunu. Böyle trencilik oynar gibi, halka şeklinde hareket ederek yol almaya çalışmak, canımı sıkıyor. Aynı noktaya hareket, yine aynı yere getiriyorsa harcanan bu enerji niye? Bitiş neresi? Başlangıç ile bitişin kesiştiği noktaya ne kadar mesafedeyiz? Ve bu yol kimin yolu. Adımlarımızı kimin için ve ne diye atıyoruz? Kabul etsem de küçüklüğümü yine de bunları düşünmeden edemiyorum."

Umudunu kesmiş olacak ki, susmuştu.

Öyle ya, cevabını bildiği soruları da sorar insan. Soruyordum, yığınla soruyordum. Oysa yığınla soru soruyor olmam, olmaya çalıştığım şeyin tam tersi değil miydi?

Becerememiştim. Becerememiştik. Ayrılmalar, gitmeleri, beklemem, geri dönmesi, olmayışı, tekrar gitmesi, artık sıradan şeyler olmuştu. Sıradan olana alışamayışım yine yakama yapışıyor, ne kadar gitse de alışamıyordum.

Artık ortak bir hayatımız yoktu. Benden adam olmayacağını anlamış ve bu kez geri dönmemek üzere gitmişti. Geriye sadece kağıt üzerindeki birlikteliğimizi bitirmek kalıyordu. Ama önemi yok, sonuçta halledilebilir bir meseleydi. O. zaman yitirmeyecek, bunu da halledecekti.

"Avukatla konuştum. Eğer anlaşarak ayrıldığımıza ilişkin bir belge verirsek, sorunsuz ayrılabilirmişiz. Buluşalım. Geriye bir şey kalmasın." En ufak bir duygu göstermeden, son derece sıradan bir şeyden bahsedercesine sadece izah ediyordu telefonda.

"Tamam. Geriye bir şey kalmayacaksa bu kağıtla, buluşalım." dedim duygusuzluğunu kopya etmeye çalışarak.

Buluştuk dışarıda. Daha önce hazırlattığı metni imzaladım. Bakamıyordum bile yüzüne. O., telefondaki ses tonunu sabitlemiş bir şekilde açıklıyordu;

"Ankara'da olursa eğer süreç uzar diyor avukat. Küçük bir ilçeye verilirse dilekçe, hem tanıdıkları varmış orada, tarih hemen verilirmiş."

Bu ne aceleydi? Gözlerimdeki soruyu okumuş olmalıydı. Cevapladı;

"Biliyorsun. Denedik fazlasıyla. Olmuyorsa, ki olmadı, daha fazla uzatmak anlamsız. Yanlış düşünmeni istemem." diye açıklamaya çalıştı.

Ne demeye çalışıyordu? Düşüncem sese dönüştü;

"Nasıl yanlış?"

"Başka şeylere yorman istemem. Sadece, denedik olmadı."

Neden açıklama gereği duyuyordu ki? Bana söylediği sözcükleri kendisi nasıl yorumlayacak diye merak edip tekrarladım söylediklerini;

"Sadece, denedik olmadı."

"Efendim?"

"Yok bir şey. Hoşça kal."

Evliliğimiz gibi sefil bir boşanmaydı. Küçük bir taşra ilçesinde, tekrar düşünmemizi isteyen hakim;

"Bakın, eğer evet diyorsanız, yazıcıdan kağıt çıkınca sizin evliliğiniz de bitmiş olacak." dedi adet olduğu üzere.

Ve yazıcıdan kağıt çıkmış, evliliğimiz bitmişti.

İKİNCİ BÖLÜM

Almak isteyip de alamadığın, yapmak isteyip de yapamadığın her şeyi alıp da yerine koy(a)madıklarına say. Başkalarınki sende dururken seninkilerin başkalarında olması şaşılacak bir durum değil. Öfkeni yen, edebinle otur. Ölüm yakın zaten.

Merhaba TAANSAŞ. Kabul eder misin beni tekrar? Teşekkür ederim...

Her şey başladığı yere dönmüş, O. artık tamamen gitmiş, bense hiçbir şeyin dokunamaması umuduyla geçtiğimiz evde, dokunmadık şey kalmamış bir şekilde tek başıma yaşamaya başlamıştım.

Nasıl bir yaşamdı?

XI.

TAANSAŞ GÜNCESİ - I

Sofadaki el feneri ışığını fark edip yatağından doğruldu. Eve hırsız girmiş olmalıydı. Ama duvar şeffaf değildi ve kapı da kapalıydı. Sofadaki ışığı yatak odasından nasıl görmüştü ki? Yatağından doğrulurken hırsızı korkutup kaçırmak için, bağırmaya çalıştı. Sesi çıkıp çıkmama arasındaymış gibi geldi kulaklarına. Korkarak kapıyı buldu ve sofaya gittiğinde rahatladı. Kediydi. Kedi, annesinin terliğini giymiş, sofada bir şeyler arıyordu. Tam yatağına dönüyordu ki kafasına takılan şey yüzünden tekrar sofaya yöneldi. Terlikler ayağına küçük değil miydi kedinin? Sıkmıyor muydu? Ve kedi, bir kedi için fazlasıyla büyük değil miydi? Ayrıca annesinin terliğinin burada ne işi vardı ki. Yıllardır annesinden ayrı, tek başına yaşıyordu. Yaklaşık küçük bir insan büyüklüğünde olan kedi, kafasında soru işaretleri yaratmıştı. Tekrar dışarı çıkınca aradığını mutfakta buldu ve haklı çıktı. Genç kız mutfakta, beceremediği belli, kocaman bir tencerede bulgur pilavı yapıyordu. Yalnız yaşadığı aklına geldi. Evinde, gece yarısı, hem de mutfakta yemek yapacak kadar evi sahiplenen birisini görmek şaşırtmıştı. Ama kız bir şey yokmuşçasına özenle pilavla ilgileniyordu. Müdahale şarttı ama sözcükleri sese bir türlü dönüştüremiyordu.

"Ne yapıyorsun burada" diyebildi en sonunda. Ekledi:

"Hem neden bulgur pilavı yapıyorsun tekrar. Koskoca bir tencere var zaten"

Evet. Koca bir tencere pilav, daha önce yapıldığı belli, duruyordu ocakta. Ama kendisi pilav yapmazdı ve yaptığını hatırlamıyordu zaten. Kafası iyice karışıyordu. Anlamaya ve kızdan cevap beklemeye çalışırken çıplak olduğunu anımsadı ve kıza gözdağı verdi mutfaktan çıkarken:

"Üzerime bir şeyler giyip geliyorum. O zaman sorarım sana."

Üzerine bir şeyler giydiğini varsayıp –giyip giymediğini kesinleyemiyor, ama giymek için gittiğine göre, giymiş olmalı- geldiğinde kız, pilavı çoktan bitirmişti. Pilav yoktu çünkü.

"Benim çikolatamı sen mi yedin" diye çıkıştı kıza.

Ne saçma bir soru! Belki, sorulabilecek en saçma soru. Ne yaptığını bilmiyordu. Ev ne kadar da değişmişti. Anlayamıyordu. Kız ne kadar da rahattı. Evin neden bu kadar pis olduğunu, bu kadar nasıl dağıtabildiğimi, temizlemek için canının çıktığını söylüyor, adeta azarlıyordu kendisini. Patronun kim olduğunu göstermenin zamanı gelmişti:

"Senin ne işin var burada?"

"Şunun babasıyla evlendim yıllar önce. Ama o hayırsız bırakıp gitti beni. Beş yıl oluyor. Kendime bir yer bulmak zorundaydım tabii"

Annesinin, yabancı birisine babası ile ilgili kötü bir tonda konuşmuş olması çocuğu incitmiş olacak ki, annesine vurmaya başladı.

"Anneye vurulur mu hiç, ona saygı göstermelisin" diyerek çocuğun kafasına tokat attı ve kızı dinlemeye koyuldu. Ama, bu çocuk yoktu ki... Nasıl da normal bir şeymiş gibi annesine saygılı olması için paylamıştı çocuğu.

Anlayamıyordu.

Olanları tekrar yerine yerleştirmeye çalışırken dizlerine yatan çocuğu baba şefkatiyle okşayarak uyutuyordu. Kız, çileli yaşamını anlatırken ev sahibesi belirdi bir anda.

Tanrım... Nasıl çıldırmasındı? Kapı neydi? Neden kimse kullanmıyordu? Nasıl girmişti içeriye bu kadın da?

"Tamam, kirayı hazırladım. Artık seninle bir alıp vereceğimiz de kalmadı" diyerek göğsündeki tomar parayı çıkarıp kadına verdi kız.

Kızıyor, kafası gittikçe karışıyordu. Kirayı daha dün yatırmıştı. Yatırmasa bile kıza ne canım. Üstelik bu kadın ev sahibesi değildi ki. Ama, anlamsız çirkin kadının, kızın ev sahibesi olduğunu ve kalan bir hesaptan söz edildiğini anladı. Bir şeyler yapması, kadına bir şeyler söylemesi gerekiyordu yine de kadını geçirirken. Salonda, kadınla karşı karşıyaydılar. Kadın, çokça çirkin perdeli ellerini ona doğru kaldırarak havalandı ve tüm çirkinliği ile kayboldu.

Anlamıştı. Ürpererek yatmaya gitti.

XII.

Oluşun sonsuzluğuna bakıp da her şeyin geçeceğini düşünme. Geçen sensin, biten de...Aymazlığın gereği yok.

Hiçbir şeyden emin değildim. Nefesimin ne zaman kesileceği artık sadece zaman sorunuydu. Hem kaçıyor, duvar diplerine gömüyordum kendimi kimse görmesin diye hem de her zamanki kendimle çelişik halimi takınıp bir şekilde yerimi belli etmeye çalışıyordum. Fişim prizden çıkarılınca, ya da çıkarırsam ben, kıyısından işaret vermeye çalışıyordum kalanlara. Hafızam olsun istiyordum kağıtlar. Çünkü artık hafızam dahil her şey her an alınabilirdi benden. Kullanmayı becerememiştim...

TAANSAŞ GÜNCESİ - II

1.

Son zamanlarda gerçeklikle düş çok anlaşılmaz bir şekilde karışıyor birbirine. Düşten gerçekliğe uyanıyorum tüm korkularımla ve algılayışım netleşene kadar, tükeniyorum. Ne zamana kadar koruyabileceğim kendimi, bilemiyorum. Şimdilik hasarsız atlatıyorum. Yada öyle sanıyorum.

2.

O.'nun öldüğünü öğrenerek uyanıyorum. Kimse söylemiş değil. Bununla ilgili bir veri de yok. Sadece, uyanıyorum ki; O. ölmüş. Böyle hissediyorum. Saatlerce ağlıyorum. Kendime geldiğimde ölmediğini anlıyorum. Ama biraz düşünmem yetiyor. Evet, O. ölüyor...

3.

Gecenin 2'si. Yine dehşetle uyanıyorum. Site boşalmış, herkes gitmiş. Her şey yıkılıyor bulunduğum yerde. Sadece ben kalmışım. Telaşla hazırlanmaya, toparlanmaya çalışıyorum, olmuyor. Elim ayağım tutmaz halde. Belim müthiş ağrıyor. Arkaya doğru kırıldı kırılacak. Evin her köşesini dolaşıyor ama terk edemiyorum. Kıyamet bu, evet. Ama ben evi terk edemem ki. Histerik bir şekilde ağlıyor, çıkış arıyorum. Hayır, O. olmadan gidemem! Hep, birlikte topladık eşyaları. Taşınma bizim için hiçbir zaman bir telaş olmamıştı. Geçmişte çok ağlamıştım ama böylesi bir histeriye tutulmamıştım. Alt çenem kırılacak gibi çarpıp duruyor üst çeneme. Az sonra ezileceğim ama yıkıntı üzerime gelse de O. olmadan evden ayrılmam söz konusu değil. Bunun düş olduğuna inanmak için sitede bir tek ışık arıyor, bulamıyorum. Herkes taşınmış. Kahrolası telefonumu da bulamıyorum. Arayıp çağıramıyorum O.'yu. Neden sonra bulup canhıraş bir şekilde mesaj yazıyorum; "Kıyamet kapıda ama ben sensiz bir yere gidemem. Evden yıkılıp ben ezilmeden, gel lütfen..." Ertesi gün işe gidebileceğimden emin değilim. Belimin ağrısı buna izin vermeyecek diye düşünüyorum kıyametten sıyrılıp. Ağlamaktan bitkin, uyuya kalıyorum.

4.

Sabah oluyor. İşe geç gidiyorum. O. aramış. Tekrar arıyor.

"İyi misin?"

"İyiyim."

"Ne oldu?"

"Yok bir şey, sadece çok kötü bir gece geçirdim."

"Şimdi iyiysen sevindim" diyor ve ekliyor;

"Eğer evden ayrılacaksan mutlaka bana haber ver. Ben de ev arıyorum. Hazır depozit de vermem. O eve ben taşınayım..."

Ve taşınacağımdan emin olmak için tekrar tekrar soruyor. Enteresan, artık kırılamıyorum da. "Tamam" diyorum. "Taşınırsam haber veririm...."

5.

Arıyor ertesi gün.

"Dün yaptığım çok büyük bir saygısızlıktı. Sen, canhıraş bir şekilde benden yardım istiyorsun. Kötü bir şeyler olduğu belli. Bense neyin derdindeyim. Kusura bakma" diyor.

Kusura bakmıyorum. Sadece, artık ev üstüme yıkılırken, altında tek başıma kalacağımı anlıyorum.

6.

Yine yola çıkıyorum. Ne gidişim kimsenin umurunda ne gelişim. İnsanlardan ne kadar uzak durmaya çalışsam da, eğer değer verdiğim ve arzuladığım bir şey varsa yolculuğa çıkarken uğurlanmak ve dönüşte karşılanmak olduğunu biliyorum. Kimsesiz bindiğim her otobüs saatler boyu hüzün oluyor. Kimsesiz dönüşler de. Terminallerin giden yolculardan çok onları geçirmek için gelenler tarafından doldurulduğunu biliyorum. Ben, tek gidiyorum, tek geliyorum. Bu, tercih değil herhalde... Sanırım oturduğum yerde üzerime aptal bir tavanın yıkılması, daha az umurumda olurdu.

7.

Sol yanıma – aşağı yukarı kalbimin biraz alt tarafı - bir ağrı giriyor. Bir an kalp krizi geçiren insanların ne hissettiğini düşünüyorum. Ölümü adım adım duyumsuyor olmalılar. Ağrı artınca bunun bir kalp krizi belirtisi olabileceğini düşünüyorum. Böyle bir sorunum yoktu. Ama o an ölseydim, gülerdim büyük olasılıkla. Yok, bu kesin. Yüzümde anlamsız bir tebessüm vardı acı çekerken. Olacaktı madem, o zaman olmalıydı. Ölüm acısına ilişkin anlatılan onca acıklı ve korkutucu öyküye karşın yüzümdeki gülümsemeyi atamıyordum. Şimdilik olmadı. Ama henüz vaktim var. Nasıl mutsuzum ve nasıl acı çekiyorum. Gülümsememse yüzüme yapışmış durumda. Olursa; böyle olacak, sanırım.

8.

Belim hâlâ ağrıyor.

9.

Düşle gerçekliğin karıştırılması ile ilgili sortileri şimdilik kazasız atlattım, en azından öyle düşlüyorum. Aksini kesinleyebilmiş değilim. Onun aksini de. Ama ne zamana kadar? Kaçıncısında aradaki bağla birlikte kaybolacağım ben de? Bilmiyorum. Sadece, bekleyişim.

10 .

Neden bilmiyorum, buradaki park yapıldıktan sonra parka gelen insanların oluşturdukları kalabalığa, park edilen arabaların oluşturduğu yığına büyük bir hınçla bakıyorum yanından her geçişimde. Sırf bu lanet kütleyi görmemek için yolumu değiştiriyorum. Bu; aslında yitikliğimin, kaybedişimin anlamsız bir belirtisinden başka bir şey değil. Öfkem bundan olabilir. Yaşama karşı, normal olana, normal algılana karşı hayretimin aslında ne kadar sıra dışı olduğunu anımsatıyor olmalıydı o kısa anlar bana olasılıkla. Bu da kesin değil tabii. Ama park yeniden düzenlenirken, buraya insanların kesinlikle gelmeyeceğini düşünüyordum açıklıkla. Hemen yanıbaşımdaki parka ben hiç gitmemişken, gitmeyi asla düşünmezken, insanlar neden kilometrelerce uzaktan kalkıp gelsinlerdi ki? Geliyorlardı ama. Beni pisliğe soksalardı tüm gün, o kadar öfke duymazdım. Kahrolası sefil yaratıklar. Bana gerçekliği! oluşturduğunuz kuru kalabalıkla, muhtemelen kabuklarını yere atacağınız çekirdekler ve aptal bir su birikintisine bakıp o aptal derin! duygularınızı kabartıp oluşturacağınız birliktelikler yada, yada, yada...ile siz mi gösterecektiniz. Allah hepinizin belasını versin. Gerçekliğiniz bir tarafınıza girer, umarım.

11.

Parkın olduğu yerde, kavşakta, kamyon, bir otomobili ezmiş. Tanrım, ne büyük mutluluk. Gözlerim fal taşı gibi. İçinde ölen var mı otomobilin, göremedim. En azından birkaç solucanın ezilmiş olmasını düşlüyor, parkın yaşattığı mutsuzluğu mutluluk olarak ödünç alıyorum o akşam.

12.

Pipom gene yandı. Öncekini değiştirmişti satıcı. "Bunu değiştiremem" diyor. "Eğer üst üste yine yanıp deliniyorsa, bu artık senin şansınla ilgilidir..." Şansımı bildiğim için, üzülmüyorum.

13.

Belim ağrımaya devam ediyor.

14.

Beni sadece A. biliyor. Anlam veremiyor bir çok şeye. Anlamsız çünkü. Evden çıkmamama, kimseyle görüşmememe, yaratık gibi yaşamama... "Seni görünce duygularımın sıradan oluşundan memnunum" diyor. Sıra dışı olan ne ki? Ben sadece, batıyorum.

15.

Uzun zamandır O. ile görüşmüyoruz. O. ile ilgili tüm kötü şeyleri kazımaya çalışıyorum zihnime, uzaklaşmak için. Sıkıyor sıkıyor ama bir yerden sonra koyuveriyorum zorunlu olarak. Uzak tutamam ki... Başka ne duyumsayabilirim?

16.

Gülemiyorum. Tanrım, bu ne hasret!

17.

Tüm dokularım paramparça. Mutluluk hormonu salgılayamıyor benliğim. Çikolata yememin de bir anlamı yok. Yüreğim, organlarım, soyut varoluşum sadece bekliyor. Neyi? Bunu sadece ben biliyorum. Paylaşamam.

18.

Belimin ağrısı geçecek diye bekliyorum.

19.

Yanımda iki kız konuşuyor. İlişkisi varmış, nasıl başlamış, nasıl devam ediyormuş, diğerlerinden nasıl farklıymış... Bok çukuru. Biri diğerini "Aaa ne kadar güzel" diye aptal aptal onaylıyor. Nasıl çirkinler; yada bana öyle geliyor. Böyle olası bir konuşmanın konusu olmamak, olmayacak olmak sevindiriyor orada beni. Sizin olsun arkadaşlar, ben almayayım. Yalan!

20.

Yeni pipom hala delinmedi. Enteresan.

21.

Geriye dönük anımsamalarım çok zayıfladı. Günlük olaylar yok gibi. İlgi eksikliğinden sanırım.

22.

Her gece gözümü kapadığımda yattığım yer hareketleniyor. Bırakırsam kendi haline, vücudumun güneybatısı yönünde, sırtüstü yattığımı var sayarsak sol ayağımın serçe parmağı yönü tam olarak karşılar, yatakta gidiyorum. Salınım yok. Kıpırtı yok. Hedef yok. Anlamı yok. Sadece o yöne yatay bir kayış. Geçmişten haber veriyor. Önceden, mutlu olduğum az zamanlarda, salınımsız bir denizde devinimsiz yüzerdim düşümde. Su çok sığ olur, boğulma korkusu duymaz, ama ayaklarım yere değmez, suyun dibini de göremezdim. Öylesi bir huzurdu ki... Böylesi düşler yok artık. Ancak aynı devinimsizlik, hareket edilen yüzeyin salınımsızlığı, uyanıkken buluyor beni şimdi. Ama olası bir duygu uyandırmıyor. Ne bir huzur, ne bir acı, ne de başka bir şey. Gidiş özdeş. Duygu yok. Grafik titremiyor.

23.

Sosyal fobim yok. Gün içinde her ortamda bulunabiliyor, eğer toplumsal bir tabakamız olduğunu varsayarsak, her kategorideki insanla gereğince paylaşabiliyorum o zamanı. Ama seçme şansına erişince, eve gelene kadar kimsenin yüzüne bakamıyorum. Duvarlar daha oturaklı sanırım. Tercih ediyorum.

24.

Pipom aynı kokuyu vermeye başladı. Tütün değil pipo yanıyor. Delinecek, biliyorum.

25.

Damarlarıma yayılan uyuşukluk aslında yığının uyanıklık dediği şeyin aynısıydı tersten. Gözlerini dört açarak işine gelen hiçbir şeyi ıskalamamaya çalışan yığınla aynılık oluşturuyordum aslında her şeye sırtımı dönerek. Fark yok. Kahrolası aynı düzlemde yer alıyorsan, ne farkın olabilir ki?

26.

Belimin ağrısı endişe verici bir boyuta geldi.

27.

Ölümden korkmadım hiçbir zaman. Korkum, birilerine muhtaç hale duruma getirecek bir hastalığa yakalanmamdı. Bunu düşünerek bel ağrımın geçmesini düşlüyorum.

28.

O. geliyor. Konuşmaya istekli bir hali var. Benimse mümkün değil. Güceniyor belki ama durum bu ise öncesi, sonrası ve şimdi hakkında konuşmamayı tercih ediyorum. Söz yok...

29.

Belimin ağrısı zirvede, gözümden yaş geliyor acıdan. Sanırım baktırmam lazım.

30.

Sonunda doktora gidiyorum. Korktuğum gibi çıkmıyor.

31.

Nihayet pipom yanıyor.

32.

Belim nedeniyle uzun zamandır yabana atılmayacak bir acı içindeyim. Yalnızlık, insan acı çekiyorken ne kadar da yaralayıcı oluyor. O.'ya özlemim, zamanların hepsinde dayanılmaz ama ağrım arttıkça yanımda olmasına duyduğum özlem tarif edilemez bir hal alıyor.

"Gel!" diyemiyorum.

33.

Belimin ağrısı ile yaşamaya alışıyorum.

34.

Ölümü denesem? Bir sürü uğraş. Ne sıkıntı. Üşeniyorum.

35.

Yaşamın alaycılığı

36.

Sevginin paradoksu![5](2)

37.

Yine yola çıkıyorum. Ev soğuk. Dönüşümde ısınabilmeyi umuyorum.

38.

Gidiyor ve dönüyorum. Bu kez duygu yok.

39.

Pipolar daha dayanıklı diye gül ağacından yapılırmış. Ama benimkiler hep yanıyor. Ama bir yol daha var; Bu kez yanmaması için lületaşından bir pipo seçiyorum. Aradığım gibi, naif bir yapısı var. Yine umut ediyorum.

40.

Ne gam!

41.

Hiçbir veri yokken ortada tekrar birlikteliğimizle ilgili, sürekli tekrar başlayacağımıza ısrarla inanırken, umut etmemi gerektirecek birçok

---

4   (1) : ....

5   (2) : ....

küçük ama önemli şey yaşasak da son zamanlarda, tam tersi umut edemiyorum daha çok. Birçok düş yaşadım. Bu da onlardan biridir diye korkuyorum.

42.

İstanbul'a gitmeden önce gerçek bir düş yaşıyorum. O.'ya dokunuyorum. Kokusunu çekiyorum içime. Ve O., uzun zaman sonra sarılırken biz, beni hissediyor, sanırım. Ama o ilk dokunuşun verdiği yasak delme rahatsızlığı gibi bir duygu ile itiyor kendisini benden. Pişman mı? Bilmiyorum. Sadece bu düşü nasıl yorduğunu merak ediyorum.

43.

Şaşkınım. Her şey o kadar kötüydü ki. Gitmeler, gelmeler, bulamamalar, bulamamalardan dolayı aramamalar ama bunun için, tersi ve düzü için yanmalar, son bulur gibi oldu. Gitmeler anlam yüklenmeye başladı dönüşümün beklenmesi umudu ile. Bulma umudum, bulma imkansızlığı ile ararken girdiğim acıyı aldı. Şimdi korkumun izin verdiği ölçüde yaşamaya çalışıyorum mutluluğu. Belki öldürürdü bu mutluluk beni, ancak bu varoluşu sürdürmem için bu sefer korkularım devrede. Botox yaptırmadım ama mimiklerim yok. Acı ve mutluluğu her an birlikte yada ayrı, her yerde hemen bekliyor olmam ne acıyı ne de mutluluğu tam yaşamama izin vermiyor. Gücüm yok.

44.

O.'nun bana eskisi gibi baktığını görüyorum. Az zamanlarda da olsa, görüyorum. Üstüme almamaya çalışıyorum.

45.

Dokunamıyorum hiçbir şeye. Sanki benim dokunmamamdan dolayı yolunda her şey. Yıkıcı bir etki yapmamalıyım, değil mi?

46.

Pipom yanmadı. Ancak kanıyor. Sanırım regl oldu.

47.

Bir insan ne kadar kaybedebilir ki? Düşünün, her kaybedişinde, "Evet, bu benim için gücümün en üst noktasındaki sınav" diyorsa ve bunu bilmem kaç kez yaşıyorsa... Tersten alın... Tanrısal kusursuzluğa erişme gücü kesin var insanın, ancak himmete muhtaç olduğu için bu olasılık kesin yok.

48.

Hep düşle gerçeklik arasındaki Araf'tayım. Hangisinden hangisine uyandığım belli değil. Belki sadece düş yada sadece gerçek. Ancak ben ikili düşünmeyi tercih ediyorum. Çünkü umut etmem lazım.

49.

Demiş ki düşünür "Evlenin, eşiniz iyiyse mutlu olursunuz, kötüyse filozof..." Benim eşim kötü değildi. Ama mutlu etmedi beni. Belki çokça mutsuz. Filozof mu?

50.

Kusmak istiyorum. Tüm organlarımı çıkarmak, üzerinde tepinmek, beni ben yapan bütün uzuvlarımı bağırsaklarımla karıştırıp püre yapmak. Nefret...

51.

Çenem kilitleniyor. Beynimde binlerce karınca, savaş içinde. Neler çıkmak istiyor dışarı. Ne kadarı çıkabilecek. Hangisi çıkarken beni de götürecek. Bekliyorum.

52.

Bir karga gördüm. Tüyleri yok. Aldırmış. Ağdacıya gitmiş olmalı. Yada kendisi almış.

XIII.

TAANSAŞ GÜNCESİ -III

1.

Umut edemiyorsun. Bulduklarından korkar hale geldin. Bu, bir şey. Biliyorsun.

2.

Bastığın toprak kayarken altından, götürmüyor seni. Yer çekiminin ihaneti değil bu.

3.

Kızını yada kendini pazarlayan kadın... Ne de kötü gözüküyor insana. Vay kahpe. Eee? Neden bu nefret? Toplamda ne önemi var ki? Boşversene...

&

Ya kendini pazarlayan o sürü? Bilgisi ile, güzelliği ile, bağlılığı ile, sevgisi ile... Eee? Hani nefret? Bunun da toplamda önemi yok. Bunu da boşver.

4.

Değersiz oluşunu katlanılabilir kılan her şeye karşı durdun. İhtiyaç ve inkar. Almaya mecbur oluşunun ağırlığını aldıklarını teker teker atarak hafifletmeye çalışıyorsun. Atarken tekrar aldıklarını görmezden gelmen boşuna. Bu bir oyun. Sense sadece...

5.

Bireysel oluştaki aksaklıklar toplumsal oluş metotlarını yaratmayı zorunlu kıldı. Hayatta kalabilme savaşı. Kime karşı? Kendimize. Neye rağmen? Galip kim? Kim kaybetmeye yazgılı?

6.

Öykünüp de gerçekleştirdiğin her eylemin sana değersizlik olarak geri dönüşü kişiliğinde derin yaralar açıyor. Yaralar nasırlaştıkça, nasırlaşmalar kişiliksizlik olarak seni iyice sağlamlaştırıyor. "Benim" dediğin şeylerin kaybolması ile herkes için olanı sahiplenirken, her şey unutulmaya başlıyor. Yedek, tarihin sonu.

7.

Bilmediğin el seni rahatlatırken rahatlatanı bulmak gibi bir düşüncen yoktu.

8.

İzafi olunanla övünen ve övünene öykünen yığın... Sen bu izafiyetin neresindesin?

9.

Yığının ortasındaki sen! Yığınla birlikte tepetaklak gidebilirsin. Bunda senin suçun olmayabilir. Kitle psikolojisi.

10.

Jöleyle yapışan saçların bir anlam bütünlüğü sağladığı varsayılıyorsa, bu ancak değerlerle bağlanan, sağlanan demek daha anlamlı, oluş kadar anlamlı olmalı.

11.

Yiyebilmek ve bunları çıkarabilmek temelinde devam eden yaşam, ilkinin hazzını ikincisinde de sonsal olarak vermiş insana. Çıkardıktan sonra iğrenerek de olsa büyük bir hazla bakarken o sona, bu kısa süreli bakış döngünün başında yiyecekle karşılaşma anında yemeden hemen önceki o kısa bakışla birdir. Bu, kısmi yaratıcılıkla ilgili. Kendi gırtlağınla ve kıçınla ilgili olduğu için sadece sana özel. Şu farkla ki; birincisi en azından ortam olarak paylaşılabilirken, ikincisinde bundan mutlaka kaçılır. Yaratılanın yaratış süreci... Aradaki tek fark, koku farkı. Bu da karışıklıktan olsa gerek...

XIV.

İhtiraslarımıza esir olup bizi yarı yolda bırakan gururumuz, ne ihtiraslarımıza dur diyebiliyor, ne de kendinden vazgeçebiliyor. Gurura ihtiyacı olmayan ve ilgilenmeyen ihtiras, tüm sevimsizliğine karşın belirleyici olmaya devam ediyor. İyiyle kötünün baş belirleyici olduğu savlanan yaşam ise iyi-kötü arasındaki çizginin silikliğine teslim olmuş şekilde, can çekişiyor. Ne gurur iyi ne ihtiras. Ne galip mutlu ne mağlup. Ne iyi haz içinde ne kötü acı çekmekte. Bu arada insan ise aranmaya devam ediyor... Neyi?

Karganın, kekliğin yürüyüşüne özenip denemesi, beceremeyip kendi yürüyüşüne dönmeye karar vermesi ancak bu sefer bunu da becerememesi ile artık hep anlamsız, kişiliksiz, paytak paytak yürüdüğü söylenir. Ben de kargadan daha umut verici bir halde değildim. Vaktiyle kendime bir anlam yaratmış, yarattığım anlamda kendimi var etmiş, sonra o anlamdan çıkıp başka şeylere yönelmiş ama onu da beceremeyip başladığım yere dönmeye çalışmıştım. Ama o da olmadı. Hilkat garibesi gibi dolaşıyordum ortalıkta. Artık ne için acı çektiğim, neye değer verdiğim, vereceğim, ne için devam edeceğim, yada edecek miyim, karmakarışıktı. Yalnızca nefes alıyordum. Almalı mıydım?

Tekrar görüşmeye başlamıştık. İkimiz de okulu defalarca uzatmıştık ve artık atılma sınırına gelmiştik. Okulla ilgili son şansımızı deniyor, telaş içinde derslere girip çıkıyorduk. Bu telaş, bir kez daha birleştirmişti bizi. Son deneme...

Geçen zamanda ne yaptığını, hâlâ onun için olup olmadığımı, araya başkalarını sığdırıp sığdırmadığını bilmiyordum. İlk gidişlerini sadece bir yol kazası olarak yormuştum. Ama her gidişi, bitiş gerçeğini biraz daha kafama sokmuş, bu mutlak sonun olabilirliğini adıma adım duyumsamıştım.

Ayrıldıktan sonra annesinin yanına gitmiş, daha sonra onun yanından da ayrılıp bir süre yalnız yaşamış, şimdi ise babasıyla birlikte yaşıyor ama rahatsız.

Rahatlatmaya çalıştım;

"Her ne kadar gitmiş olsan da biliyorsun ki bu kapı sana her zaman açık. Ne zaman istersen gelebilirsin. Eğer bir gün istersen, çık gel. İster sevgili, ister eş, istersen ev arkadaşı olarak, gelmeyi düşünürsen, buradayım ben. Gitmiş olmanın ağırlığını taşıma sakın."

Zaman ilerliyor, bana daha sık geliyordu. Ne önceki birlikteliğimize ilişkin sorgulamalara girişiyor, ne ben yokken ne yaptığını soruyordum. Babasının yanında rahatsızlığı arttıkça, bana daha bir sokuluyordu. Yakınlaşmasının benden ziyade evle ilgili olduğunu biliyor ama hala bu tür basitlikleri O.'ya konduramıyordum. O.'nun her şeye hakkı vardı... Beni daha fazla da batırabilirdi.

"Babamla konuştum. Sana gelmek istediğimi söyledim ancak tekrar evlenmeden birlikte oturamayacağımızı söylüyor."

Anlamamıştım. Sordum;

"Eee?"

"İşte, 'gelsin konuşalım' diyor. Bu sefer bari bazı şeyleri atlamayalım."

Nasıl yani? Sordum tekrar;

"Eee?"

Hâlâ aynı dilde konuşuyordu.

"Ee'si bu. Konuşur musun babamla?"

"Bu, bir şey değil. Sen ne düşünüyorsun?"

Düşündüğünü söyledi;

"Burada olmak istiyorum."

Burada olmak istiyor... Benimle birlikte değil. Ve bunun için evlenmeye bile razı. Tanrım, ne oluyorduk? Dikkatini çekmek istedim; "Daha birlikte bile değiliz. Aşka dair, bizimle ilgili tek söz söylemedin. Sıralamada bir hata yapmıyor musun? Yapmıyor muyuz?" Derdimi anlamıştı. Hiçbir şey anlatmasa da her şeyi anlayacağımı biliyordu ve sadece konuşmuş olmak için söyledi;

"Biliyorsun çok şey yaşadık!"

Nasıl devam edeceğini bilemedi bir an. Çıkmaza girdiğini sezmişti.

"Her şey eskiye dönebilir belki. Zaman ver bana." diyebildi belli belirsiz.

Artık hiçbir şey bilmiyordum. Ne değişmişti? Geçen onca 'zaman,' zaten bizim için değil miydi? Zamanların hepsini önceden ve sonradan koparıp kendimiz için ayırmamış mıydık? Bu yetmezken birlikteliğimize, şimdi benim verebileceğim zamanın neyi onaracağını bekleyebilirdim ki? Beklemiyordum. Hiçbir şey beklemiyordum. En fazla bir daha kaybederdim. İstenen oyunsa, öyle olsun... Kabul ettim.

Oyun oynanmış, perde inmiş, birlikte yaşamaya başlamıştık. Bir oyun olduğunu bilsem de, benimle, önceki gibi esrikleştiren bir ruh kaymasından değil tamamen ihtiyaçlarından dolayı aynı mekanı paylaştığının farkında olsam da, aynı yatakta yatıyor olmamıza rağmen bana dokunamayacak kadar yabancılaştığını geceler boyu saatlere eş dakikalarda yaşasam da, 'belki bir gün' diyebilmeme olanak sağlayacak aşktan artık hiçbir şey taşımadığını görsem de, en azından bu kadarı da bir şey diyerek rolümü kabul ediyordum. O.'dan başka herkese karşı gösterdiğim katı tavır O.'ya gelince siliniyor, bir gün tekrar gidecek olmasının kesinliğini olası bir davranışa dönüştüremiyordum. Bir yandan korkularımı beslerken tekrar, bir yandan da O.'suz kurduğum ve bir şekilde devam ettirmeye başladığım hayatımın orta yerine girmesine izin veriyordum.

Bu, nasıl hastalıklı bir adanmışlıktı? Bu nasıl bir bitimsiz geriye dönüştü? Ve ben neye dönüşmüştüm? Nereye gitmişti yücelttiğim oluş çözümlemelerim, nereye gitmişti kusursuzluğun karşısında tek engel olarak kadını, kadına yönelen erkeği, erkeği kadına yönelten Tanrısal oluş yasalarını görüşüm? Nereye gitmişti gördüğünü sandığı şeyin üzerinde yükselip her şeyi, herkesi mahkum eden yüce ben? Hani en farklı ben olacaktım? 'Sen kimsin ki koskoca bir tarihe, bu koskoca tarih içinde dizayn edilen ilişkilere, süregelen dengelere, ne neyse öyle eden oluşa kafa tutacaksın' mı deniyordu karşı koyduğum her şeye dönüşmemle? Gücünün farkına var, edebinle otur mu deniyordu bana yoksa? Ah ruhuma taktığın kibir hortumuyla kanımı emen egom! Vazgeçmeyeceksin değil mi? Gene kendine yontacaksın her şeyi en düşmüş halinle bile. Gene alçalmışlığını bir yığın kutsala atıp kendini temize çıkarmaya çalışacaksın. Yetmez mi? Yetmedi mi?

Yetmemişti... En ufak bir hatayı bile affetmeyen, özellikle tutarsız olana asla tahammülü olmayan ben, kendi içinde onca tutarsızlığı barındırmasına rağmen bu şekil birlikteliğini sırf bir şekilde O. ile ilişkili diye kabul ediyordum.

Artık sessizdim. Her şeye saldırmam, 'yanlış her şey, bak doğrusu bu' diye uzun uzun konuşmam son bulmuştu. Sözlerimle zihnimde ve zihninde yıktığım her yapıyı kanımla canımla kendimden verip kurmam, sözden korkar hale getirmişti beni. Suskunluğum dikkatini çekti;

"Ne o. Soruların mı tükendi yoksa cevaplardan mı kaçıyorsun?" dedi yarı alayla.

"Belki." dedim sesiz bir ciddiyetle.

"Ne çok sorardın. Ne çok cevap verirdin. Verdiğin her cevap soruydu aynı zamanda. Sorularının tükendiğini sanmıyorum."

Kendinden emin bir hali vardı. Neyi öğrenmeye çalışıyordu ki? Tanımıyor muydu beni? Yada ne kadar iyi tanıdığını mı anlatmaya çalışıyordu. Ne önemi vardı artık tüm bunların? Rahatlasın bari;

"Tükenmese ne çıkar? Cevap vermek soruyu ortadan kaldırıyor mu? Sorusu ortadan kalkan cevap neye tutunabilir ki? Kendi varoluşu buna yetecek mi? Yetmiyor nitekim. Var olan her şeyde en baskın şey kendini koruma, varlığını devam ettirme duygusu. Bu, sorularla cevaplar arasındaki ilişki için de geçerli. Cevaplar da devam etmek için sorularını hep var ediyor. Ben, sadece paravan olmaktan vazgeçtim. Hepsi bu." Yüzündeki alay ifadesi kaybolmuştu. Bu sefer daha ciddi; "Sorularından koptuğunu sanmıyorum yine de. Daha çok sorduğunu biliyorum. Ancak, artık açık etmiyorsun. Gördüklerinden korkar hale geldin. Ama sen de biliyorsun, bir kere girmeyegörsün zehir. Atamazsın. Ve yine seni tanıdığım için söyleyebiliyorum; atmak da istemiyorsun."

"Boşversene... Gördüğün her şey kopmana neden oluyorsa gördüklerinden, bir yerde bir yanlış var demektir. Ben de ne gördüysem koptum dehşetle. Hem gördüklerimden, hem kendimden. Neden ısrar edeyim ki? Kendini devam ettirmeye istekli var olanlardan biri değil miyim ben de? Düşünmeye bile gerek yok" dedim.

Neden 'ben normalim bak' diye çırpınan biri durumundaydım. Normal yada değil. Kime neyi ispat edecektim?

İnanmıyordu;

"Yanlış var derken aksine biçtiğin pay umut olsun istiyorsun sana ama buna sen de inanmıyorsun."

Ah... Sonuçta karşımda herhangi biri değil O. vardı. Sır verir gibi fısıldadım;

"Ne için katlanıyorum yaşama. Ya da yaşam ne için bana. Bunlara cevap veremiyorum. Aramıyorum da. Ne aramak, ne bulmak, ne kaybetmek, ne de kazanmak... İstediğim şey değil. İstemek için bile yetersiz gördüğüm algılamam, bana kendinden öte pay biçmiyor. En nihayetinde, biliyorum. Yok olacağım."

İstediğini elde etmişti. Zafer naraları atabilirdi şimdi. Atıyordu;

"Bu mu soruları ortadan kalkmış halin? Sorularından vazgeçemeyeceğini biliyordum. Her zaman olacak bu. Değişmeyeceksin."

Daha mutlu olsundu o zaman; daha mutlu etmek için onu içinde onlarca yoklukla ilgili öykü, cevapsız soru ve sorusuz cevap barındıran anlamsız mantık yürütmelerle dolu, tamamen retorik gevezelik ürünü bir sürü şey söyledim. Korkmuş ve çekilmişti. En sonunda yokluğa vurgu yaptığım zamanlarda takındığı tavrını aldı, sustu.

Karıştırıyor olabilirdi, ilgili gözükmemeye çalıştım.

XV.

Umudun tükendiği yer, nefesin kesildiği. Küçültül-
mesi imkansız olan geçmişe yönelik parantezlerin
yıkıcılığından kurtulmak için onları yok saymaya ça-
lıştığın anlar. Unutmaya çalışıp derinlerine gömdü-
ğün parantezlerin birikmesiyle büründüğün, zorunlu
yazgı da denebilir,   geometrik tarifi imkansız görü-
nüşün. Etrafına sıktığın sis perdesi belki kapatabilir
pürüzleri. Ya sonra?

Sonrası yoktu işte. Öncesi, sonrası ile ilgili yeteri kadar haber ve-
riyordu. Başlangıçta, sırf gelirken böyle konuştuğu için adet yerini
bulsun diye ne zaman evleneceğimizi soruyor, bense sadece durumu gösterip zaman gelince beklemeyeceğimi bildiğini söylüyordum.
Güya o zamanın gelmesini bekliyorduk. Bekliyor muyduk? Ben, bir
yandan istememe rağmen olmayacağını bildiğim için, o ise zaten
gerçekte böyle bir şey düşlemediği için, ikimiz de bekliyor sayılmaz-
dık. Aramızda sanki konuşulması bile yasak ama uyulması şart bir
anlaşma varmış gibi devam ediyorduk.

Ve bir yandan da hep oluğu gibi, zaman geçiyordu. Babası ile ara-
sının iyice bozulması nedeniyle görüşmemeye başlaması, babasının
isteği nedeniyle ara sıra düşünüyormuş gibi yaptığı evlilik olasılığını
gündemimizden tamamen düşürmüş, en azından daha bir gerçeklere dönmüştük.

Ve gerçek, daha önce de gösterdiği şeyi daha iyi anlamamız için bir
kez daha gösterecekti.

Artık her akşam eve 'bu oyun ne zaman bitecek' diye düşünerek dönüyor, beklediğim ama zamanını kestiremediğim o son perdenin açılmasını, açılmaması umuduyla kestirmeye çalışıyordum. çok beklemem gerekmedi. Sofada beni bekler buldum O.'yu. Üstünü bile değiştirmemiş, mevzisini almış, söyleyeceklerini hazırlamış, sabırsız bekliyordu. Söylemesine gerek yoktu. Anlamıştım.

"Evet, dinliyorum. Bir şeyler olduğu belli."

Ne çok sinirlenirdi kendisi söylemeden hissedip ben dinlemeye başlayınca. Hazırlığına bu durum da eklenince o son perdeyi keskin bir prologla açtı.

"Böyle olmuyor. Bu evden ikimizden birinin gitmesi lazım."

Bu ne?

Bekliyordum ama bu kadarını değil. Bir an düşündüm; gerçeklerle bağımı bu kadar mı koparmıştım? Yanlış mı hatırlıyordum? Daha düne kadar bu evde ben yaşamıyor muydum? O., benden aldığı cesaretle ve davetle benim yanıma gelmemiş miydi? Ortada 'ya sen gideceksin ya ben' denebilecek bir durum var mıydı? Bu nasıl bir arsızlıktı? Bu nasıl bir kötülüktü? Bu nasıl bir bencillikti? Bu, nasıl bir acımasızlıktı? Karşıdakinin her şeyini feda edebilecek kadar seviyor olması, bunu gücü ölçüsünde yapması, sevileni bu kadar acımasız, duyarsız, çiğ yapabilir miydi? Önceki gidişlerinde her 'gidiyorum' sözüne 'İstersen ben gideyim. Yeniden mücadeleyse bunu ben yapayım. Sen, burada kal' diye karşılık verir, onun gidişinin yükünü üzerime almaya çalışırdım. O. kabul etmez, gitmeyi seçerdi. Son bir hamle daha yapar, 'Kitaplarıma dokunmamak kaydıyla istediğin her şeyi alabilirsin.' derdim. Ve O., ne isterse onu alır, nasıl isterse öyle giderdi. Ama bu kadarı fazlaydı artık. Bana bile fazlaydı.

Bir yandan o korktuğum anın gelmiş olduğunu görerek acı acı gülüp, bir yandan da O.'nun bu kadar nasıl çiğleşebildiğini anlamaya çalışırken, yırtılırcasına kahkaha attım. Gülüşüm, gülüş değildi. Pespayeliğin, çiğliğin, saygısızlığın bu kadarını her şeyin çok kötü olduğu gerçeğiyle bile açıklayamamaktan çıkan hıçkırıklı kahkaha kılığında. O.'ya kondurmuş olacağım ki bazı şeyleri, ilk kez diyebildim:

"Eğer gidecek biri varsa evden, o sen olacaksın."

Ama hâlâ açıklamak, O.'yu kırmamak telaşındaydım. Yumuşatmaya çalıştım ifademi;

"Biliyorsun. Senden sonra hep en büyük süreyi kendimi toparlamaya harcadım. Bunu ne kadar yapabildim bilmiyorum. Ama en azından bir akış tutturdum hayatımda. Sen her zaman içimde olduğun için, bu akışın da doğal ortağı olabilirdin, oldun. Ama bu kez müsaade et."

Ancak bu şaşırtabilirdi O.'yu. Alışmıştı aşkımın vermeye hazır haline, her şeyi ve her zaman. Ne kadar çekinmese beni sevmediğini göstermeye, benim sevmemi, olan, olabilir her şeye rağmen sevmemi kanıksamıştı, anlamaktan çok.

Beklemediği cevabı mecbur kabul etti;

"Tamam, ben ev arayayım o zaman."

Verdiğim cevaba ve az önce gösterdiğim katı tavra yabancılaşmış, hem O.'ya hem kendime açıklama yapıyordum;

"Bu evin her tarafı seninle, anılarımızla dolu. Sen yokken, bu anılara, sana ihanet edecek hiçbir şey yapmadım. Bir gün geleceksin ve hiçbir şeyin dokunamaması hayali ile yerleştiğimiz bu evde, seninle tekrar birlikte olacağız diye umutsuzca bekledim. Onun için bir yere gitmedim, burada kaldım. Bu olasılık da kalmadıysa, ki artık kesin yok, ben de sen taşındıktan sonra çıkacağım buradan. Ama kusura bakma, sana bırakamam. Sen, benden sonrayı yaşayacaksın bu evde ve aptalca belki ama her tarafına seni kazıdığım, umutlarımla, umutsuzluklarımla kutsallaştırdığım burada senin başkalarıyla birlikte, yaşayamadıklarımı yaşamanıza   katlanamam. İzin veremem buna."

Anlamaz gözlerle bakıyordu bana.

"Artık beni anlamanı beklemiyorum. Sadece kararım bu."

Her zamanki gibi yine ekledim;

"Kitaplarıma dokunmamak kaydıyla istediğin her şeyi götürebilirsin."

Kahır...

Ama bu da yetmemişti bana. Ondan çok ben bakıyordum uygun bir ev bulmak, o sıkıntılı ev arama sürecini ben üstleniyordum O.'ya sıkıntı adına ne varsa dokundurmamak için. Ev bulunmuştu. Kim temizleyecekti evi peki? Kim taşıyacaktı eşyaları? Kim yerleştirecekti? Kıyamıyordum tüm bu gereksizliklerle O.'nun uğraşmasına. Tabii ki o 'kim'in cevabı, bendim. Varsın anlamasındı eşyaları yerleştirdikten sonra evimin yolunu bulamamamı o gece. Varsın habersiz olsundu, evinden çıkarken kendimden neleri bıraktığımı orada. Hâlâ onun için bir şeyler yapabilmiştim. Yeterliydi. Yeterli miydi?

Kaçarcasına boşalttım O. gittikten sonra evimi. Daha sonra ise bir eve gereksinmem olmayacaktı. Tutsaklık günlerim başlıyordu çünkü.

ÜÇÜNCÜ BÖLÜM

XVI.

Çırpınarak geçirdiğin tüm zamanların ardından geriye, bu çırpınışların varlığını sarmalayan nasırları kalıyor. Ve bağladığın nasırların ağırlığıyla daha bir bilge hissediyorsun kendini. Duyu organlarının duyarlılığının azalmasını "Her acıya teşne oldum artık." bilgeliği ile algılıyorsun. Rahatlama... Seni hiçbir şey acıtamaz artık. Ateşin yakacak kadar yakına gelmemesini yanmaya karşı gösterdiğin direnç olarak algılayıp, ısınarak tadını çıkaran sen. Ya ateş içine düşerse...

Tutsaklık günlerimi, belki kendi tutsaklığımı göz ardı ettirebilecek bir şans olarak yorumlatabilecek kadar büyüktü hayal kırıklığım. Seve seve kabul ettim önceden olsa yıkım olarak göreceğim özgürlüğümün alınmasını. Ne görebilirdim ki artık? Ne acıtabilirdi beni bundan sonra? Hayatı algılayışımı, durduğum yeri yok sayarak her şeyi yeni baştan yaratmaya girişip sayısızca hayal kırıklığı ile kendime yabancılaştıran o zorlu sürecin yanında, kendi kendimi tutsak ettiğim, çıkmaya çalıştıkça daha kalın parmaklıklar ördüğüm dünyamla karşılaştırdığımda yeni hayatımın ne zorlayıcılığı olabilirdi?

Ah, yine yanılmıştım. Öyle değildi işte. Ne kadar da uzağındaymışım meğer yaşadığım toplumun. Tamam, çok hareketli bir hayatım, insanlarla dolu bir çevrem yoktu ama yine de uzaktan da olsa içinde olduğum halkı çok iyi tanıdığımı sanırdım. Tek fark, tanıdığım bu insanlarla birlikte olmamayı seçmemdi. Ama bu yeni bir durumdu. En galiz küfürlerin hiç çekinilmeden söylendiği, argonun tek üslup olduğu, anlık parlamaların ve kavgaların o hızla yatışıp bir şey yokmuşçasına her şeyin kaldığı yerden devam ettiği, incelik adına, asgari nezaket adına, asgari insani duyarlılık adına bir şey bulunmayan yepyeni bir sanrılar dünyasıydı mecbur kaldığım bu yeni dünya. Ama gerçekti. Althusser'in dediği gibi sanrılar da aynı gerçek olarak kabul ettiğimiz şeyler gibi birer olgu değil miydi? Peki bu olgulardan hangisiydi asıl gerçek? Alışmaya çalışıyordum.

Alışmaya çalıştığım bu yeni dünyada dikenli tellerin dışındaki görece özgür hayattan çok, bir 'merhaba'ya, bir 'müsaade eder misiniz'e bir 'lütfen'e hasrettim. Daha iyi anlıyordum Dmitri Karamazov'un sancısını. Cezasını çekmek için Sibirya'ya gidecekken kendisini kaçırmak isteyen kardeşlerine, orada karşılaşacağı her şeyi hak ettiğini söylemesi ve yaşayacaklarını ruh olgunluğuna erişmesi için bir yol olarak görerek ısrarla kaçmaya karşı çıkması, her şeyi olgunlukla göze almışken; 'Kaçmalıyım... Çünkü orada bana 'Sen' diye hitap ederler' diye fikrini değiştirip kaçmaya razı olmasını... Özgürlükten daha çok istiyordum incelikli bir ruhu, içinde 'lan' yada 'sen' bulundurmayan seslenmeleri, kapıda karşılaştığım zaman bana öncelik tanıyan birini, yada öncelik tanıdığım birinden duyacağım teşekkürü. Ne bekliyordum ki? Sadece toplumsal hikayeyi okuyabildiğini sanan ben, daha önceleri defalarca olduğu gibi yanılmaya, şaşırmaya devam ediyordum. Yaşadığım kültür şoku, daha önce karşılaşmadığım bir durumdu. Aynı topraklarda böylesi bir yabancılık... Böylesi bir şaşkınlık. Böyle olmamalıydı. Tamam, tutsak olma gerçeğimiz belli davranış biçimlerinin kümelendiği bir sınıfın varlığını da zorunlu kılıyor olabilirdi ama umut ediyordum yine de. Bulamıyordum. Ve her zamanki gibi kitaplara kapandım.

Dostoyevski'nin hapishane ve kürek günleri, Althusser'in beyninde, Melville'in denizlerdeki tutsaklığı yeni bir umut oluyor, tutsaklık günlerimde "Olsun, felsefenin kuşu alacakaranlıkta uçar.[61-] Ben de bundan kendi payıma düşeni alacağım. Bekle, sabret ve yarat." yanılsamasını sokuyordu beynime. Bu avuntularla benim olmayan bir hayatı yaşayarak tutsaklık günlerimi geçiriyordum.

Ama hepsi bu da değildi tabii. Bu arada O., her zaman olduğu gibi yine benimleydi. Yine aradığım, özlediğim ne varsa O.'da somutlaştırıyor, hem buradaki eksikliklerimi hem de O.'da bulamayıp yaşadığım hayal kırıklığını yine paradoksal bir şekilde hâlâ O.'da tamamlamaya çalışıyordum. Bu paradoks, özlemimi daha katlanılmaz yapıyor, daha erişilmez kılıyordu. Yetmemişti. Yaşattığı onca şey, tutsaklıktan önce görüştüğümüzde bir ilişkisinin olduğunu, evlenmeyi düşündüğünü söylemesi rahatlıkla ve bu ilişkisinin benimle oturduğu zaman başladığını, evden ben gitmiş olsaydım birlikte o evde oturacaklarını itiraf etmesi, böyle bir şey yapabilmesi bir yana beni ne kadar inciteceğini bildiği halde bana söyleyebilmesi kayıtsızca, söylediği zaman kendimden geçip ilk kez ona karşı ağza alınmayacak sözler söylemem yetmemişti O.'dan yüz çevirmeme. Ben, nereye gitmiştim? Nasıl bir kayboluştu bu? Nasıl bir karşıtına dönüşmeydi? Tanrısal kusursuzluk tasarımı bir yana, insan olma durumunu bile kaldıramayacak kadar nasıl gerilemiştim? Aşka duyduğum apriori tiksinti bu sonu sezişten mi kaynaklanıyordu? Ve fakat, içinde bulunduğum durum buydu. Kabul etmesem de, gerçekti her şey.

Yaptıklarını unutmamaya çalışıp, öfkemi diri tutarak kendimi korumaya çalışsam da O.'dan, öylesine zayıftım ki söz konusu O. olunca... Ah, bu çelişkiyi her yanıyla görüp, gördüğünden titrercesine iğrenip devam ettiren birisi nasıl çıldırmasındı? Çıldırmıyordum ama. Ne iğrenmekten vazgeçiyor, ne iğrendiğim şeyi terk etmekten, ne de yaptığım şeyi kanıksıyordum. Mr. Hyde'den kurtulamayan Dr. Jekylle gibi çırpınıyordum kendi açmazımın içinde. Ben mi yaratmıştım bu sefil 'ben'i? Kurtulabilecek miydim? Kurtulabilmem için daha ne kadar batıracaktı ki beni? Tiksinti yaratmadığı hangi uzvum kalmıştı? O.'ya tutsak edip kendimi geriye dönünce, bu tutsaklık için kendimden nefret edebileceğim hangi davranışım eksikti? Kafka ne-

[1-] Hegel

den geliyordu hiç yoktan aklıma? Milena'nın konuyla ilgisi neydi? Neden Kafka'yı yazdığı vıcık vıcık aşk dilenen mektuplarından sonra terk edişim bir anda yerleşiyordu zihnime? Bu zamansız usavurmalar, yaşadığım tutsaklık nedeniyle O.'ya tek ulaşabilme yolum olan mektuplardan olmasındı sakın?

XVII.

Değersiz geri çekilmeler yada değersizlikten geri çekilmeler. Duygusal varoluş...

Bir yandan kaybedişimi kabul etmeye çalışıp kayıplarımdan O.'yu sorumlu tutarken, öte yandan her şeyi üstüme alıyor, ne olursa olsun O.'ya karşı kötü konuşmamam gerektiğini düşünüyordum. Evleneceğini söylediği zaman nasıl da kaybetmiştim kendimi. Neler yapmıştım öyle. Ne söylerse söylesin, ne yaparsa yapsın benden asla çıkmamalıydı öyle sözler. Çıkmıştı ama... Belki hala üzgündü daha önce benden duymadığı sözleri söyleyebildiğim için, belki hala tedirgindi daha ne yapacağımı bilmediği için, belki hala korkuyordu. Deli olmalıydım. Rahatlatmaya çalıştım. Yazdım;

20 Nisan

Söylediğim o sözler sadece bir anlık cinnetin sonucuydu. En nihayetinde senin biricik hayatın. Mutlu olmayı seçeceksin. Yaptığın her şeyden bağımsız, senin için tek şey dileyebilirim; mutlu ol. Ve o sözler için, çok üzgünüm.

Ses yoktu. Olumlu yada olumsuz cevap yazmamıştı. Ah, rollerin dağılımında yine bir hata olmalıydı. İncinmiş olması gereken, en azından bir özür bekleyen neden ben değildim? Neden yine ben onarmaya çalışıyordum? Onarılacak ne kalmıştı ki? Kesip atmam için yeterince sebep vermemiş miydi bana? Cevabını bildiğim benzer yüzlerce soruyu davranışa dönüştüremeyecektim yine de. Devam ediyordum yazmaya;

26 Nisan

"Size kızmak mı Nastenka? Parlak, sakin mutluluğunuza kara bir gölge çekmek mi! Acı kınamalarla kalbinizi kırmak, gizli bir vicdan azabıyla kıvrandırmak, tam mutluluk anında hüzünlere boğmak mı! Düğün gününüzde kara saçlarınıza taktığınız çiçeklerden birini bile soldurmak mı! Yo, asla, asla. Sizin gökyüzünüz hep bulutsuz, güzel gülümsemeniz hep parlak ve daimi olsun. Yalnız ve şükran dolu bir kalbe verdiğiniz mutluluk ve sevinç için sonsuza değin mutlu olun" *(Dostoyevski, Beyaz Geceler)*

Büyük yıkıntı ve kaybetmişlikte bile bu sözleri söyleyebilmek, söylediklerini hissedebilmek... Maalesef, her ne kadar farklı olduğumu düşünsem de, beslendiğim topraktan daha fazlasını ifade edemedim. Kaybedişim bile ne kadar soysuz ve seviyesizceydi. Üzgünüm...

Bu kez yanıt vermişti. Ah sefil yaratık, mutlu ol!

1 Mayıs

Yanıt verip vermeme konusunda tereddütte kaldım... Bana hayatta özür borçlu olmayan ve olmayacak tek kişi olduğunu daha önce söylediğimi anımsıyorum. Biliyorsun ki, idealize insanlar ve özendiğimiz soylu davranışlar ancak kitaplarda oluyor. Sadece yazılması mümkün onların. Yaşamak çok başka bir şey. Dostoyevski'nin bile yazdığın satırlarda dillendirmiş olduğu soyluluğun onda birine sahip olduğunu düşünmüyorum.

Sana gelince; kitaplarda yalandan tasvir edilen (TASVİR EDİLEN HERŞEY KOCA BİR YALANDIR ÇÜNKÜ) soyluluktan çok daha üstün vasıflara sahipsin. Bana saydığın kelimelerin hepsini senin nazarında hak etmiş olabilirim. Bir durum yada bir olgu farklı yerlerden bakıldığında bambaşka şekiller alıyor çünkü. Duyduğun sevgiden şüphem yok. Saygını kaybetmiş olabilirsin belki.

*Üzgün olma artık. Vicdanım şimdilik suskun... Azap çekecek
duruma geldiğimde, beni senin bile rahatlatacağını sanmıyorum.*

O.

Gerçeklerle bağlarımı tamamen koparmıştım. Uyaranlar birbirine
karışıyordu. Neye hangi değeri yükleyeceğimi bilmiyordum. Aptalca
bir af dileme yarışına dönüştü sonraki tüm mektuplarım. Daha fazlasına layıktım. Daha batırabilirdi. Daha da batıyordum yazdığım her
kelimeyle. Gerçeklere dönünce kendi yüzüme bakabilecek miydim?
Umurumda değildi. Her zamanki gibi O.'ydu söz konusu olan ve
bendim O. söz konusu oldu mu her türlü soysuzluğa gebe.

12 Mayıs

*Umarım vicdanın, azap çekecek duruma gelemeyecek ka-
dar mutlulukla meşgul olur hep. Boş versene azabı. Ölüyoruz an be an. Azapsa, sonrasında zaten fazlasıyla bekliyor
bizi. Şimdilik mutlu kal.*

Ah! Kendimle boğuşmam yetmiyordu sefilliğimi bitirmeme. Devam
ediyordum;

19 Mayıs

*Sana olan saygımın kaybolması mı O.? Sana olan sevgi-
min beslendiği en yüce kaynağın yara alması mı? Ruhum....
Asla ve hiçbir zaman. Senin içimde aldığın yerin ulaşılmaz-
lığına, ne varolanların dünyasının sözleri, ne de bu lanet
dünyanın nitelemeleri -ve bu kelimeleri kullanan zavallı la-
netliler!- ulaşabilir mi, yaklaşabilirler mi sanıyorsun? Aynı
düzlemde mümkün mü O.? Seni düşünürken sen sadece
sevgili yada eş değildin benim için. Yaşamla kurduğum ya-
kınlığın, umut ettiysem şayet bu umudun tek ve yeter sebebi... Birlikte, hesap kitap yapmadan alacağım son nefese
kadar yaşayacağım-yaşayabileceğim-yaşamak istediğim tek*

insan, tüm hücrelerimi kanatırcasına sürdürdüğüm yaşamda kalma uğraşımı -ki bu uğraş benim için ne zordur, bilsen.

"Yaşıyor" olabilmek belki herkesin çok kolayca üstesinden geldiği, farkında bile olmadıkları bir edimken benim için tam bir mücadele alanı olan bir çaba- ne zaman ve nasıl istersen olduğu yerde kesebileceğim tek insan... Yani ruhum, yani her şeyim... Yani sen...

Bir ilişkide -İlişki... Aramızdaki bağı "ilişki" klişesi ile ifade etmek ne büyük bir aptallık- "saygı", belki çoğu insan için çok da anlamlı ve belirleyici değil. Çünkü varolanların dünyasının gerçeklikleri, yeter sebepleri çok farklı ve asla aşkın özüne dokunmayan tali şeyler. Ama benim için, biliyorsun...

Peki, çoğu insan için dikkate bile alınmayacak, alınsa bile en kolay göz ardı edilecek şey olan saygıya bu kadar önem veriyorsam ve diğerlerini lanetliyorsam, onlardan daha pespaye bir davranışta nasıl bulundum? O kelimeler kimden çıktı? Hem de sana karşı...

Bunu ne kadar düşündüm bilsen ve her düşündüğümde nasıl utandım. Bunun açıklaması olabilir mi? Ama ben yine de yapmaya çalışacağım...

Seni kaybediyor olmak... Adım adım... Göz göre göre... Her anını damarlarımdan dikenli teller çekilircesine (ki ölüm acısının böyle bir şey olduğunu söyler Gazali...) bir azapla izlemek bu kaybı. İçinde olmak, bu kaybın bir parçası olmak ama önüne duramamak, önüne çıkmaya her çalıştığında üstünden silindir geçmişçesine ezilip yere serilmek ve tekrar kalkıp umutsuzca, arsızca, ısrarla tekrar tekrar süreci tersine, eskiye çevirmeye çalışmak ve her seferinde daha çok kayba uğramak, bitişe durması için dokunamamak... Yani seni kaybetmek O. Belki benim kadar seviyor olsaydın; böylesi bir kaybın ne kadar yıkıcı, ne denli mantıktan, hatta seni sen eden şeylerden, özünden uzaklaştırıcı olduğunu anlardın. Ussallaştırmaya çalışmıyorum hiçbir şeyi, kesinlikle. Sade-

ce, anlaşılmaz olanı anlatmaya çalışıyorum. (Aynı anda an-
lamaya da çalışıyorum. Çünkü şaşkınım. Bunu kendime de
izah etmem lazım.) Kahretsin ki, en nihayetinde insanım.
Ve insan soyunun taşıdığı tüm zayıflıklar da fazlasıyla bulu-
nuyor bende. Evet, bu pespayelik de çok insani bir şeydi.
Kesinlikle reddettiğim bir insanilik. Sebepler, süreç, ne olur-
sa olsun.

Şimdi, af dilemek mi? Neyi çözer? Nasıl arınabiliriz? Daha
fazla ağlayarak mı? Kahır katsayısını yükselterek mi? Kana-
tırcasına her hücremizi azap çekerek mi? Hepsini o kadar
yaşadım ki... Daha fazla azap mı? Var mı? Geriye ne kaldı
O.? Sensizlikten başka....

Elimde ne var? Sadece tamamen sana adanmış bir ben.
Hepsi hepsi sadece ben... Sana, kendimi sunabilirim ancak,
sundum, sunuyorum. Biliyorsun; ama ben yine yinelemek-
ten geri durmayacağım. Her zaman seninim... Al, ne ya-
parsan yap. İstersen özenle rafa kaldır, ister yırt at, ister baş
tacı... Başka ne diyebilirim ki? Seni seviyorum... Hasretle.
Her zaman hasretle.

Bir kere sınırı aşan için artık sınır yoktur derler. Ben de onursuzlukta
sınırı aşmıştım. Sorularım yoktu. Hızla düşüyordum. Yanıt gelme-
mesine rağmen, devam ettim.

26 Mayıs

Başlangıcı ne? Sonu ne? "Büyük yüreklilik; ölüme oldu-
ğu kadar ışığa da gözlerini kırpmadan bakabilmektir" der
Camus. Düşünüyorum; Elimde ne var? Sanırım,-çoğu kez
kaybetmeme neden olan, sadece büyük yüreğim...(Sence
öyleydi değil mi? Ya çok saf olmalıydım yada kocaman bir
yüreğe sahip...) Camus'dan ödünç alırsam düşüncesini, za-
manların hepsinde ölüme ilişkin olana gözlerimi kırpmadan
bakmamı sağlayan 'Büyük yüreğim!' seninle ışığa yönel-
mişti açıkça... Ah ne kadar karanlık bir ışık! Ve bu kapkara
ışığa gözlerimi kırpmadan bakıp seni düşlerken yine, sana,

senden bana eskisi gibi yönelecek sesini umut etmiyorum aslında. Ama yine de düşlüyorum. Çünkü az biraz daha ışığa ihtiyacım var nefesim tükenmeden önce.

İçimdekileri bilebilsen, anlatabilseydim sana keşke. Kavrayabilseydin yada sen. O. dediğim zaman sesimdekini duyabilseydin, sana dokununca, tenin, o dokunuştakini gerçekten hissetseydi, sana baktığım zaman sadece rengi değişen gözlerimden öte neler gördüğümü görebilseydin, sana her yönelişimin nasıl tamamen ruh olarak, önceden ve sonradan bağımsız bir akış olduğunu kavrayabilseydin, belki bu satırlar dahil yaşanmaması gereken birçok şeye gerek olmayacaktı. Ve ben, farkına varmak için daha çok, cennetimin yitmesini mi beklemeliydim? Yitmesini beklememeliydim. Evet, sanırım asıl cennetlerin yitirilen cennetler olduğu doğru.

Artık ne yapabilirim? Cennetimin cehennemle sarılmış hali, ışığımın kör eden karanlığı... Her şeyi hızla tüketip sona yaklaştıran zamanın yıkıcılığına karşı... Ancak iflah olmaz bir arsızsam, düşleyebilirim... Ve düşlüyorum...

Sen; iyi ol. Daha fazla bir dileğe, dokunamam...

Bir anlamı varsa, seninim...

Bir anlamı yoktu tabii. Bilmiyor muydum aramızdaki ortak anlamın bittiğini? Biliyordum ama ısrarla, düşme kabiliyetimin daha nereye kadar varabileceğini merak ediyor, kendimi sınıyordum.

2 Haziran

O.,

Ne çok severdim ismini söylemeyi...Ne çok severdim O. ile ilgili tüm detayları, kokunu çekmeyi içime, nefessizce- Ki senin korktuğun o her nefesi içimde tutma anlarımda bir gün bu kokuyu duyamayacağım gerçeğini duyumsayarak kokunu içimde hapsedip kendimce savaşa girerdim yazgımla.

Senin "Nefes al" demene kadar geçen sürede ben amansız
bir savaştaydım, bilsen...-

Bunların hepsine, sayamadığım daha fazlasına O. demiştim
ben. Ve O.'yu ne çok sevmiştim. İfadelerimdeki zaman kipi
ne kadar anlamsız aslında. Geçmiş zaman, yeterli değil asla.
Bunu böyle anlamanı umut ediyorum... Sana sadece bir
anlık dokunuşumu veya bakışımı düşün her şeyden bağımsız. Aslında geri kalanın laf kalabalığı olduğunu göreceksin.
Ve aslında bu; benim susmamı da gerektiriyor. Ama..

Adım adım ama hızla kopuşumuzdan düştüğüm panik, ta-
rifsizdi. Keşke, o anlarımda yanımda olabilseydin... Geceler
ve günler boyu kopuşunu duyumsarken yaptığım yalpala-
maları, seni beklememi, anlaşılır olanı anlamayan (basitti
çünkü, yoktun...) anlamak istemeyen (İstemiyordu çükü
öyle olmamalıydı...) beynimi binlerce olasılığa yönlendirip
bir ışık aramamı... Keşke yanımda olsaydın...

Her şeyi görmüştüm. Bitiş, başlamıştı ilk ayrılışımızla. "Tanrının kusursuz dünyası" devam ediyordu nitekim... Bizse
çırpınıp duruyorduk. Ne acz...

Belki her şeyi "Tanrının kusursuz dünyası"na refere edip ra-
hatlayabilirdik bir yere kadar.

Etmeli miydik?

Seni bilmiyorum ama ben edemiyorum.

Geçen zamanda tükettiğim umutlarım adeta topraklama yapar gibi aşkımı güçlendiriyordu... Hâlâ da... Ama artık seni
aramaya gücüm yok. Şimdi sadece düşünüyorum. Eğer
söylendiği gibi karşımızdakinin hisleri dediğimiz şey kendi
sevgimizin çarpıp geri dönüşüyse... Hayır, yine de umut etmiyorum. Sadece bir yerlerde, belki başka ama çok başka
formlarda seninle tekrar karşılaşacağımı düşlüyorum.

Yaşayacak bir şeyimiz kalmadı maalesef. Bunun farkındayım artık. Çektiğim acıyı dereceleyemiyorum. Seninleyken

yaşadığım hazzın tersini düşün bunun için. Her iki uçta da
yaşanılabilir olanı gösterdin bana. Teşekkür ederim.
Sevgiyle kal...

Köpekleşmemin sonu yoktu. Kendime rağmen engelleyemediğim
bir oyunun içindeydim. Deniyordum. Daha nereye kadar alçalabi-
lirdim? Merhamet, aşktan daha mı güçlüydü? Belagatımın etkisi var
mıydı en duyarsız olana karşı bile? Günlerce kapıda bekleyip uluyan
köpeğin önüne sussun diye atılan bir kemik gibi, kısa, anlamsız bir
yanıt geldi;

12 Haziran

Ne diyeceğimi bilmiyorum. Yazdıkların beni çok üzdü. Duy-
gularını bilmiyor değilim. Ama bazı şeylere gücüm yetmedi.
Kusura bakma...

O.

Ah, uslanmaz bir arsızdan başka neydim? Sanırım her şeyi hak ediyordum. Yazdım yine;

16 Haziran

Ve neden sonra senden, içinde "duygu" bulunan bir mektup
alıyorum. Bunu nasıl yorumlayacağımı, nereye koyacağımı
bilemeyerek, sadece geçmişe gidiyorum. Saatler boyu sen-
den duygu akarken tüm sıcaklığınla; şimdi neye yoracağımı
bilemediğim iki satıra bakakalıyorum...

Hangi kapısı açık kalmıştı? Daha nereden zorlayabilirdim O.'yu?
Pis bir hesapçılık içine giriyor, daha önce yazın üzerine saatler boyu
attığım nutukları göz ardı edip, sırf yumuşak karnı diye yazma üzerinden götürüyordum bu kez dilenmemi. O.'ya okuttuğum bir şey
olmamasına rağmen "Bak beklemedin ki" gibi çocukça, aptalca bir
koz sürüyordum önüne. Artık önemli değildi bu tutarsızlıklarım.

24 Haziran

Yazardım... Yazdıklarımda (Yazma ediminin kendiliğinden-liğine inat-doğasına bir küfürdü bu aslında-) tek bir tetik-leyici güdü vardı. Senin tarafından beğenilmek. Bir gün "Gerçekten güzel olmuş" dediğini duymak... Bu ne kadar aykırı gözükse de yazmanın doğasına, yazanın aşkın haline.. Hepsinden öte tek güdü "O. ne diyecek?" idi. Aslında ters-ten bakılınca çok da şaşılası bir durum değildi bu. Çünkü tek bir nesneye yönelen özne, tabii ki her davranışını ve bu arada yazıklarını da o nesneye, oluş nedenine adayacaktı. Onun için yazdığım her şeyi sana sunup onayını beklemek ve onayını alınca "evet" demek ancak, anlaşılır bir durum değil mi? Bunu bir düş olarak yaşatmam ve bu düş eksiksiz gerçek olsun diye hep geriye atmam.

Ve fakat... Yazıyorum hala. Yazdıklarım sana adak... Ama yazarken seninle paylaşamamak... Bu; hayatımı sana adar-ken senden uzak yaşamak kadar acı verici ve en az o kadar yıkıcı...

Bazen uyanıyor, "Ben ne yapıyorum" sancılarıyla baş başa kalıyor-dum. Bu durumda bile hemen O.'ya yöneliyor, hiçbir şeyi geriye döndüremeyeceğimi görüp (Ne bekliyordum ki, "ah çok güzel yaz-mış, döneyim tekrar" mı diyecekti?) belki hala kendi yüzüme baka-bilecek kadar saygım kalır kendime diye düzeltmeye çalışıyordum durumumu.

1 Temmuz

Tamam, çok seviyorum. Ve bu sevgimi "Güçlü kalemimle!" ne yaman anlatıyorum. Tekrar çakarak kafana "Bak O., ne kaybettiğinin farkında mısın? Umut yok diyorum ama umut etmemi sağla... Anla işte" diyerek en alt perdeden, alçak-ça hala umut dileniyorum. Ahlayıp oflamalar ve bir sürü laf ebeliği. En alt tabaka köylü kurnazlığı, en bayağısından şarklılık. Açıkça ve alçakça...

Ben, ne yapıyorum?

Çok sevebilirsin... Sevgin kaybedişinle birleşince o ölçüde yıkıma da yol açabilir. Ama eğer asalet diye bir şey var diyorsan ve bunu kendinde var kabul ediyorsan, eğer zorlama değilse bu sezişin, öyle olmalısın sonunda da.

Eee? O zaman ben ne yapıyorum?

Ne; kaybettiği sevgilisini son bir kez daha kollarına alabilmek için sevgilisinin evini yakan ve alevler arasında sevgilisini kollarına alıp dışarı çıkan adamın gözü pek, çılgın, ölçüsüz aşkı, ne; kendisini sevmeyen eşi ile ayrı yatmaktan bıkmış, bir kez olsun ona candan yaklaşmayan eşinin eve hırsız girmesiyle korkup kendisine sokulması ile hırsıza binlerce minnet duyan adamın talihinin belki bir gün yine böyle bir aksilikle bir vuslat daha yaşatacağına dair umutsuz bekleyişi, ne; yaşamını kaybettiği sevgilisini sırf bir kez daha görmek için tüketmeyen adamın sessiz sabrı, ne de "Aşkımla var oldum ben, yoksa o, daha fazlasını istemiyorum" diye hayatını sonlayan adamın kararlılığı...

Eee? Peki ben ne yapıyorum?

Umudu tükenmiş bir halde "umut" bir daha. Hâlâ hesapkitap. Ben... Yakalandım. Tamam, bitiriyorum her şeyi, ama bitirmeden önce son bir sorti daha umuda... Kahrolası bir hesapçılık. Hâlâ... Tüm bu aşağılık davranışlarım; "Antikahraman olamayacak kadar kahraman, kahraman olamayacak kadar silik, normal olamayacak kadar naif, altta yada üstte izole olamayacak kadar normal, bitiremeyecek kadar yaşama bağlı, sürdüremeyecek kadar isteksiz ve nefret dolu" olmamla açıklanabilir mi?

Kelimeler oyuncağım, dil metresim. Sözün sınırı yok

Ama bu mudur? Ne yapmalıyım?

Yakalıyorum kendimi... Cesaretsizliğimi umursamazlıkla maskelememi, kaybedişimi kaybı kutsayışımla ussallaştırmamı, beceriksizliğimi bir şekilde Tanrı'ya refere edişimi, bitimsiz hatalarımı pişmanlıkla rahatlamaya dökmemi (ne ihtiyaç!), kesip atamayışımı "aman, az sonra olacak" kandırmacasına yem etmemi... Yakalıyorum. Herkesten öte, kendime yakalanıyorum. Ve zehrim akıyor içime. Geber... O.'nun artık ne sorularıma ihtiyacı vardı ne de cevaplarıma. Daha önce olduğu gibi sorularımı yine kendim cevaplıyordum. Ama bir yandan da kendimden emin, yazmasını bekliyordum. Sanki yazacak, her şey için özür dileyecek, affetmemi isteyecek, tutsaklığımın bitmesini sabırsızlıkla bekleyip tekrar benimle olacaktı. Ama, yazmıyordu. Kızıyordum, ama yine ölçülü:

15 Temmuz

Yazdığım onca mektuba karşılık olarak sadece son derece soğuk, yasak savarcasına iki cümle... Kızgınlık mı? Kırgınlık mı? İnat mı? Sevgisizlik mi? Sebebi ne olursa olsun... Nezaket cevap gerektirir. Kabul yada ret...

Kendime dönmem için fazla bir şeye gerek yoktu aslında. Sadece O.'dan, bu kahredici bağımlılıktan kurtulmam yeterdi. Bir yandan bunu biliyor, bir yandan da engellenemez şekilde O.'dan vazgeçemiyordum. Neyse ki O. beni yok sayıyor, zorla da olsa beni durduruyordu. Uzun süre yazmadım. Aradan aylar geçmiş O. da yazmamıştı. Hâlâ, hiç olmazsa benim önemsemediğim ama O.'nun çok önemsediği doğum günümde yazar umudunu taşıyordum. Yazmadı yine. Ve ben son defa yazdım;

17 Eylül

Tabii ki senden doğum günümü kutlamanı beklemiyorum. İnceliğin (!) göz önüne alındığında böyle bir beklenti içine girmiyorum kesinlikle. Ama bana tuhaf geliyor. Bir zamanlar her şeyimi paylaştığım birisinden, böylesi bir günde zoraki de olsa herhangi bir ses çıkmaması...

Aman, saçmalama değil mi? Sanırım tüm bunları düşünmek için hiç vaktin yok... Hoşça kal.

XVIII.

İlkelerin için yaşayacak kadar idealist olman, ilkelerin anlamsızlığını duyumsayamayacak kadar sığ olmanda anlam kazanabilir belki. Doğru ile yanlış birbirini tamamlamak zorunda. İlkelerin doğruluğu! Sığlığın yanlışlığı! Tersi de olabilir. Doğru ne? Yanlış ne? Arz talep meselesi.

Tutsaklık günlerimin sonuna yaklaşıyordum. Bir yandan tekrar O.'dan bana doğru yeni anlamlar yaratmaya çalışırken bir yandan da başladığım yere dönüyordum. Kılıfımdan çıkıp yarattığım anlamlar dünyası O. ile var olup yine O. ile dağılırken, sürekliliğin zorunluluğu, başlangıçta yaptığı gibi yeni kılıflar hazırlıyordu bana. Ama muhtemel kılıflarım artık devam ettirmeye değil, iyice çekilmeye, debelenircesine çıkmaya çalıştığım yaşamla ölüm arasındaki boşluğa doğru çekiyordu beni. Bitmişlik duygusu içindeydim. Toprak çekiyordu. Ne kadar yakınsam toprağa, o kadar dingin, rahat oluyordum. Bu yüzden, oturuş yerimi ve şeklimi hep toprağa daha yakın olacak bir şekilde seçiyordum. Gerçekleşmiş miydi her şey? Buraya kadar mıydı? Tanrısal kusursuzluğu kurmaya çalışırken zihnimde, bunun için yükselmeye çalışırken varolanların dünyasının gerekliliklerinin hepsinden, bu yükselişin önünde gördüğüm en büyük engel olan karşı cinse duyulan aşkla tahayyül sınırımın bile üstünde düşmüştüm aşağılara. Aldığım mesafeyi düşününce, bunun bir süreç sorunu olmadığını anlıyordum. Milat yoktu. Milat yoksa, tamamlanmış da olamazdı. O zaman beni sarmalayan bu duygunun anlamı neydi? Diğer tarafta; toprak ne kadar çekiyorsa, sıcaklığa karşı özlemim de o boyuttaydı. Sanırım çok yakında her şey bitecek. Toprağa çekilişim, içinde yer almakla; sıcaklığa özlemim, ateşle son bulacak. Mutlak karanlık, toprak ve ateş. Bekliyorum...

XIX

İçimden çıkararak yaktığım ışığın aydınlığıyla görülebilecek her şeyi gördüm. Yaşanabilecek her şeyi yaşadım, en uçlara kadar gittim. Mutlu oldum. Zaman zaman rahat ettim. Görece lüks içinde yaşadım. Hızla beni terk etse de coşkunluklar tattım. Artık ışığım sadece kötülükleri, sıkıntıları, iç hesaplaşmaları, iğrençlikleri yani hüznü ve derin kaybedişlerimi gösteriyor bana. E, o zaman neden kapatmıyorum ışığı? Klik sesiyle birlikte bana gösteremeyeceği tüm o "şey"lerden neden kurtulmuyorum? Mutlak karanlıktan neden hâlâ kaçıyorum? Umut mu hâlâ arsızca? Gelecek bitti oysa. Hadi, biraz cesaret. Görülebilecek iyi bir şey kalmadıysa artık...

SON